REGENERATIVE FICTIONS

REGENERATIVE FICTIONS

POSTCOLONIALISM, PSYCHOANALYSIS, AND THE NATION AS FAMILY

BY
ALEXANDRA W. SCHULTHEIS

REGENERATIVE FICTIONS

First published 2004 by
PALGRAVE MACMILLAN™
175 Fifth Avenue, New York, N.Y. 10010 and
Houndmills, Basingstoke, Hampshire, England RG21 6XS
Companies and representatives throughout the world

PALGRAVE MACMILLAN is the global academic imprint of
the Palgrave Macmillan division of St. Martin's Press, LLC and of
Palgrave Macmillan Ltd. Macmillan® is a registered trademark in the
United States, United Kingdom and other countries. Palgrave is
a registered trademark in the European Union and other countries.

ISBN 1–4039–6308–8 hardback

Cataloging-in-Publication Data is on file at the Library of Congress

A catalogue record for this book is available from the British Library.

Design by Newgen Imaging Systems (P) Ltd., Chennai, India.

First edition: January, 2004
10 9 8 7 6 5 4 3 2 1

Printed in the United States of America.

For Chloë

Contents

ACKNOWLEDGMENTS

This project would not have been possible without the support and guidance of many people, and to them I am profoundly grateful. At every stage, James Longenbach offered thoughtful and sustained critical readings, encouraging me to clarify my thinking and writing whenever they were murky. In addition, I have tried throughout to apply his generous insight that one's own good ideas develop because, rather than in spite of those of others. Bette London and Janet Wolff provided valuable responses to earlier drafts of the full manuscript; the chapters on Salman Rushdie and Darryl Pinckney also benefited from the readings of Vikram Chandra and Robert Samuels, respectively. My thinking about the relationship between psychoanalysis, postcolonialism, and aesthetics evolved through discussions with all of them as well as with David Rodowick, John Michael, and Ali Behdad. The late Roger Henkle of Brown University first taught me how literary studies could be not just pleasurable, but socially necessary. Ed Bock of Syracuse University encouraged rigorous yet supple thinking that I hope I have upheld. Faye Moskowitz and Nina Mikhalevsky, of the George Washington University, ensured I had time and institutional support when I most needed it.

Kirstin Hotelling Zona has been unstinting with her friendship and intellectual fierceness over the past ten years. The combination has enriched every aspect of my work.

My family, Howard and Miriam Engelson, Erik Engelson, Kathy Engelson, Susan Engelson, Nancy Craft, and Bill Schultheis, have provided everything from unflagging encouragement to room to write to needed breaks. My father, Rob Schultheis, and grandmother, Eugenia Barnett Schultheis, continue to teach and inspire me with their artistic and social passions and intellectual freedom.

I could not have completed this without the love and kindness Ben Moore has offered from the bleakest days of 2000 to the joys of the present. And, finally, I owe my deepest gratitude to Tad Welch for this life "Off the Trail," "where the wild will take us."

I am grateful to the editors of *Jouvert* and *Twentieth-Century Literature* for permission to reprint portions of this manuscript. Chapter 5 first appeared as "Family Matters in Jamaica Kincaid's *The Autobiography of My Mother*," *Jouvert* 5.2 (Winter 2001). A portion of chapter 4 appeared as "Postcolonial Lack and Aesthetic Promise in *The Moor's Last Sigh*," *Twentieth-Century Literature* 47.4 (Winter 2001): 569–95.

I would also like to thank the following for permission to cite copyrighted material: Extracts from "The Schooner *Flight*" from *Collected Poems* by Derek Walcott. Used by permission of Faber and Faber Ltd. Extracts from *The Autobiography of My Mother* by Jamaica Kincaid published by Jonathan Cape. Used by permission of The Random House Group Limited. Extracts from *The Holder of the World* by Bharati Mukherjee, copyright © 1993 by Bharati Mukherjee. Used by permission of Alfred A. Knopf, a division of Random House, Inc.

Reprinted by permission of Farrar, Straus and Giroux, LLC: Excerpts from *The Autobiography of My Mother* by Jamaica Kincaid. Copyright © 1996 by Jamaica Kincaid. Excerpts from *HIGH COTTON* by Darryl Pinckney. Copyright © 1992 by Darryl Pinckney. Excerpt from "The Schooner *Flight*" from *Collected Poems* by Derek Walcott. Copyright © 1986 by Derek Walcott.

Introduction
Regeneration of the Nation as Family

At the beginning of Derek Walcott's "The Schooner *Flight*," the speaker Shabine prepares to set sail from Trinidad's "slums of empire" to escape pervasive colonial and neo-colonial degradation which renders him little more than "a dog on these streets." His name, "the patois for any red nigger," makes him representative of all those simultaneously produced and forgotten by colonial empires; it reminds him, "either I'm nobody, or I'm a nation," and locates his struggle for recognition at the intersection of subjectivity and national identity. As he leaves home, the baptismal image of Shabine's "sea-bath" takes on literary and historical connotations: he takes the helm of the English language, searching for the terms with which to create a valued social identity.

The sea for Walcott always offers an ahistorical respite from the narrative of imperialism as well as a history of slave-trading, colonial exploration and exploitation. Nation-building separates these two narratives of the sea; it is where History begins, as Walcott writes in "The Sea is History," and Shabine rides its crest. His flight north through the islands linking the Americas is less an attempt to escape the history that created and imprisons him, a predictably futile goal, than a poetic journey to reclaim for himself the central images of that history. Once adrift, he realizes, "I had no nation now but the imagination," and he pledges to craft a narrative of imaginative renewal, as opposed to one of domination, out of his journey:

> when I write
> this poem, each phrase go be soaked in salt;
> I go draw and knot every line as tight
> as ropes in this rigging; in simple speech
> my common language go be the wind,
> my pages the sails of the schooner *Flight*.

Freedom from the oppressive legacies of empire, Shabine suggests, necessitates recognition of how one is constituted by the historical forces that shape subjectivity and the nation in tandem *and* of the imagination's power to heal the wounds those forces inflict. Healing occurs through the imaginative reclamation of history and language. As Salman Rushdie writes in " 'Commonwealth Literature' Does Not Exist," the language of domination is transformed into one of self-determination as "peoples who were once colonized by the language are now rapidly remaking it, domesticating it, becoming more and more relaxed about the way they use it—assisted by the English language's enormous flexibility and size, they are carving out large territories for themselves within its frontiers" (64). Rushdie, Walcott, and the other authors I discuss turn tools of colonization—voyages of self- and geographic exploration and the occupation of linguistic territories—into those of self-determination.

As one whose subjectivity and national identity are indissolubly forged, Shabine turns his poetic eye to the metaphors that bind them and to their historical contexts in order to see them anew. Central among those metaphors is the image of the family. For Shabine, his immediate family is what he loved "as poets love the poetry/that kills them, as drowned sailors the sea." At the same time, his mixed Dutch, African, and English lineage renders him invisible to history, and thus provokes his flight: "I met History once, but he ain't recognize me." Family is at once a source of identification as well as of marginalization, disappearance, or death. Shabine's vision, in contrast to History's, is transformative in its awareness of his corporeal and historical foundations rather than in spite of them. For example, the Middle Passage of his journey calls forth cultural memories of his ancestors that range from European explorers to African slaves, but concludes neither with the horror of slavery nor a promised paradise of opportunity in the United States (Shabine makes it as far as the northern rim of the Bahamas). Instead he celebrates

> [t]he bowsprit, the arrow, the longing, the lunging heart—
> the flight to a target whose aim we'll never know,
> vain search for one island that heals with its harbour
> and a guiltless horizon[.]

Only in the imagination can such refuge exist; yet this realization insists upon rather than negates the value of the imaginative journey itself. Imagination, specifically through the conscious reworking of aesthetic terms, offers an escape both figurative and potentially real from oppression.

While the poem seems to end pessimistically with "Shabine sang to you from the depths of the sea," it simultaneously resists the implied futility of an anonymous death at sea. In that last line, which reconnects Shabine to an unsung genealogy ranging from drowned slaves of the Middle Passage to more recent Haitian and Cuban refugees, the speaker refuses to accept anonymity or silence as his fate. In his final gesture, naming the addressee ("you"), he implicates the reader in the poem's journey, asking him or her to bear witness to the passage of "The Schooner *Flight*" and those revealed in its wake. This connects reader and speaker in the common project of revising History, of curing what Judie Newman calls "the amnesia which is America's second name" (74).

Shabine's journey underscores the promises and pitfalls of this project. His journey insists on the need to revise the dominant metaphors that structure our worlds as well as on the impossibility of ever crossing that "guiltless horizon." I have chosen to focus here on the image of the patriarchal family because it plays a central role in Western narratives of subjectivity on the one hand and postcolonial literature and theory on the other. As an integral component of modernity, even as modernity assumes varied forms depending on its cultural context, the patriarchal family—understood through gender-coded signifiers of power and value—has been and continues to be invoked in political, literary, and scientific realms to "explain" global phenomena; therefore, it plays a key role in maintaining inequity.

Feminist responses to this metaphor and the practices accompanying it are widespread and range from Marilyn Waring's analysis of patriarchal biases implicit in international accounting standards (in *Counting for Nothing: What Men Value and What Women are Worth*) to much of the more recent work on culturally specific alternative modernities. As just one among many possible examples, Anouar Majid, in *Unveiling Traditions: Postcolonial Islam in a Polycentric World*, presents a particularly timely argument in his call for a conception of Islam whose "ultimate goal is a culturally 'polycentric' world founded on economic socialism and gender equality" (102). This kind of theorizing disrupts the hegemonic political discourse in the United States today that posits a lone superpower (masculinized as militaristic, capitalistic, technologically advanced, and rational) against a world of supposedly ineffectual allies and wily, yet archaic enemies. As Geoffrey Galt Harpham shows in his reading of the first President Bush's rhetoric on the eve of the Gulf War, such a model, while eliding the difference between the secularity of Iraq and the perceived threat of a strong, Islamic Middle East, works "to relegate Iraq [. . .] to the 'jungle' of the Third World, and then to eliminate that World, so there would be simply one, resolutely modern and enlightened, world, in which fundamentalism and ethnocentrism would simply have vanished in the course of the inexorable evolutionary advance of Homo sapiens and the legitimate destiny of freedom" (140).

The ease with which political rhetoric dispatches (in this case) Iraq from "the family of nations" and, thus, "the world," suggests that learning to recognize and value postcolonial subjects and nations, whether from the inside or outside, demands a willingness to re-examine the importance of the family metaphor in our collective memory, history, and identifications. Bharati Mukherjee, Darryl Pinckney, Salman Rushdie, and Jamaica Kincaid bring the complexity of this process to the forefront as all four blur the line, in different ways, between American and postcolonial subjects. Rather than dismiss their work as inauthentic because of the authors' own mobility (all four live outside their country of origin), I argue that they reveal the far-reaching effects of the family metaphor and, in doing so, render questions of authenticity and purity suspect if not obsolete. As part of the project of working toward alternative modernities, I look at the ways these authors respond to the pressures of the patriarchal family from positions that complicate the center–periphery model of postcolonialism. These authors have achieved critical success in the Western literary marketplace, their work is often taught in university classes, and their subversions of dominant literary tropes stem from facility with them. Yet from these ostensibly conservative aesthetic positions come narrators, plots, and writing that disrupt the legacy of what Paul Gilroy terms Euro-American modernity: The postcolonial subjects and authors of these novels challenge the legacy Paul Gilroy describes of Euro-American modernity:

> this legacy conditions the continuing aspiration to acquire a supposedly authentic, natural, stable "rooted" identity. This invariant identity is in turn the premise of a thinking "racial" self that is both socialized and unified by its connection with other kindred souls encountered usually, though not always, within the fortified frontiers of those discrete ethnic cultures which also happen to coincide with the contours of a sovereign nation state that guarantees their continuity. (30–1)

The lead characters of Mukherjee's *The Holder of the World*, Pinckney's *High Cotton*, Rushdie's *Midnight's Children* and *The Moor's Last Sigh*, and Kincaid's *The Autobiography of My Mother* all possess a self-reflexive awareness of the reciprocal constitution of subjects and nations even as they contend with a variety of forces, historical and psychoanalytic, which challenge the unity of those (their own) identities. Each character strives to define and maintain social standing despite prevailing social ideologies that would render each one, like Shabine, invisible, marginal, or forgotten. The characters seek social recognition at once within and against the images of the nation as family at their disposal.

My readings of the texts follow their search for stable subjects, nations, and histories. The novels all address the movement from yearning for stability to finding of both power and pleasure in provisionality. What they ultimately reveal is that an embrace of provisional over stable constructions of subject and nation provides the most effective challenge to the strictures of normativity. This process simultaneously destabilizes more comfortable identifications while enabling those who hold them to learn to value identities otherwise shunned. The novels also trace a historical continuum of colonization, independence, and neo-colonialism that stretches over the past 500 years and includes America, the Caribbean, and India. With these far-ranging texts, I want not to universalize the experience of colonization itself, but to read the pervasiveness of the patriarchal family metaphor across traditional literary and geographic boundaries in relation to its particular cultural deployments.

As a primary goal of the argument is to show how wrestling with this metaphor in different cultural contexts potentially expands the range of alternative modernities, the grouping necessarily departs from more traditional literary categories of geography, history, literary style, or authorship. Instead the five novels share, in addition to their contemporaneity, a preoccupation with the nation as family and a perspective that quite self-consciously is neither acquiescently reflective of what Kaja Silverman calls the dominant fiction nor starkly resistant to it. Each author contends with the effects of patriarchal ideology while maintaining a critical distance from it, thereby concretizing anthropologist Katherine Pratt Ewing's argument for a theoretical space between "hegemony as a control over public discursive space" and "consciousness" (5). It is this space or critical distance that I seek to reveal and expand in my readings of the novels. Locating critical distance within this range of postcolonial texts means dismantling the opposition between the Western modern self and the other.

Focusing on the nation as patriarchal family illuminates the metaphor's circulation through the overlapping discourses of national identity and subject formation, and asks us to rethink our easy acceptance of its terms. The role of the family, and with it gender identifications, in structuring "normative" subjects is a central tenet of Freudian and Lacanian psychoanalysis. Given that our conceptions of modern subjects and nations arose simultaneously, it is perhaps unsurprising that the metaphor plays a primary role in national identity as well. Predicated on the division of gender, the family metaphor, as Anne McClintock writes in *Dangerous Liaisons*, helps explain the nation's conflicted, yet continuous, identity through time. By ascribing to women representation of the nation's "atavistic and authentic body of [. . .] tradition" and to men its "progressive, or revolutionary, principle of discontinuity" (92), the family metaphor provides a convenient, seemingly "natural" model for reconciling violent historical change. The image of the patriarchal family is so widespread, McClintock adds, because it "sanction[s] national hierarchy within a putative organic unity of interests" while also offering a "'natural' trope for figuring national time" (91). The metaphor works to the extent that it can provide a common image for collective identification through a conflation of gender roles, cultural motifs, and national history. In this way we experience what Deleuze and Guattari term the "imperialism of Oedipus."

Although it is not uncommon to hear that the nation is fast becoming obsolete as a political and social category, sidelined by the ostensibly invisible superstructure of the market, such arguments ignore the ways in which the metaphors that hold together our worlds remain largely unchanged. Feminism suffered a similar challenge in the 1970s when, just as women began to lay claim to powerful subject positions, the subject itself was declared "dead." The danger of ignoring the prevailing metaphors of social life, as Donna Haraway pointedly warns, is that "we end up with a kind of epistemological electro-shock therapy, which far from ushering us into the high stakes tables of the game of contesting public truths, lays us out on the table with self-induced multiple personality disorder" (*Simians, Cyborgs, and Women*, 186). Even if the nation is declining as a primary form of social identification, and this is debatable, we need to understand its effects in order to imagine new, more equitable ways of seeing ourselves and our worlds.

In the chapters that follow, I examine the intersections between poststructuralist psychoanalysis, focusing primarily upon the work of Kaja Silverman and Judith Butler, and postcolonial theory. The latter field grows increasingly complicated as it responds to the evolution of countries that are no longer newly postcolonial, the increasing circulation of global capital and the English language (each with imperial tendencies), and the needs of those communities traditionally omitted from the grand narratives of either nation or subject. To chart a path through this theoretical labyrinth, I draw mostly on the work of those postcolonial scholars, such as Homi Bhabha and Anne McClintock, among others, who share some of the concerns if not the methodologies of psychoanalysis. I also bring my own background in the study of history and national planning to bear in situating the theoretical and literary readings in specific historical contexts.

While the intersection of the two theoretical fields in the metaphor of the patriarchal family provides the foundation of my project, it is a foundation frequently under siege from novels. What I argue, and what the novels reveal, is that possibilities of re-imagining subjectivity and nationhood exceed the bounds of the very theoretical approaches that enable my readings. While the nation as family continues to proliferate through contemporary fiction, that fiction simultaneously regenerates, revises, and subverts the metaphor itself. Thus, the real power of my argument is located in the aesthetic. Although the aesthetic realm in each of the novels may promise a wider range of possible identifications than are available in other daily forums, as in Walcott's poem that promise is always circumscribed by historical context. The aesthetic functions here not as an ahistorical, transcultural category of set standards, but as aspects of each text which hold its deepest affective charges; those charges, moreover, derive their power from the social context of both text and reader.

The aesthetic, like psychoanalysis, is inseparable from the order it critiques. Harpham defines the aesthetic through this "theoretical confusion": "the undecidability between object and subject, freedom and repressive law, critical and uncritical passages, grievous and necessary misreadings, even art and ideology" (135). Yet out of this paradoxical and ambivalent relationship comes the possibility of achieving, through the workings of the imagination at the deepest levels of belief, not just a sense of our own limitations, but what Alan Shapiro describes as "that empathetic power of entering into the moral experience of others." He adds that this "capacity for ethical discrimination [. . .] can alter the very conventions which inform it" (11). I focus on the aesthetic precisely because its current conceptions arose contemporaneously with those of the subject and nation, such that all three work together to define modernity on the broadest level. My critique of the workings of the family metaphor in characterizing modernity thus stems from the ability of the ethical imagination to render "what we know best into something strange and puzzling, thereby enabling us to see our lives, the apparent givenness and stability of our arrangements, as only a way of living, as a contingent set of possibilities always open to reform or corruption" (Shapiro 26).

The Holder of the World introduces the gendered terms of the patriarchal family that are foundational to a Western understanding of modern identity, predicated on autonomy and individual rights. The novel manifests the seemingly unquenchable desire for a unified subject and nation even as it initiates their undoing. As a revision of Nathaniel Hawthorne's *The Scarlet Letter*, *The Holder of the World* emphasizes the link between canon formation, the control of knowledge, and national identity. Mukherjee's goal is to revise all three by incorporating the ethnic or racial other—the product of colonization—into the nation as family. Drawing on the aesthetic terms of the American romance and of Mughal miniature paintings, she moves from mimicry (in aesthetic and psychoanalytic terms) to reinvention of American national identity.

Both *The Holder of the World* and *High Cotton* emphasize the contemporary legacy of America's colonialism, slavery, and imperialism. Pinckney moves beyond Mukherjee in his critique of that legacy by focusing on the marginalization of a distinct community (African Americans) rather than on the promise of seamless integration. He also unmasks historical trauma, expressed in terms overdetermined by gender and race, as integral to the provisionality we *all* hold. Learning to accept both that common provisionality and a communal identity frees the African American narrator from the oppressive desire for dominant whiteness. This conclusion, although it remains within the nation as family model, undermines its traditional racial bias.

The metaphor of the nation as family becomes more explicit as well as more complicated in Rushdie's *Midnight's Children* and *The Moor's Last Sigh*. Both novels are constructed around the literalization of the metaphor as the main characters' lives correspond to national history. At the same time, the patriarchal model of the nation as family, a legacy of colonization, competes with the matriarchal image of Mother India to hold the subjects' identifications. In the end, dissolution of narrator and nation, though both cling to familial forms, results in a privileging of the imaginative aesthetic as the site of meaning and pleasure. It seeks to heal the wounds of the subject and the nation. In *Midnight's Children*, the oral narrative, which Rushdie invokes throughout the novel, serves as the regenerative antidote to the narrator's decline. *The Moor's Last Sigh*, with its depiction of great murals, portraits, abstract art, and, finally, popular culture, insists on a much broader reading of the aesthetic as the glue that holds national culture together.

Finally, in *The Autobiography of My Mother*, Kincaid provides the most damning critique of the (white, patriarchal) nation as family, insisting that it *always* enslaves and silences its marginal members (people of color and women). She opposes Shabine's flight from history, as she argues for both an accounting and a conscious rejection of the nation as family metaphor, although she stops short of offering an alternative to it. The novel's negative conclusion at once demands a critical distance from the nation as family and finds less solace in the text's own aesthetic workings. *The Autobiography of My Mother* insists on the post-colonial subject's need to claim and wield power in order to re-imagine, as the title suggests, the relationship between self and other.

The novels continually remind us of the limits of theory. No single identificatory image or model, even one as widespread in both literary and theoretical texts as the nation as family, can fully account for the entire range of identities and agencies subject or nation may assume at a given historical moment. While my focus here is on modern subjectivity and national identity's common topographies, a term that incorporates both metaphors and mechanisms of identification, this focus does not preclude learning to see otherwise barred images to which subject or nation may also lay claim. The malleable precision to convey meaning or emotion that language possesses exceeds any singular image or ideology, whether aesthetic, historical, or theoretical. Even if, as I argue here, subjectivity and national identity share an ideological framework based upon certain culturally determined discursive limitations, the subject constituted in and by that discourse must always find his or her own words with which to speak.

In *The Psychic Life of Power*, Judith Butler defines these two forms of discursive power comprising subjectivity as ideologically connected, but not identical: "Power considered as a condition of the subject is necessarily not the same as power considered as what the subject is said to wield. The power that initiates the subject fails to remain continuous with the power that is the subject's agency" (12). While ideology may delineate the range of the subject's speech and the forms of its social existence, it cannot account for every expression of that existence because the complexity of human experience supersedes any pre-given set of representations. The resulting flexibility does not come close to outweighing the force of prevailing ideologies which structure our "reality," making it recognizable and thus "real," but it nonetheless exists and forms a basis for challenging normative representations. What the novels illuminate is that this goal necessitates the subject having achieved critical distance from his or her own governing ideologies. To help create that critical distance, I focus here on the ways in which the aesthetic, working through the stimulation of memory and desire, both depends upon and disrupts the texts' foundational metaphors—those of the family that bind subjectivity and national identity.

CHAPTER 1

SUBJECTIVITY, NATIONAL IDENTITY, AND THE AESTHETIC

> To articulate the past historically does not mean to recognize it "the way it really was" . . . . It means to seize hold of a memory as it flashes up at a moment of danger.
>
> Walter Benjamin, *Theses on the Philosophy of History, VI*

Political Foundations

As building blocks of a modern ideological framework, subject and nation are united in form and function. In *Political Theory and Modernity*, William Connolly describes how subject and nation are indivisibly linked in the project of modernity, yet always compete over which holds "the privileged site of agency" (3). The constitution of subjectivity and national identity through a shared symbolic order and their dependence upon one another keep their competition in check in order to maintain ideological continuity. The expression of the relationship between nation and citizen-subject as a division of public and private further protects that continuity. Two sides of the same coin, public and private delineate supposedly separate sets of identifications and agencies throughout the subject and nation's mediating spheres of civil society, including the market and the family. Mutually dependent yet nominally distinct, public and private function analogously to the two forms of power Butler defines within subjectivity. For even as she notes that the power the subject possesses to act on its desires is not the same as that which inaugurates it, she insists on their inseparability: "To desire the conditions of one's own subordination is thus required to persist as oneself" (*PLP*, 9).

Connolly describes a parallel situation on societal level. "We begin to discern," he explains, "how the institutions of civil society constitute the forms through which we achieve identity and how reconciliation to the imperatives of this institutional matrix is essential to maintaining and perfecting that identity [. . .]. It is the state experienced as an external entity, understood to act upon the self, but not yet understood to enter internally into the very constitution of the self and the ethical life which holds the totality together" (PTM, 118). The sense of coherence comes not from state apparatus that tries to enforce it, but from a belief in the nation as "a people" implicitly comprising unified subjects who have relinquished to the state a measure of their intrinsic sovereignty. The state guarantees the safety of its citizen-subjects, tries to instill sense of solidarity, and promises to protect private differences in exchange for public allegiance. For allegiance to become national unity, however, depends upon constituents, in Ernest Renan's apt phrase, "being obliged to have forgotten" the fractures in their communal history. As Benedict Anderson remarks in his reading of the passage, Renan's syntax "suggests, in the ominous tone of revenue-codes and military conscription laws, that 'already having forgotten' ancient tragedies is a prime contemporary civic duty. In effect, Renan's readers were being told to 'have already forgotten' what Renan's own words assumed that they naturally remembered!" (200).

As Anderson's reading points out, memory produces potential disruptions to the ideological continuity of subjectivity and national identity. Required to fulfill simultaneously public and private functions within a model based on the division of those two spheres, memory continually threatens to collapse the distinction between them. Even as subjects "forget" the violence foundational to national unity, they face daily reminders of state aggression, directed both internally and externally, aimed at maintaining a unified public. The more state power to regulate social life is challenged by international economic forces or by intra-national community interests, the more often the state, Connolly writes in Identity/Difference: Democratic Negotiations of Political Paradox, "sustains collective theatrical displays of punishment and revenge against those elements that threaten to signify its inefficacy. It launches dramatized crusades against the internal other (low-level criminals, drug users, disloyalists, racial minorities, and the underclass), the external other (foreign enemies and terrorists), and the interior other (those strains of abnormality, subversion, and perversity that may reside within anyone)" (206). Sovereignty becomes increasingly dependent on maintaining normative representations despite the fact that it derives from a promise to protect (private) individual differences.

The theoretical models engendering this project similarly bring this tension between public and private to the fore. While much political, and more specifically postcolonial, theory focuses on the historical and material conditions of modernity as imperialism, psychoanalysis often lays claim to the supposedly universal (and, therefore, timeless) subject's internal life. Each theoretical model alone runs the risk of reducing the flux of experience to fit within a singular understanding of what counts in defining subjectivity; and that danger may be compounded by an attempt to combine strands of postcolonial and psychoanalytic theories into a single determinant narrative. Katherine Pratt Ewing, in her recent anthropological study of Sufi mysticism in the context of modernity and psychoanalysis, warns of these methodological dangers:

> in theories that posit the past hegemony of an overarching colonial discourse and the ever-tightening hegemony of modernity, the postcolonial has been identified as the ruptured subject par excellence, survivor of a political domination and supposedly hegemonic order in which the subject was interpellated as a radically subordinate "other" to the Western "self." Such postcolonial subjects—for whom "tradition" has been devalued and frozen—would seem to face a rupture with the past and a slide into a condition of rootless modernity. This postcolonial subject has been characterized as a new, distinctly modern phenomenon, severed from its cultural roots by the behemoth of a global capitalist system, its consciousness sundered by the persuasive power of identities shaped by a divisive discourse of nationalism that generates newly imagined communities based on supposedly primordial ties of language, religion, and ethnicity. (7)

Whether read internally or externally, the postcolonial subject's experience is reduced to terms recognizable by the theoretical models. Despite their seemingly opposite domains, moreover, both theoretical approaches begin with an assumption of imperialism as foundational to understanding contemporary postcolonial subjects. Unsurprisingly the methodological language reinforces this assumption, for a postcolonial subject or nation, as such, is defined in relationship to colonial experience that is itself an integral aspect of modernity. Similarly, the discourses of both modernity and (post-)Freudian psychoanalysis, with their focus on change, progress, and self-determination, present models of consciousness which the experiencing subject either achieves or, if "held back" by tradition or neuroses, wants.

Ewing combines Gramsci's conception of public hegemony with Lacanian psychoanalysis to distinguish between subjectivity and discursive positions. Her goal is to separate the subject's potential for critical distance from modernity. According to Ewing's reading of Lacan, the lack occasioned by the subject's entry into the Symbolic Order (by the subject's "giving up" of him- or herself in order to become recognizable in social terms) produces a space in which the subject may escape the dictates of that order. Subject formation then, takes places during the mirror stage, the recognition of oneself as other and the internalization of an imaginary sense of coherence, prior to entry into the Symbolic Order of cultural representation. She brings together Gramscian and Lacanian modes of understanding experience to argue for "the possibility of a critical distance, from which the subject—the 'organic intellectual'—may recognize the condition of its own constitution" (36). This critical distance results from the multiple discourses surrounding the subject at any given time and not from modernity itself. Self-consciousness read as an effect or indication of modernity, she argues, renders the pre-modern subject grossly unaware of ideology, "a presumption that itself reproduces the tradition–modern dichotomy that deconstruction of Western discourse so decisively undercut" (20). Critical distance also depends upon her reading of a chronology of subject formation, such that subjectivity pre-exists its socially determined terms of identification.

The novels I discuss in the following chapters share Ewing's insistence on the broad range of formative experience and on self-reflexivity that transcends historical markers of modernity and tradition. In *The Holder of the World*, the female protagonists in both America and India, from the early seventeenth century to the present, consciously challenge normative practices through such diverse means as their choice of clothing, sexual partners, and language. *High Cotton* presents contemporary self-consciousness and critical distance as a result of the lasting impact of the historical violence of slavery; self-consciousness, therefore, overruns any particular historical moment. Rushdie's novels confuse all boundaries between tradition and modernity through the sheer excess of characters who themselves could not and do not make any such distinctions. Rushdie parodies any such discussion of national representations as "the endless talk about *the West as problematic* and *the myth of authenticity* and *the logic of the dream*" (*MLS*, 201). These parodies do not obviate questions of historical and cultural difference, but warn instead against any assumption of a specifically modern self-consciousness, accessible only to those who have embraced a particular version of modernity. In *The Autobiography of My Mother*, Xuela achieves critical distance from and some semblance of mastery over the social structures that seek to deny her all forms of love, power, pleasure, and meaning. She does so without recourse to nostalgia or tradition, yet while emphasizing the historical roots of her oppression.

Although the novels support the goals of Ewing's approach, they also call into question the division between public and private upon which her theoretical model rests. Maintaining that division limits an understanding of just how pervasive ideology is, how its success depends on the ability to fit the contours of the subject's life, how subjectivity always occurs within culture, and how difficult it is to recognize and to act within a critical distance, regardless of historical context. Sunil Khilnani provides an excellent example of the complex effects of imperialism on subjectivity and identification in *The Idea of India*. Those effects include the way the postcolonial nation-state creates its own categories of subjects, defining the terms with which subjects identify themselves and seek social recognition rather than self-consciousness in and of itself. Arguing that the "idea of India" is modern in that it derives from "agencies" of "European colonial expansion, the state, nationalism, democracy, [and] economic development," he points to the newly created realm of state politics as the site where this idea is realized (5). In contrast to the United States Constitution, which defined a relationship between individual rights and state power, the Indian Constitution, Khilnani writes, "established a language of community rights" that simultaneously produced bearers of those rights (36). That Constitution provides its fullest benefits to Indians who identify themselves as members of distinct, protected communities, rather than as individuals with discrete rights. Subsequent political development has transformed these traditional religious and social groups into vehicles of political agency. We can see one of the clearest examples of this in the electoral success of the Hindu nationalist Bharatiya Janata Party (BJP) and the internal popularity of its recent nuclear tests. Khilnani attributes this trend to the decline in the secular Congress Party's efficacy following Indira Gandhi's "Emergency" (the suspension of civil rights in 1975–77). Community identities, protected by the Constitution, rose in the vacuum left by the Congress Party's reorganization on the local level and then its loss of national power. Khilnani concludes "the fact that such identities were less significant for four decades after independence, and then surged into national politics, only shows how much they are creations of modern politics, not residues of the past" (59).

Khilnani's reading of the political basis of "the idea of India" works with Ewing's argument to underscore the difficulty of disentangling traditional and modern identities, even though both describe the effects of imperialism on contemporary subjects. In order to pursue their goals without re-inscribing the line between public and private, I want to see how critical distance can arise not from the space between hegemony and consciousness, nation and subject, or history and psychoanalysis, but from the topographies those categories share.

* * *

Psychoanalytic Foundations

Throughout this book, I argue that subject and nation depend upon mutual agencies that together form the foundation for primary forms of social identification in American, British, and, often, postcolonial nations. If we define the modern nation as having a shared sense of belonging that rests on a state apparatus ensuring autonomy, self-determination, economic development, global standing, and national planning, then their subjects must necessarily reflect or embody the nation's "individuality." In order to see these terms as ideologically deployed rather than as natural expressions of historical "progress," we need to examine their constitutive role in the very formation of subjectivity and in structuring paths of identification.

In *Male Subjectivity at the Margins*, Kaja Silverman provides a model of subjectivity, drawn from Althusser and Lacan, which emphasizes the cultural context of subject formation and all of the subject's subsequent identifications. Silverman's objective is to divorce psychoanalysis from paternal law as the inevitable ontological foundation of the subject and to examine ways in which male subjectivity may subvert what she calls the dominant fiction of patriarchy. The dominant fiction is a supra-ideology, encapsulating the privileged signifiers which structure the Lacanian Symbolic Order as well as subjects' "imaginary affirmation" of the cultural images within which they recognize themselves (*MSM*, 24); it is, thus, the "primary agency of social consensus" and incorporates ideologies of class, race, and sexuality (*MSM*, 28). Integral to both subject formation and material existence, the dominant fiction connects psychic and social life through a set of privileged ideological signifiers, foremost among them in Western culture, the phallus. I argue, with Silverman, that those privileged signifiers of subject and nation create the conditions of their own undoing by producing subjects who may consciously breach the layered ideologies of the dominant fiction.

The usefulness of Silverman's model in this regard comes from its separation of paternal law as an ideology playing a constitutive role in subject formation from paternal law as an essential marker of subjectivity. Following Lévi-Strauss, she argues that, while the incest taboo functions universally to distinguish nature from culture, and therefore designates kinship a primary model for understanding subjectivity, the incest prohibition itself takes various forms depending upon cultural and historical context. As she explains in *The Subject of Semiotics*, "[s]ince in Western societies, the forbidden alliances are those between father and daughter, and mother and son, unconscious desire most frequently takes an Oedipal form" (73). The subject's very existence is driven by desire (to achieve social standing) and depends upon entry into the social order of kinship and language. The universal Law of Language demands that the inauguration of subjectivity take place through "castration or lack [which] entails both the loss of being, and the subject's subordination to a discursive order which pre-exists, exceeds, and substantially 'speaks it' " (*MSM*, 35). In other words, in order to become socially viable, the subject attempts to satisfy his or her most basic desire by identifying with the images made available through the symbolic order: entry into language inaugurates subjectivity by creating the conditions of its expression. The form that the Law of Language takes, however, is neither universal nor essential, but ideologically coded by the incest taboo and its normative terms, in Western culture, of the Oedipus complex, the Name-of-the-Father, and phallic power. This means that the subject's fundamental desire (Lacan's "petit objet *a*"), the desire for what must be sacrificed in order to "exist" within the social structure, is inevitable, yet ideologically scripted. That foundational desire, forever insatiable, triggers the subsequent unconscious and conscious desires that drive mental activity.

For my purposes, the key aspect of Silverman's description of the dominant fiction is the way its privileged signifiers, drawn from the paternal family of the Oedipus complex, function on multiple ideological levels to create our understanding of the world. As Silverman notes, "our present dominant fiction is above all else the representational system through which the subject is accommodated to the Name-of-the-Father [. . . and whose] most central signifier of unity is the (paternal) family." This unity depends upon a binary gender opposition which functions metaphorically to produce "many other ideological elements, such as signifiers like 'town' and 'nation,' or the antithesis of power and the people" (*MSM*, 35). The paternal family forms the basis for the Western subject's experience of the world and the identifications that make that subject socially recognizable. Thus, we see the terms of the paternal family reproduced in discourses of modernity, race, nationhood, and capitalism; those terms provide the glue that holds our sense of "reality" together.

While Silverman focuses on how the dominant fiction shapes subject formation, her explanation of the central role of the family and paternal power in connecting psychic and social life dovetails with Connolly's description of nationhood and political modernity. In both Silverman and Connolly's models, we can see how the dominant fiction naturalizes its effects through the illusion of a public–private division. Silverman details how the subject's supposedly interior, essential life depends upon the same set of terms as its social contexts; Connolly similarly emphasizes the way in which civil institutions such as family and market create ideological continuity between what we call the public and private experiences of the citizen-subject.

The image of the family provides a key bridge between these two theoretical approaches, located, as it is in both, at the intersection of public and private. In *Dangerous Liaisons* and *Imperial Leather*, Anne McClintock focuses on this intersection in her analysis of the relationship between the family and modernity. The temporal disjunctions between the nation's timelessness and its development are "typically resolved by figuring the contradiction in the representation of *time* as a natural division of *gender*" (*DL*, 92). Integral to McClintock's analysis of the gendering of the nation as family is the way the metaphor contributes to imperialism and, in doing so, makes imperialism a defining attribute of Western modernity (*IL*, 5). Not only did the image of the family tree of man, popularized by Darwinism at the height of the British Empire, legitimate (naturalize) a notion of progress predicated on whiteness and masculinity, but this image, when applied to nation-building and imperialist expansion, "enabled what was often murderously violent change to be legitimized as the progressive unfolding of natural decree [. . .]. The trope of the organic family became invaluable in its capacity to give state and imperial intervention the alibi of nature" (*IL*, 45). McClintock insists we recognize how the nation as family is itself a historical construct, a specific vision of domestic life arising out of nineteenth-century European economic and philosophical developments, and how it operates through and subsumes metaphors of gender and race; at the same time, she insists that we remember the material effects—the nonmetaphorical consequences—of the nation as family as ideology.[1]

Jacques Donzelot, Ann Laura Stoler, and Amit S. Rai, among others, expand upon McClintock's argument in crucial ways by showing how the family functions not merely as a model for governmentality in imperial centers and colonial outposts, but also as a mechanism or instrument of it. Writing about the role of the family in the development and maintenance of the bourgeois order, Donzelot, in *The Policing of Families*, notes that the family is "indispensable" to that order: "This is owing to [the family's] function as an anchorage point for private property and its function of reproduction of the ruling ideology, for which purpose alone its authority is recognized and mandated" (xx). Subsequent chapters describe the "transition from a government of families to a government through the family," whence the family serves as a mechanism for enforcing economic and social normativity (92). This is not to say that the family simply reproduces or functions as a simulacrum of the ruling ideology, but, on the contrary, that it is most effective in its ability both to contain deviance and inspire political acquiescence (93–4). Donzelot reads the " 'psy' discourses" as complicit with this trend in the ways they position the family as at once "the only model for socialization and the source of all dissatisfactions" (230). In agreement with and response to this criticism, I argue throughout these chapters that psychoanalytic theory, while complicit with the orders I use it to critique, also holds a means of resistance to those orders. By insisting on the paternal family as an ideological construct, we gain the distance necessary to begin to separate ourselves from its symbolic functions, ultimately deconstructing the very models upon which psychoanalysis currently rests.

Stoler and Rai argue that Donzelot's "policing of families" becomes, in colonial contexts, a fundamental tool of social control in what Stoler calls, "colonial politics of exclusion" (345). She examines the ways in which such politics were enacted through the regulation of domestic arrangements, defined by race and gender, of both European colonials and colonized subjects. Guaranteeing white, middle-class privilege in the colonies depended upon economic and legal control of marriage and concubinage of both the colonized and those white women who were either allowed or encouraged to join white men there. The family thus became an instrument of imperialism in fostering the "embourgeoisement of colonial communities" through the "sharpening of racial lines" (351). Rai looks specifically at the role of sympathy, "the first of all domestic affections" (13), in these colonial processes, arguing that historically, sympathy has been inseparable from policing even as he suggests alternative relationships between sympathy and humanitarianism (166–7). These approaches to the family—as an instrument of governmentality—share an insistence that metaphor alone fails to account for its crucial role. While I agree that reading the effects of the nation as family metaphor does not fully explicate the workings of colonial governmentality, I believe it elucidates its ruling ideology and makes possible various forms of resistance to that ideology. These approaches, despite the wariness Donzelot and Stoler express toward psychoanalysis, work well in tandem to show how ideology maintains the allegiance of its subjects and reproduces itself materially; at the same time, they suggest two possible avenues of resistance.

Reading imperialism as integral to modernity and the nation as family as its primary instrument and metaphor runs the risk, as Ewing warns, of reducing postcolonials to exemplars of damaged subjectivity. In *Monsters and Revolutionaries*, Françoise Vergès emphasizes this danger in her critique of the Lacanian psychoanalysis in the postcolonial context of the island of Réunion. In her reading of the application, by French psychiatrists, of Lacan's three orders to Creoles on Réunion, Vergès shows how easily Lacanian psychoanalysis may be made complicit with colonization. The psychiatrists' relegation of the Reunionnais to an Imaginary realm defined by primitivism and the inability "to think in concepts and ideas" as opposed to the doctors' own rational, Symbolic realm inevitably provided a racist logic for the continuation of colonial power (229–30). Silverman's work helps us avoid this re-inscription of the opposition between Western coherence and postcolonial lack by emphasizing the lack at the center of *all* subjects. By focusing on the metaphor of the nation as (paternal) family as a key ideological stress point upholding the dominant fiction, we can read discourses of the modern subject and nation against themselves, across the divide of public and private, and across the political spectrum of colonial and postcolonial power. Such counter-reading reveals the ways in which the metaphor fails to produce the coherent subjects and nations it promises and, in the cracks in coherency, enables us to rediscover valuable identities our dominant fiction otherwise bars. In each of the novels I discuss, cultural difference and historical trauma, both of which are consistently gendered, disrupt ideological continuity, repeatedly illustrating weaknesses in the narrative of modernity as a conflation of patriarchy, capitalist power, and progress.

The Holder of the World, set in colonial Salem and India and contemporary Cambridge (Massachusetts), marks the limits of the "modern nation" and its narratives. The contemporary narrator, Beigh, culls her story from traditional historical sources (shipping records, paintings, letters, newspaper reports, etc.) and from a virtual reality "re-creation" of historical events. As a revision of *The Scarlet Letter* that locates itself in the gaps in Hawthorne's chronology, the novel explicitly raises the question of what it means to write the nation and how the literary canon as a storehouse of shared discourse is implicated in national identity. In Mukherjee's version, however, the threat female desire poses to social stability is compounded by its trespass of racial boundaries—the "A" for

Adultery here becomes "I" for Indian lover, though Mukherjee celebrates rather than condemns illicit desire. Memory plays a dual role in rethinking the connection between desire and identity in the novel. *The Holder of the World* revises the literary canon, a kind of national memory bank, to include the liberation of female desire across racial and cultural barriers and, therefore, to make ethnic diversity an integral component of national identity. The resurfacing of colonial Hannah's repressed childhood memories, of the identifications that society forbids, in moments of intense psychological excitation (Freud's cathexis) drives this revision. Hannah's unleashed desire, which descends seemingly genealogically to present-day Beigh, ultimately fails to disrupt the narrative of modernity as (white) paternal power: the novel ends with the containment of desire by a masculinized fantasy of cultural assimilation, historical mastery, and capitalist expansion. Despite the final triumph of the nation as family metaphor, with all of its complementary economic and political effects, however, *The Holder of the World* presents strategies for contesting that metaphor and expanding the literary canon and the nation's memory to include "other" kinds of Americans.

High Cotton locates the connection between whiteness and paternal power in US history in the novel's examination of the lasting effects of historical trauma. The African American narrator struggles to come to terms with the contemporary material and metaphoric legacies of slavery. Pervasive racism serves as a continual reminder of the fissures in the nation's history that the nation as (white, paternal) family metaphor attempts to elide. The narrator's own experience reflects an ongoing disjunction between the identities he would claim intellectually for himself and those ascribed to him based on the corporeal "evidence" of race. In recognizing that the governing social metaphor conflates masculinity and whiteness, thereby relegating him solely to negative identifications, the narrator learns to look again at his own bodily and discursive positions in order to move beyond the identities proffered by the dominant fiction.

In *Midnight's Children* and *The Moor's Last Sigh*, Rushdie's narrators function as spokesmen for, and symbols of, the nation's history, and their bodies and families reflect national events. Rushdie's extravagant style, his "teeming" narratives underscore the inadequacy of the family trope, whether based on the patriarchal model of European colonization or the popular image of Mother India: both fail to create unitary subjects or a singular image of the nation. The metaphors barely hold together the flamboyant plots they generate. In *Midnight's Children*, the fantasy of nation creation and self-creation is personified in Saleem as author, narrator, subject, and nation. At the same time, Rushdie reveals the fantasy itself as flawed: Saleem's memory is faulty, his telling meandering, his genealogies false, and his body on the verge of shattering into "specks of voiceless dust," which will be "sucked into the annihilating whirlpool of the multitudes" (552). *The Moor's Last Sigh* is in many ways a sequel to *Midnight's Children*, though here the narrator, the Moor, represents just one facet of the nation's history and competes with other characters to present himself as the face of the nation. Both novels end with the simultaneous dissolution of nation and narrator, suggesting that neither the metaphor nor the theoretical models used to describe it is wholly capable of explaining contemporary identities. To offset the despair of dissolution and fragmentation, however, Rushdie offers his fantastical aesthetics that strive to provide the coherence and continuity the nation as family itself cannot deliver. These aesthetic realms are at once idealistic and aware of their limitations, seeking above all else to provide access to the memories and desires necessary for imaginative renewal, if not renewal itself.

The Autobiography of My Mother demands a rethinking of how we depend on the nation as family metaphor for a sense of historical and individual coherence. Like Rushdie, Kincaid explores maternal and paternal genealogies while simultaneously refusing any return to essential gender, racial, or national identities. This approach forbids any nostalgic return to pre-colonial identities even as it valorizes the self-aware and powerful female subject. The narrator, Xuela, insists on the centrality of the nation as family in structuring her own subjectivity even as she tries to move beyond it. Thus, I argue in chapter 5 that adding maternal to paternal power does not in itself expand the range of identities we commonly recognize; rather, Kincaid's novel underscores our need to reconfigure radically our idealizations in order to see ourselves in those separated from us by historical trauma, gender, or race. Her novel works with the theoretical perspectives to define my central concern: *how aesthetics may bring the terms of our governing ideologies to the forefront while enabling us to see beyond them.* At the same time, the novel elucidates the failure of postcolonial and psychoanalytic theories to conceptualize the alternatives they, and the novels, demand. The theoretical models do not provide a lens through which to read the fiction; rather, the fiction explicitly invokes the models and their conceptual limitations.

In all five novels, the narrators gradually come to question their relationship to prevailing social ideologies as the identifications most readily available fail to reflect their own understanding of their experiences. The crises in identification become most acute as heretofore buried memories surface (or "new" memories are imagined), giving shape and substance to those experiences in ways unsanctioned by the dominant fiction. In these instances, "reality," or the subjects' perspectives of themselves and their worlds, falters and creates a space for the critical distance Ewing describes. While the outcomes and historical circumstances among the texts differ, all work toward the denaturalization of the nation as family within narratives of imperialism and (as) modernity.

* * *

Subjectivity and Critical Distance

The question remains of how literary subjects, their authors, and readers may achieve critical distance from the very terms that define their worlds. Even if we see critical self-consciousness as a faculty that subjects may develop throughout history, we need to account for the way that faculty may challenge the subject's situated identifications rather than subjectivity itself. This problem is both political and methodological. If, on a political level, subjectivity only makes sense in the ideologically coded terms of the dominant fiction, then how can a subject come to transform or even reject what renders his or her own consciousness possible? We must ask the same question of the psychoanalytic methods that define this problem, methods themselves embedded in the cultural contexts they critique. In their readings and revisions of fundamental Freudian and Lacanian psychic topographies, Kaja Silverman and Judith Butler address both questions. In different though complementary ways, Silverman and Butler show us how psychoanalysis may be used, in a sense against itself, to examine the subversive potential of the very subjects the methodology itself produces. By focusing on both the ways in which subjectivity, identification, and desire are culturally constructed as well as the limits of understanding these processes from within them, Silverman and Butler achieve a critical distance from their own approaches. That critical distance helps rescue psychoanalysis from its own sexist and racist history (its privileging of the white, heterosexual male as the universal subject), making it useful in understanding a complex array of social phenomena.

Drawing primarily on Freud's *The Interpretation of Dreams* and *Beyond the Pleasure Principle*, Silverman, in *The Subject of Semiotics*, provides an overview of one of Freud's earliest models in order to describe the inseparability of subjectivity and signification. Even though Freud's own model changes in his later writing, and Lacan's work builds on those changes, this early description of the psyche illustrates simply the subject's ideological construction and potential to exceed the conditions of its own making. Dividing psychic topography into memory, the unconscious, and the preconscious, Freud describes how perception generates memories that leave imprints, or mnemic traces, in sensory form on the mind. As, in Silverman's words, the "raw signifying material" of the unconscious, mnemic traces also contain the mind's most powerful emotional reservoirs (SS, 55). The unconscious, as the storehouse of these affective traces, holds all the subject's repressed material. Defined by its repressed contents, the unconscious is as culturally determined as preconscious and conscious activity. The preconscious, meanwhile, functions as the sieve for cultural norms, filtering out trace images that do not assume culturally acceptable forms before allowing unconscious material to become conscious.

What remains behind in the unconscious are those mnemic traces which, at least in their current form, cannot pass the mental censors and which hold the highest affective value, while the material reaching the preconscious assumes a less affective and more narrative presentation. That presentation contributes to the easing of the mind's tensions (cathectic relief), according to the dictates of the pleasure principle, by presenting a limited range of psychic and affective material and thus assuaging the excitations initiated by desire. Silverman explains that, "[w]hereas [the unconscious] strives to recover the full sensory and affective value of the desired mnemic trace, [the preconscious] tries to exclude sensory and affective values in favor of the connections between that mnemic trace and those adjacent to it; it attempts to recover the relationships between one memory and those related to it logically or chronologically" (SS, 59). Since desire, the catalyst for mental activity, is always a desire *for* something, and thus arises from an awareness of lack (a lack both Freud and Lacan separate from biological need or instinct), the subject negotiates the dual demands of desire and narrative satisfaction. The pleasure yielded by preconscious filtering and arranging of these traces, what Freud calls the secondary process (*The Interpretation of Dreams*), comes at the expense of the deep, yet inexpressible affectation of what remains unconscious.

Even in this early topography of the subject, before Freud reworks his terms into the id, ego, and super-ego, we find two crucial components for understanding subjective experience: the key role of the body in the formation of mnemic traces (through perception) and the inseparability of subjectivity and culture. Together they insist that we recognize corporeality itself, marked by race, gender, and an unlimited host of other physical attributes, as culturally coded. When Freud discusses mnemic traces in *The Interpretation of Dreams*, he notes that, although the perception itself has no memory, it "provides our consciousness with the whole multiplicity of sensory qualities" (578). There are two processes through which sensory-bearing memories may generate mental activity. Through the unconscious workings of the mind, what he later terms the primary process, those images, when called forth by desire, are condensed or displaced onto alternative images, similarly laden with libidinal or affective weight and with sensory data, in an attempt to bypass the prohibitions of socially regulated consciousness. The alternative images, selected by condensation and displacement, have metaphoric and metonymic relationships, respectively, to the original memories. Emotionally rich yet fragmentary in nature, the alternatives offer only fleeting or hallucinatory satisfaction. The other process, "[t]he preconscious," Silverman notes, "is 'born' of disillusionment with the solutions provided by the unconscious" (*SS*, 59). In both processes, however, the sensory material initially derived from and transferred to mnemic traces remains an important stimulant of the subject's mental activity. The role of sensory material in spurring and providing the terms of mental activity emphasizes the inseparability of the subject's material conditions and his or her psychic life.

Sensory material plays an even greater role in the Lacanian description of subject formation with the centrality of the mirror stage, in which the child recognizes his or her ideal (coherent) image as both reflective of and apart from him- or herself. The glance of self-recognition is based on a sensory awareness of one's corporeality, and Silverman insists that we understand both that glance, and the experience of the body accompanying it, as culturally informed. Since the mirror stage and entry into the Symbolic Order together produce the lack at the core of subjectivity (the recognition that the coherent image is identification, in Silverman's words, "at a distance"), lack itself is culturally determined according to the laws of the Symbolic Order; lack describes what the child forever abandons at the constitutive moment of subjectivity within the Symbolic Order. Both the understanding of the reflected image as "ideal" and Lacan's description of the mirror stage as only comprehensible retrospectively, after entry into the Symbolic Order, make it clear that the subject's body and the experiences it perceives are "always already" (Althusser) social.

This reading of the mirror stage and its impact on subject formation differs from Ewing's interpretation by collapsing the distance (spatial and chronological) she finds between the subject and the Symbolic

Order. Whereas Ewing suggests that the subject's ability to challenge the restrictions of the Symbolic Order comes from the lack that is apart from that order, here I argue, following Silverman, that the challenge comes from lack that is culturally delineated. If lack constitutes the most basic and general form of the desire catalyzing mental activity, and if, as Freud describes, desire is only either temporarily and imaginarily satisfied by the primary process of the unconscious or satisfied at the expense of deep emotion by the secondary process, then access to libidinally charged mnemic traces may reveal the otherwise hidden cultural parameters of lack. In other words, we may begin to trace the outlines of lack (which itself remains always unthinkable), and, therefore, of the origins of desire, from the ramparts to contain it built by the Symbolic Order. Because the novels work simultaneously from colonized and colonizer postcolonial perspectives, portraying memories of both, they reveal the commonalty of lack across political boundaries. At the same time, they demand an accounting of cultural and historical specificity of ideological responses to lack.

Silverman responds to the demand to incorporate such specificity into psychoanalytic models in *The Threshold of the Visible World*. There she expands her analysis of bodily sensations in the mirror stage to emphasize the ways in which race, gender, and sexuality are all integral to subject formation within culture. Since ego formation in Lacan's model takes place during the mirror stage, the ego itself is "the representation of a corporeal representation" (*TVW*, 10), a bodily representation comprehensible only in social terms. Silverman focuses in her reading of the mirror stage on the ways in which the reflected and internalized visual image (which is also understood tactilely and kinaesthetically) not only constitutes the idealized, yet forever removed coherent subject, but also the limits of that subject: "the bodily image [described by Lacan in *Seminar I*] plays this including and excluding role with respect to other images, specifying those which are acceptable loci of identification, and those which are not" (*TVW*, 11). This drawing of boundaries means that the "normative ego allows only those identifications which are congruent with its form" (*TVW*, 12).[2]

What Silverman makes clear is that the culturally scripted idealizations, the moments of coherence or wholeness the subject experiences, depend upon a unity of the sensational (both corporeal and psychic) ego and visual ego. In other words, coherent identity only occurs when the two images of the subject line up. Coherence is vulnerable to attack from the same cultural values at work in subject formation, for those values instill in the subject the images available for idealization and thus identification. Again, by looking at how culture deploys the privileged signifiers of valued subjectivity, we may begin to understand the desires they simultaneously produce. These signifiers also code the foundational memories of mental activity, since they come from the experiencing and sensational subject, such that the mnemic traces may provide further access to understanding the subject's founding and potential.

In her reading of Lacan's *Seminar XI*, Silverman notes that subjectivity denotes being recognizable as well as recognizing one's self in the images culturally available. Using Lacan's terminology, those images are presented on the cultural screen (the range of possible identifications) and illuminated by the gaze, the figurative light that blinds us to its own source while making possible our cultural vision and, therefore, existence. In Silverman's words, "In order to emerge within the field of vision, the subject must not only align him- or herself identificatorily with the screen, but must be apprehended in that guise by the gaze" (*TVW*, 18). Race, gender, and other corporeal markers may disrupt this three-way process of identification by presenting markers not of the ideal, but of its negative. Thus, the coherent ideal subject has as its opposite, not a fragmentary image, but a negative one caught in the slippage between the visual and sensational egos (*TVW*, 20). Moreover, since the subject always holds a multiplicity of identifications and discursive positions, even when those positions operate in ideologically connected contexts, such slippages occur regularly. They continually displace the subject from culture's idealizing terms (or reveal the potential for variability of those terms), spawning the desire for restitution and recognition.

Even though ideology works by naturalizing its terms, the subject's repeated experiences of displacement produce the conditions of self-reflexivity and possibly critical distance that Ewing demands. Self-reflexivity entails, then, awareness of one's own position within the dominant fiction as well as one's ability to challenge its normative ideals. At the same time, the subject's subversive potential is limited: self-reflection must always stop short of comprehending lack itself, what Butler terms the "loss that cannot be thought, cannot be owned or grieved, which forms the condition of possibility for the subject" (*PLP*, 24). Instead of attempting to satisfy lack, the subject may challenge its *effects* through the critical distance. Cultural narratives (particularly those such as the novel, poem, or film which privilege affective content) can foster this attempt by offering both the compensation the subject desires (as discussed above in the context of the secondary process) and, potentially, access to the mnemic traces that spur the desire for narrative pleasure.

In the novels I discuss in the following chapters, the lead characters achieve a measure of critical distance where desire, corporeality, and memory intersect. *The Holder of the World*'s colonial heroine, Hannah, first questions her own relationship to Puritan Salem when, in a dream-like fit, she remembers her own mother's illicit desire for her Native American lover. While we never learn the source of the mother Rebecca's passion, we see its seemingly hereditary effects throughout the novel in Hannah and then Beigh's desire for "Indian" men. The significance of these desires comes not from the danger or excitement of the taboo but from the way in which they produce in Hannah and Beigh a new critical perspective capable of altering the relationship between self and "other." In *High Cotton*, desire, corporeality, and memory have a more complicated relationship. The narrator's yearning for recognition manifests itself across the spectrum of his social relationships. Whether trying to prove his virility, his social conscience, or his academic prowess, he finds himself limited by the historical legacies of slavery imprinted on his skin. His race itself serves as a historical legend, inscribing him in socially determined ways. It is only when he reclaims that history, rather than trying to escape it, that he can consciously revise his identifications. In Rushdie's novels, desire and memory constitute the subject both corporeally and psychically. With each ebbing of hope, desire, historical memory, or narrative strength, the cracks running along Saleem's body widen, threatening him with complete dissolution, while the Moor's fantastical growth and aging threaten him with premature death. The narratives themselves attempt to stave off annihilation even as they reflect the impossibility of a singular, coherent, complete history. Critical distance emerges from Saleem's cracks, Aurora's paintings, and the Moor's writing, from the space between desire and narrative satisfaction as well as between the recognition of author/artist as at once authoritative and deeply flawed. Xuela, finally, achieves critical distance in the recognition that controlling her own sexual pleasure and the English language enable her to disrupt the narratives of oppression that otherwise script her life, though this distance fails to produce happiness.

* * *

Critical Distance, Melancholia, and Subversive Agency

The examples above illuminate the kind of critical distance made possible by Silverman's model; however, they are not the only kinds of self-reflexive agency the novels produce. Judith Butler, in *The Psychic Life of*

Power, provides added insight into how the subject possesses and uses self-reflexivity to challenge the cultural norms within which he or she exists. To do so, Butler takes us even deeper inside the psychic topography, as it were, while still insisting on its ideological foundations. Her focus is on the way in which subjectivity entails both subjection (*assujetissement*) to power matrices in Foucaultian and Althusserian senses and becoming an instrument of power. One of Butler's great contributions to our understanding of the conditions of subjectivity comes from her own language: drawing on theorists ranging from Hegel to Foucault, she uses the materialist language of power and agency to describe psychoanalytic functions. This combination makes it impossible to presume any division between public and private or social and psychic conditions because the language she uses to describe any one of these is thoroughly implicated in the others.

Butler's explication of subject formation shares with Silverman's an emphasis on the way subjectivity is bounded by ideological context yet initiates the potential to challenge that context. Whereas Silverman speaks of the lack occasioned by entry into the Symbolic Order and its effects on the subject's subsequent identifications, Butler focuses predominantly on the agency of psychic processes at work within subjectivity. The processes they define are parallel: entry into the Symbolic Order parallels Butler's concept of subjection; lack parallels foreclosure; identity-at-a-distance parallels the condition of self-reflexivity of "one who can take oneself as an object" (22); and, the dominant fiction parallels the social regulatory power the self-reflexive subject may contest.

Butler invokes subjection, foreclosure, self-reflexivity, and the social regulatory power, all of which resonate materially and psychically, to explain the duality of subordination and empowerment within subjectivity:

> Agency exceeds the power by which it is enabled. One might say that the purposes of power are not always the purposes of agency. To the extent that the latter diverge from the former, agency is the assumption of a purpose *unintended* by power, one that could not have been derived logically or historically, that operates in a relation of contingency and reversal to the power that makes it possible, to which it nevertheless belongs. This is, as it were, the ambivalent scene of agency, constrained by no teleological necessity. (15)

The subject's agency, while it knows no predetermined limits, nevertheless remains grounded in the condition of subjection, what Butler calls the condition of "either/or": "To claim that the subject exceeds either/or is not to claim that it lives in some free zone of its own making. Exceeding is not escaping, and the subject exceeds precisely that to which it is bound" (17). While Silverman explains how the subject constituted within a regulated discourse simultaneously finds subversive potential among the slippages of those regulations, Butler notes that, "[b]ound to seek recognition of its own existence in categories, terms, and names that are not of its own making, the subject seeks the sign of its own existence outside itself, in a discourse that is at once dominant and indifferent" (20). The two explanations of the subject's agency, as arising from the inability of ideology to make sense of all experience and from the subject's capacity to use the discourse which founds it, are not identical but complementary; together they express a greater range of subversive potential than each one does alone.

Silverman and Butler's models of subjectivity work especially well to denote subjectivity as a form of social conscription and liberation, as entry into the normative world and into the condition of alterity from it. Both models also locate the source of agency, and, ultimately, conscience, in the subject's foundational loss. Silverman categorizes this loss as shared by all subjects, a topographical feature that refutes the possibility of coherent subjectivity as anything other than an ideological wish. For Butler, loss similarly inaugurates subjectivity and remains inscrutable and irreplaceable. Following Freud, she describes how it generates melancholia that "rifts the subject, marking a limit to what it can accommodate. Because the subject does not, cannot, reflect on that loss, that loss marks the limit of reflexivity, that which exceeds (and conditions) its circuitry" (23).

The lack Butler describes here remains inaccessible because it derives from foreclosure rather than repression. Following the distinction Freud makes between the two forms of prohibition, Butler notes, "a repressed desire might once have lived apart from its prohibition, but that foreclosed desire is rigorously barred, constituting the subject through a certain kind of preemptive loss" (23). Whereas foreclosure is unknowable, repressed material remains in the unconscious and may either emerge in altered forms or generate desires that bear the mark of their source. Foreclosure, the prohibition that initiates the subject into the symbolic order, leaves only the illegible mark of absence or limitation on the subject. We can only begin to approach this absence through the desires it produces secondarily, through the Symbolic Order and the mechanisms of conscious and unconscious activity; its desires are knowable only through the identifications and narratives deployed to satisfy them. By approaching the limits between conscious and unconscious (repressed) material, between what is presentable and prohibited, we may find ourselves at the edge of the abyss, able to reflect on its effects though never to assuage the loss or to see into its depths.

According to Butler, the melancholia produced through foreclosure creates a psychic topography capable of and, indeed, defined by conscience. When foreclosure initiates subjectivity, it creates an insatiable, unknowable desire that is subsequently displaced through the terms of identification available in the Symbolic Order. Those desires find various degrees of partial fulfillment (for complete satisfaction is impossible given the subject's foundational lack) in the stimulation of unconscious and conscious activity, respectively: the displaced and condensed substitutions of prohibited identifications and their more narrative, less affective versions. Since the satisfaction of desire is socially regulated, as the split between the unconscious and conscious or the id, ego, and super-ego make clear, we can see, following Butler, "that this prefiguration of the topographical distinction between ego and super-ego is itself dependent upon melancholia. Melancholia produces the possibility for the representation of psychic life" (*PLP*, 177).

The irony of Butler's analysis is that it shows us, once again, how psychoanalysis eventually comes up against its own limits. Butler's reading of melancholia leads to a psychic topography defined by the split between the ego and super-ego on the one hand and the power constituting the subject and that which the subject wields on the other. At the same time, the topography itself cannot represent its most fundamental feature: the loss at its center. We have instead a blueprint in invisible ink, whose dimensions and intentions appear only in its effects, in the identifications it leads us to build.

In reading those identifications, particularly those loaded with the greatest reservoirs of affective value, we may begin to grasp a second irony of Butler's analysis of psychic topography: the melancholia that produces the schism between ego and super-ego simultaneously produces the critical faculty to challenge the super-ego's dictates. As the repository of cultural normativity and the product of mirror stage identification, the super-ego, like the ideal image the child internalizes, presents itself as the locus of both idealization and punishment. Freud locates this duality within the framework of the Oedipus complex, and Silverman explains its effects: "[The super-ego's] relation to the ego is not exhausted by the precept: 'You *ought* to be like this (like your father).' It also comprises the prohibition: 'You *may not be* like this (like your father)—that is, you may not do all that he does; some things are his prerogative' " (*SS*, 135). Lacan, Silverman, and Butler build upon Freud's work to show how the role of the father described above is a symbolic one functioning in various forms throughout society. As Silverman notes, "Freud here draws attention not only to those values which define the paternal position—repressiveness, privilege, potency—but its institutional supports: the state, the church, the education system and texts" (*SS*, 135).

Butler pushes Freud's model to its logical limits. She argues that it is precisely the dual nature of the subject's relationship to the ideal image (the internalized yet distant image the subject loathes and loves) that creates a subject capable of critical distance from that image. "The 'price' of such an identification," she writes, "[. . .] is that the ego splits into the critical agency and the ego as object of criticism and judgment" (*PLP*, 180). Since loss, the source of melancholia, cannot be thought, the subject makes the closest substitutions it can within the parameters of the Symbolic Order. The subject attempts to ease the melancholia of foreclosure when it "withdraws into the psyche a configuration of the social world [. . .]. The ego thus becomes a 'polity' and conscience one of its 'major institutions,' precisely because psychic life withdraws a social world into itself in an effort to annul the losses that world demands" (*PLP*, 181). This restatement of the subject's entry into the Symbolic Order reinforces the importance of ideological features on psychic topography. At the same time, those constraints produce the conditions of their own vulnerability because the subject with critical agency is the subject who looks at him- or herself from a distance. The desires driving mental activity continually demand that critical agency be turned "inward," a turn that, given the normative role of the super-ego, can only be simultaneously social or "outward."

Social and psychic losses are interactive and inseparable in this reading, and both yield critical agency. The subject's conscience reflects and enacts that of the wider social body, such that the two forms work together to ensure ideological continuity. Butler explains how this relationship between subject and social conscience goes beyond analogy to mutual dependence:

> This super-egoic conscience is not simply analogous to the state's military power over its citizenry; the state cultivates melancholia among its citizenry precisely as a way of dissimulating and displacing its own ideal authority. This is not to suggest that conscience is a simple instantiation of the state; on the contrary, it is the vanishing point of the state's authority, its psychic idealization, and, in that sense, its disappearance as an external object. The process of forming the subject is a process of rendering the terrorizing power of the state invisible—and effective—as the ideality of conscience. Furthermore, the incorporation of the ideal of the

"Law" underscores the contingent relation between a given state and the ideality of its power. (*PLP*, 191)

Conscience not only reinforces the state's authority, but also in doing so creates the illusion of a separation between public and private authority. In her reading of conscience, Butler stresses its negative power of censure, calling it an "instrument of psychic terror" which threatens the subject's existence (191). While the loss stimulating melancholia may be that of an ideal such as "a country, a concept of liberty," it creates a conscience notable here for its capacity for violence (196). Our understanding of the relationship between subject and nation grows if we remember how the internalized ideal image that forms the basis for the super-ego is an image hated and loved. Conscience wields the power of affirmation and condemnation; it ought not to be defined solely by its terrorizing potential. Since subjectivity only makes sense through the process of identification, and since any single identification only makes sense in relation to others, the selection or regulation of the process is at once destructive and productive of social standing. Rather than separate the loved and hated aspects of the ideal into what has been forever lost and what regulates all possible compensation, respectively, we might find both within conscience.

The novels also reveal the need for a theory of conscience which incorporates its dual functions. Just as all of the narrators strive to redefine the terms of social standing, they simultaneously idealize and are bound to existing images of subjectivity and national identity. For example, it is Mukherjee's bid for inclusion into the literary canon that spurs her revision of *The Scarlet Letter*. Her motivation, while it carries with it a desire to transform the canon to reflect a diversity of subject positions, underscores a faith in the nation as a construct which can accommodate that diversity. She envisions an America whose founding mythologies need to be altered but not rejected. Similarly in *High Cotton*, we follow the narrator's attempt to stake a claim for himself within contemporary middle-class life. Again the subject's response is transformative rather than revolutionary, as he vows to forge his own terms of social acceptance once he realizes his exclusion from existing ones. Although this strategy will, of necessity, alter social values, it does not seek to overthrow them. This response does not indicate a failure in the subject's will or his critical agency, but rather the way in which the inaccessible ideal of nation or subject continually drives the desire for narrative compensation. Rushdie's novels and his ongoing political predicament serve as another poignant example of the tension contained within conscience.

For it is his narrative abundance, the way in which his work strains against the limits of its own form that produces both aesthetic pleasure and political reprisal. In an interview with Linda Hutcheon in *Other Solitudes*, Michael Ondaatje affectionately described Rushdie's writing as "rather like a creaking ship carrying everything it can take across the ocean" (200). That ship most often represents the idea of India which constantly threatens to sink under the weight of its own multitudinous cargo. In the response to *The Satanic Verses*, particularly the banning of the book in India, Rushdie found one of the limits of the nation's tolerance. Kincaid's Xuela also negotiates the dangerous territory between defeat and domination. Refusing to be either a victim or a heroine, she claims some attributes of patriarchal, white, colonial power for herself in order to criticize its historical legacy.

The strategies adopted by the narrators in Mukherjee and Pinckney's novels reflect the limits conscience may abide by in order to maintain the subject's existence. In Rushdie's case, we see the both the aesthetic and political danger of trespassing those limits. Kincaid dispels any possible remaining idealizations of the nation as family through a narrator who claims its weapons for herself in a desperate bid to avoid complete objectification. Xuela succeeds in securing her survival, but fails to construct an alternative ideal herself. She represents conscience in its most painful form. Conscience is, by Butler's definition, an "internalized ideality," but it maintains its status through the threat of psychic violence. The subject avoids self-destruction by giving him- or herself over "from the start to social terms that are never fully one's own" (197). At the same time, social interpellation produces the subject's own agency and, in doing so, "fails to determine such a subject exhaustively in time" (197). Thus, the sequence of novels gives us characters that wield more and more power, at greater and greater costs. For Butler, it is the iterability of the subject—its discursive power and constitution—that endows him or her with agency founded by, yet exceeding the terms of conscience. The novels demand that we take her model one step further to see how the critical agency which conscience produces may bestow both love and hate.

* * *

Conscience, National Identity, and Social Change

The full potential of critical distance depends upon a third kind of power within subjectivity as figured by Butler. In addition to the power that subordinates the subject (the process of *assujetissement*) and the power the subject gains (*pouvoir*), we find the power of critical self-reflexivity. It is Butler's *pouvoir* (the subject's discursive potential) combined with her notion of conscience. With discursive tools whose applications extend beyond their original intent and conscience, which turns back on itself to examine its own foundations, the subject should be able to deploy this combined third power, critical conscience, to challenge social ideals and identifications. Critical conscience suggests that even if we cannot fully understand the source of our deepest desires, we can learn to take responsibility for their effects, for the identifications they privilege and condemn.

Critical conscience arises out of the contingency of social power. Despite the existence of a social ideology that creates its own willing subjects, we are reminded that the power of "the Law" demands and depends upon its own repeated invocation, that the Name-of-the-Father in our culture only exists within each instantiation of its principles. In other words, the Name-of-the-Father does not exist outside the social psychic network it produces. The contingency, in Butler's words, "between a given state and the ideality of its power" means that the identifications to which subject and nation lay claim must be constantly reproduced and reiterated. Since we all hold multiple identities, depending on our immediate context, we constantly shuffle our identifications as guided by our desires. While each identification, each reiteration of subjectivity, carries forth its ideological foundations, each also holds the potential for change. Condensing her work on gender performativity in *Gender Trouble* and *Bodies that Matter*, Butler explains this paradox succinctly in "Imitation and Gender Subordination": "For if the 'I' is a site of repetition, that is, if the 'I' only achieves the semblance of identity through a certain repetition of itself, then the I is always displaced by the very repetition that sustains it" (311).

Unsurprisingly we find this same tension between producing and subverting identity in discourses on the nation. All of the novels I discuss here invoke shared discourse as constitutive of national unity, though the forms of that discourse vary depending on the context. Whether the text invokes the literary canon (*The Holder of the World*), the *Bildungsroman* (*High Cotton* and *The Autobiography of My Mother*), or the shared language that makes imagining national identity possible (*Midnight's Children* and *The Moor's Last Sigh*), discourse plays a constitutive role in national identity. As Benedict Anderson argues in *Imagined Communities*, modern nations coincide with the spread of print capitalism and a common language, both of which enable people to imagine themselves simultaneously as part of a national collective. Such simultaneity also leads to the "conviction that languages (in Europe at least) were, so to speak, the personal property of quite specific groups—their daily speakers and readers—and, moreover, that these groups, imagined as communities, were entitled to their autonomous place in a fraternity of equals" (84). Common discourse, in this context, becomes a method of social equalization rather than cultural warfare.

Anderson's emphasis on discourse in fostering an imagined community of the nation underscores the shared topographies of subject and nation. Those topographies convey a sense of uniqueness within and among their subjects, such that submission (Butler's "subjection") to hegemony seems like a benefit rather than a cost to the subject. The Symbolic Order, which regulates subjectivity, similarly orders other forms of identification, such that both subjectivity and national identity find their primary means of expression through discourse. Whatever shared loss the nation's subjects experience, whatever the form of the ideal nation, continually displaced, that produces melancholia, loss must take place on a common discursive ground. That commonalty allows the ideal of the nation to coexist with the coercive potential of the state, paralleling the two facets of conscience; together they produce subjects who think of themselves simultaneously as individuals and as national citizens.

The nation as family metaphor facilitates the subject's concomitant identification as individual and citizen by bridging his or her nominally private and public roles. We have seen how it circulates in discourses of the nation to naturalize its own historical effects and, therefore, to present the subject with seemingly organic rather than ideological identifications. In this discursive realm, the nation as family metaphor is vulnerable to memories that penetrate the veneer of domestic (national) unity. Such memories may render the subject unable to sustain uncritically his or her original allegiance to the prevailing social order. The metaphor also functions in the psychic topographies outlined by Silverman and Butler to capture the ideological, Oedipal foundations of conscience. On the level of the psyche, critical conscience may emerge from the disparities between the various identifications we hold, the constant need to reassert them, and their social values.

We find a third invocation of the nation as family metaphor, and its relationship to critical conscience, in Edward Said's *The World, the Text and the Critic* where he describes the social networks accompanying the rise in modern nations in terms of a transformation from the filiation of shared birth to an affiliation of shared consciousness. Affiliation (chosen association) takes place, Said suggests, when filiative networks fail to provide the connectedness necessary for communal identification and through institutions of civil society. In his reading of T. S. Eliot's *The Waste Land*, for example, Said sees Eliot's pessimistic portrayal of Western culture as a sign that "the aridity, wastefulness, and sterility of modern life make filiation an unreasonable alternative at least, an unattainable one at most. One cannot think about continuity in biological terms [. . .]. The only alternative seemed to be provided by institutions, associations, and communities whose social existence was not in fact guaranteed by biology, but by affiliation" (17). For Said, modernist aesthetics promise a "compensatory order that [. . .] provides men and women with a new form of relationship, which I have been calling affiliation but which is also a new system" (19). Shared discursive pleasure, in other words, contributes to the foundation of new "imagined communities."

Not only do filiation and affiliation apply to social belief systems and to aesthetics, they also, according to Said, denote distinct critical perspectives: "My position [. . .] is that the contemporary critical consciousness stands between the temptations represented by two formidable and related powers engaging critical attention. One is the culture to which critics are bound filiatively (by birth, nationality, profession); the other is a method or system acquired affiliatively (by social and political conviction, economic and historical circumstances, voluntary effort and willed deliberation)" (25). Adopting an affiliative critical consciousness, then, means recreating "the bonds between texts and the world," a process built out of "genuine historical research" and out of taking deliberate responsibility for the effects of criticism (175). The image of the scholar-critic caught between contesting allegiances suggests that filiative associations remain central to the social order of nations, thereby re-inscribing the nation as family metaphor itself. At the same time, Said's argument for affiliation as an alternative challenges the authority of that metaphor.

In arguing for an affiliative critical consciousness, Said wants to break down barriers between scholarly disciplines (barriers that, he says, make individual disciplines into miniature filiative networks whose authority derives from the exclusion of "outsiders") and, thus, to make responsibility for critical positions an integral part of such consciousness. This self-reflexive consciousness comes from stepping outside the familiar and, ironically, intentionally forging a wider system of inclusivity. In *Imperial Leather*, Anne McClintock supports the overall goal of creating a self-reflexive critical consciousness, yet she reads Said against himself to show how the family metaphor functions as a central organizing trope for Western culture across its various disciplines. As discussed previously, that metaphor, at the level of the nation, naturalizes often violent internal and imperialist aspects of national history. The pervasiveness of the image of the nation as family suggests we add another dimension to Said's concept of affiliative critical consciousness. In order to see how such consciousness necessitates a deliberate look "back" at the dominant filiative consciousness, we might focus on the ways in which it reproduces itself through time and across cultural spheres. Affiliation would not necessitate getting beyond or outside filiation, since that order is foundational to Western culture; rather, affiliation ably captures the process of denaturalizing filiation, of recognizing how we are implicated in its circulation and how we may consciously work to subvert it.

Said's concept of affiliation as a critical position finds a counterpart in the other theoretical approaches invoked here. Silverman and Butler argue for a psychoanalytic approach which is fully aware of the limits imposed by its own history and terms (which continually deploys the terms of the normative Oedipus complex and phallic power even as it tries to subvert them, e.g.). We may read Said's filiative and affiliative networks similarly for the way in which they depend on one another and, thus, produce the same identities he seeks to dismantle.

I turn to Homi Bhabha's analysis of national identity in *The Location of Culture* (particularly the chapters "DissemiNation" and "How Newness Enters the World") to complete the theoretical project of rethinking affiliation. First, he shows how Anderson's "homogeneous empty time" of the nation describes not a horizontal simultaneity of subjects' experiences but the continual reiteration of the ideal of the nation; secondly, he looks at ways in which reiteration itself introduces the possibility of subversion. Just as Butler describes subjectivity in terms of fleeting, repetitive identifications of the "I," Bhabha describes narrative instances of the nation. Noting the instability of the term, Bhabha writes of the nation: "As an apparatus of symbolic power, it produces a continual slippage of categories, like sexuality, class affiliation, territorial paranoia, or 'cultural difference' in the act of writing the nation. What is displayed in this displacement and repetition of terms is the measure of the liminality of cultural modernity" (140). While we have focused up to this point on the ways in which those various levels of cultural identification are stitched together by threads of a common ideological framework and the common metaphor of the nation as paternal family, Bhabha urges us to look at the edges of that social fabric. The ideal itself, the image beyond the discursive order, the image for which the narratives of the nation try to compensate, remains forever lost; nevertheless, Bhabha argues that through "another time of *writing*" the nation, we might learn to see the ambivalence of both our desires and the narratives they spawn (141).

Looking back on the eve of Indian independence, Saleem of *Midnight's Children* captures this sense of the nation as an ideal made possible not through decree, a constitution, war, or election, but which exists only in its imaginary form, "by the efforts of a phenomenal collective will— except in a dream we all agreed to dream" (130). Bhabha's explanation of the temporality of writing the nation helps us understand how the ideal combines intention and the unconscious or, as Rushdie writes, will and dreaming. Bhabha divides the "production of the nation as narration" into two temporalities: the performative and the pedagogical. While the pedagogical turns the "scraps, patches and rags of daily life [. . .] into the signs of a coherent national culture, [. . .] the very act of narrative performance interpellates a growing circle of national subjects" (145). In other words, the "nation as narration" continually produces both its own "story" and its designated reader-subjects. It only maintains its adherents, who turn toward the narrative to substitute for the unlocatable, indefinable ideal, through repeated interpellations. This "double-time" of the nation creates the sense of ahistorical continuity and of present-ness. Its people, Bhabha writes, "are the historical 'objects' of a nationalist pedagogy, giving the discourse an authority that is based on the pre-given or constituted historical origin *in the past*; the people are also the 'subjects' of a process of signification that must erase any prior or originary presence of the nation-people to demonstrate the prodigious, living principles of the people as contemporaneity: as that sign of the present" (145).

For Bhabha, as for some subaltern studies critics, cultural difference disrupts the "nation as narration" in productive ways through the introduction of community identifications into the equation of nation and subject. Given our understanding of how subjectivity occurs within a regulated symbolic order, the idea that community identification would be *necessarily* subversive seems, to me, overly hopeful. Khilnani's discussion of how community identifications are redefined and redeployed in the bid for national power provides an example of how the dominant fiction may both confound and co-opt alternative paths of identification. At the same time, Bhabha's emphasis on enunciation suggests that, since the subject holds multiple identities simultaneously and the social order values those identities unequally, each enunciatory moment of subject and nation potentially brings the tensions within the constitution of both to the fore. The novels bear this out, as the characters derive their subversive power from slippages between the dominant fiction and their own narrations of memory, desire, and cultural difference.

Bhabha's enunciatory moment finds a parallel in Butler's theory of gender performativity, and both suggest that we might more productively read the internalization of the ideal (what Lacan encapsulates in the mirror stage) as an ongoing process rather than a singular event. While what may constitute an ideal always revolves around culturally defined, libidinal images such as the paternal figure and the phallus, the instability of our resulting cultural identifications (the fact that we must continually engage in the process of identification and that those identifications vary) would seem to indicate that the ideal is itself, however slightly, variable. The continual (re)production of subject and nation, the need for reiteration, ensures that "adding *to* does not add up" (The Location of Culture, 162) and will, therefore, always produce the melancholia of the missing ideal as well as the desire for narrative compensation. At the same time, this impossibility of lasting coherence should encourage us to take responsibility for the identifications we unconsciously make and ultimately, therefore, for the parameters of the ideal itself.

* * *

The Role of Aesthetics

Reading the "nation as narration," which produces its own subjects, requires a closer look at exactly how such textual affiliations work to satisfy our deepest longings. In order to establish the kind of critical distance or conscience so many critics call for in various forms, we need to find a new perspective from which to view our relationship to the discursive compensation we seek. In *The Threshold of the Visible World*, Silverman presents a reading of the aesthetic that fosters this perspective. Her goal is to show how "we might be carried away from both ideality and the self, and situated in an identificatory relation to despised bodies" through an understanding of aesthetics' effects on our fundamental desires (*TVW*, 2). Silverman founds her argument on the idea that, through the stimulation of desire with libidinal images, the aesthetic may facilitate identifications that are not sanctioned by the dominant fiction. Moreover, since "we cannot idealize something without at the same time identifying with it," responsibility for our identifications can only come from a conscious re-vision of the ideal images structuring subjectivity and driving its desires (*TVW*, 2). Responsibility and critical conscience are therefore inextricably linked.

According to Silverman, the aesthetic may foster intervention into the normative processes of identification by making our most affective images, both those accepted and those normally barred from consciousness, available for conscious scrutiny. As the realm of emotional charges and libidinal satisfactions, the aesthetic crosses the boundaries between the conscious and unconscious and is, therefore, able to make otherwise barred images "present" to the subject. Since aesthetic texts, in Silverman's words, "have the formal and libidinal properties of highly charged unconscious memories," we may learn to read backward, so to speak, from textual compensation to its instigative desires to their foundational memories in order to see what otherwise remains hidden by the censoring mechanisms of the psyche (*TVW*, 4). Although aesthetic texts exist within the same symbolic and ideological contexts that structure subjectivity, they provide access to the privileged signifiers of those contexts. By taking advantage of that access, we might begin the long and difficult process of learning to identify with those who are precisely "not us." Because idealization, unlike sympathy, necessitates identification, this process obviates the problem Rai defined of the link between sympathy and policing in humanitarian efforts.

Silverman argues that the subject who learns to accept his or her own innate provisionality, and thus to recognize the distance and deferral inherent in any identification (beginning with that in the mirror stage), might also learn to revise those identifications consciously. To capture the specular features of identification, its corporeal and psychic attributes, she turns to cinematic imagery. Her concept of the "productive look"—the conscious re-visionary apperception that bestows love and affection on bodies previously shunned by the dominant fiction and negated by the psychic censors—incorporates those spatial and temporal lapses necessary for alternative and subversive identifications. The "productive look" is anything but a passing glance; rather, it is the laborious result of learning to look from one's corporeal and cultural context and, in doing so, to denaturalize the identifications of the ego. The "productive look" means "to *confer* ideality, not to *find* it," to illuminate those who would otherwise be hidden in the shadows cast by normative images (*TVW*, 78).

We have already seen the way in which cultural normativity imprints itself on the subject at its inauguration. When the subject looks in the mirror for images to substitute for foundational lack, he or she is confronted with a range of identifications delineated by the predilections of the Symbolic Order. In its subsequent identifications, the performative and reiterative acts Butler and Bhabha describe, the subject is "under cultural pressure to apprehend the world from a preassigned viewing position, and under psychic pressure to see it in ways that protect the ego. The look is exhorted from many sides to perceive and affirm only what generally passes for 'reality' " (*TVW*, 3).

While the pressure to conform comes in part from the super-egoic conscience and the psyche's censoring mechanisms, it is crucial to remember that these mechanisms are driven by the subject's unconscious desire to overcome its own constitutive lack. This means that cultural ideals derive their staying power from the subject's libidinal investment in them. The aesthetic may interrupt this process of libidinal regulation because it, like the process of idealization itself, works simultaneously on conscious and unconscious levels. The images endowing the aesthetic text with affective power, in other words, may include those that would otherwise be barred from view but, through their close association with valued images, have sneaked by the psychic censors. When the creative process calls forth a rich array of representations, illuminating images which otherwise remain hidden in the unconscious, those images ultimately appear on the surface of the aesthetic text, rather than in the realm of the imaginary or the unconscious. Once a part of a working aesthetic, they are available for conscious scrutiny, analysis, and ethical consideration.

Central to learning to idealize an identity heretofore shunned is recognizing that all identifications, including that of the ego itself, take place "at a distance." In order for the subject to idealize an alternative, barred, or subversive identity, then, he or she must learn to love what is precisely outside or not, him- or herself. Since idealization revolves initially around the internalization of the mirror image (and subsequently the cultural images purveyed by the same symbolic order that regulates the visual and sensual ego in the mirror), re-visionary idealizations depend upon a profound understanding of the temporal and spatial lapses in the entire process. Silverman describes these lapses initially as the *distance* between the subject and the ideal and the continual *deferral* of a stable, unitary identity, both of which create opportunity for the "productive look." Out of the distance and deferral of identification arises the critical distance necessary to alter the terms of social value.

The process of forging a conscious relationship to society's privileged signifiers, of trying actively to reconstruct what passes for "reality" through one's own vision, begins with memory. To return for a moment to the earlier discussion of the organization and cathexis of the psyche, perception provides the unconscious with memories that are catalysts for mental activity. The desires awakened by memory spur the subject to seek compensation in culturally sanctioned representations, and the social-psychic network regulates the compensatory process by dictating which memories may and may not reach consciousness. Meanwhile, the unconscious reworks mnemic traces into forms most likely to bypass the censors.

Aesthetic texts, according to Silverman, intervene in the manipulation of these traces in two ways: by illuminating memories that the dominant fiction seeks to repress and by forging "new" memories at the level of the unconscious which may then stimulate conscious intervention into normative representations. Because aesthetic texts are aligned closely with the workings of the pleasure principle, they work by implanting " 'synthetic' memories—libidinally saturated associative clusters which act like those mnemic elements which, as a result of a psychic working over, have been made the vehicles for the expression of unconscious wishes" (185). The memories produced by the aesthetic do not function alone, Silverman continues, but in conjunction with those already active in the unconscious. The synthetic memories have already become conscious representations, yet their affective power derives from the unconscious. They may, therefore, "put marginal elements of the cultural screen in contact with what is most meaningful to a viewer or reader, and thereby validate what would otherwise be neglected or despised" (185). In other words, those memories, in displacing the subject from predetermined identifications, must also displace the subject from him- or herself; they must introduce the " 'not me' into my memory reserve" and thus make it available for self-reflexive identification (185).

Silverman's aesthetic theory has profound implications for the way we understand our own subjectivity and national identity. She outlines a process through which we might look to the pleasures produced by cultural texts in order to understand and, then, to refigure the desires they reflect. Through analysis of the mnemic elements of aesthetic texts, we might learn to recognize the privileged signifiers of our dominant fiction as constitutive to ourselves yet, in their need for constant reiteration, always yielding the potential for alterity.

* * *

The Limits of Theory

Up until this point, I have focused on subjectivity and national identity's mutual topographies in relatively abstract terms. By turning to the novels themselves, I would like to see how their aesthetic values enable us to rethink the kinds of historically specific subjects and nations they present. To do so requires that we develop an added dimension to Silverman's aesthetic theory in order to endow it with the same potential for critical consciousness as that possessed by the other theoretical approaches. That is, we must insist on the historical contexts of both the aesthetic pleasure the texts offer and their driving memories. In their unveiling or production of memories, aesthetic texts initiate a chain reaction of desire and identification through which otherwise barred images may satisfy, and thus revise, the objects of the subject's desire. These memories are, by definition, bound to the historical fissures in the nation and subject's unity, and they derive their affective value from that lack. Conscious revision of the identifications made possible through the aesthetic, then, entails a concomitant revision of the subject and nation's histories.

The novels demand a strict accounting of those histories; in the process they push the limits of the theoretical approaches that enable my readings. Because memory both produces and challenges the subject's relationship to the nation, it turns the psychoanalytic and postcolonial approaches back on themselves. For example, we read the psychic splitting induced each time Pinckney's narrator remembers when he, as a black boy, was cut off from the rewards of the dominant fiction in the same psychoanalytic terms which have themselves a history of racist exclusion. The separation he feels between his intellectual identifications and his material conditions parallels the psychoanalytic split between self and other which, historically, presupposes a white ideal subject. Recognizing the terms through which he ultimately hopes to move beyond this binary opposition means accounting for and moving beyond the limits of the psychoanalytic model itself.

A similar paradox exists in the postcolonial approaches as we try to read alternatives to modern nation with theories that privilege it as a primary locus of social identification. As Khilnani notes, "The choice seems stark. On the one hand, the old opposition between the monochromy of the post-imperial imagination and that of nationalist histories of a unified people; and on the other hand, set against both, [. . .] ever more ingeniously trawling and re-reading the archives for examples of 'resistance' (textual or practical) to the ideas of nation and state" (3). This either/or dilemma, as a problem of representation, appears in the novels as well, both in the difficulty of reformulating their central subject-nation alliances and in understanding the relationship between aesthetic pleasure and the nation. When the Moor's mother, Aurora, exhibited her pluralistic paintings during Indira Gandhi's authoritarian return to power, for example, the critics

> turned upon Aurora Zogoiby and savaged her as a "society artist," out of tune with, and even "deleterious" to, the temper of the age. On the same day the lead story on every front page was that of the dissolution of Parliament after the disintegration of the post-Emergency, anti-Indira coalition government; and several editorials made use of the contrast in the two old rivals' fortunes. *Aurora Plunged Into Darkness*, said the headline of the *Times's* op-ed page, *but for Indira, Another New Dawn.* (261)

The aesthetic possibilities of national identity, as Rushdie makes clear, are constrained by their historical and political contexts.

In *The Holder of the World*, the memory of illicit desire introduces female agency and ethnic difference into the story of colonial settlement and nation-building in America and India and, in doing so, revises the image of the nation as family. Even as the novel alters this vision of the nation, it reproduces the central metaphor in the genealogical transmission of disruptive desire from seventeenth-century Hannah to contemporary Beigh Masters (who shares more than just initials with the author). By integrating the aesthetic traditions of Mughal painting and American Romance, Mukherjee inserts cultural difference into the nation's identity. This integration works less to subvert the dominant fiction, however, than to underscore its absorptive capacity as the intertwined ideological strands of gender, ethnicity, and class that uphold the dominant fiction of the modern nation remain intact.

High Cotton presents a greater challenge to our understanding of how the dominant fiction structures subjectivity and nationhood. Because the narrator faces daily reminders of his lack of social standing, and because he refuses to align himself with a black community defined in opposition to the recognition he seeks, he breaks down the self-versus-other terms of both subjectivity and the nation. Pinckney's parodies of the *Bildungsroman* and of other forms of self-identification, ranging from the Black Panthers to Marxism, underscore the difficulty the narrator (and the psychoanalytic model of subjectivity) faces in finding terms with which he is recognizable to himself and others. With him, we must, finally, account for rather than ignore the legacies of slavery that continue to mark him in order consciously to forge a new relationship to them.

In *Midnight's Children* and *The Moor's Last Sigh*, Rushdie literalizes the nation as family metaphor in order to examine its most debilitating effects. This strategy not only reveals the ways in which the nation as family threatens the very viability of subjects who challenge its authority, it also shows the inability of the metaphor itself to encompass all the identities produced by colonial and postcolonial histories. Rushdie offers his own extravagant style as an antidote to the singularity of the nation as family and to the theoretical approaches built around it. His obvious awareness of contemporary theoretical trends, and his playful invocations of them, serve as constant reminders of the diversionary, potentially disruptive, power of the aesthetic. At the same time, just as his use of the nation as family unveils its coercive power, Rushdie's own aesthetic promise is limited by the retaliation it provokes from existing political forces.

The Autobiography of My Mother brings us back to the inescapable lack we all "hold." It is the hole at the center of nation as family that promises to render any subjective or national identity incomplete. Xuela provides the most negative critique of the metaphor, and with it the theoretical models, as even her mastery of its terms brings only power without pleasure. This conclusion turns us back to the aesthetics of the text itself in order to re-imagine social value.

CHAPTER 2

MIMICRY AND REINVENTION: FEMALE DESIRE AND NATIONAL IDENTITY IN BHARATI MUKHERJEE'S *THE HOLDER OF THE WORLD*

> It is the story of North America turned inside out.
>
> Bharati Mukherjee, *The Holder of the World*

"I am one of you now," Bharati Mukherjee writes provocatively to her American audience in a *New York Times Book Review* essay ("Immigrant Writing," 1). Her statement unsettles and challenges the reader's identity as much as the author's. Who defines "American"? Who can claim to belong? Insisting upon an ethnically inclusive American identity as her own, Mukherjee concludes her transformation from what she calls expatriate detachment to immigrant engagement. I borrow the title of my chapter from the essay in which she describes this process. Mimicry and reinvention, she explains, capture the two options available to a postcolonial writer composing in English for an American audience: "I felt my entire writing and life bounce off those two words. I am always mimicking and hoping to break out of the mimicry and into reinvention" ("Mimicry and Reinvention," 147). Mimicry here indicates an imitation that, rather than reinforces the model, simultaneously destabilizes authority of model and mimic. Reinvention thus applies to both as well, and nowhere is this clearer in Mukherjee's writing than in *The Holder of the World* (1993). The novel offers a rewriting of Nathaniel Hawthorne's *The Scarlet Letter* that stretches the history and effects of colonialism from Hawthorne's Salem to Moghul India to contemporary Boston. Located in the historical elisions of *The Scarlet Letter* and American national mythology, *The Holder of the World* presents feminized desire as an alternative to the masculinized appetite that drives colonization. While Mukherjee's alternative fails to complete the transformation of the nation as family metaphor it launches, it does insist upon a rethinking of that metaphor in our contemporary lives.

The American mythology of assimilation and profit in the "New World" is predicated upon gender-coded signifiers of national identity. The fantasy of cohesion that provides a sense of collective identity often takes place through the domestication (in fiction as well as other realms) of gender opposition: feminized nature, natives, and new lands and masculinized culture, capitalism, and knowledge. My aim throughout this project is to investigate contemporary manifestations and subversions of this opposition in order not to abandon the concept of nationhood but to begin to re-signify it. Mukherjee's position as a postcolonial and American writer makes her an apt guide to begin the process. She insists repeatedly in her critical work over the last 20 years, "I am an American. I am an American writer, in the American mainstream, trying to extend it. In other words, my literary agenda begins by acknowledging that America has transformed me. It does not end until I show how I (and the hundreds of thousands like me) have transformed America" ("Four-Hundred-Year-Old Woman," 25). While committed to her American present, however, she does not abandon the Bengali mythologies, language, and religion with which she was raised. Mukherjee's criticism and fiction negotiate the uneasy spaces between these two aesthetic traditions through mimicry, revision, and reinvention in order to expose the foundations of national unity and integration. Her work insists upon an engagement with the aesthetic and ethical terms of national identity even as it renders them suspect. It is through her commitment to immigration as "fusion," which she develops most profoundly in *The Holder of the World* (1993), that we see the subversive potential as well as the limitations of aesthetic techniques spawned by mimicry.

As she describes herself in "A Four-Hundred-Year-Old Woman," Mukherjee occupies an ambivalent position within the postcolonial worlds of North America and India, and her own aesthetic emerges from that ambivalence:

> I was born into a city that feared its future, and trained me for emigration. I attended a school run by Irish nuns, who regarded our walled-off school compound in Calcutta as a corner (forever green and tropical) of England. My "country"—called in Bengali, *desh*, and suggesting more a homeland than a nation of which one is a citizen—I have never seen. It is the ancestral home of my father and is now in Bangladesh. Nevertheless, I speak his dialect of Bengali, and think of myself as "belonging" to Fardipur, the tiny green-gold village that was his birthplace. I was born into a religion that placed me, a Brahmin, at the

top of its hierarchy while condemning me, as a woman, to a role of subservience. The larger political entity to which I gave my first allegiance—India—was not even a sovereign nation when I was born. (24)

Concluding this passage with "I am an American [. . .] my investment is in the American reality," Mukherjee points to the slippages between homeland—a private realm of ancestry, nostalgia, mythology, and language—and nationhood with its legal rights and restrictions and explicitly public membership. Distinctions between home and nation, private and public begin to blur as she constructs an aesthetic approach incorporating Indian tropes to detail the mutually transformative effects of immigration on contemporary America and its new citizens. This wary alliance of national mythologies—Indian and American—combined with the epic theme of immigration challenges the familiar center–periphery model of colonial and postcolonial/indigenous authority and complicates its standards of identity and difference.

Development of what Mukherjee might call an aesthetic of fusion corresponds to her own move from Canada to the United States. Prior to that, she writes, "I had thought of myself, in spite of a white husband and two assimilated sons, as an expatriate. In my fiction, and in my Canadian experience, 'immigrants' were lost souls, put upon and pathetic. Expatriates, on the other hand, knew all too well who and what they were, and what foul fate had befallen them" (Darkness, xiii). She characterizes her "Indianness" at that time as a something both "fragile" and exotic. Both attributes identified her as a target of "the paradox of prejudice" which "renders its victims simultaneously invisible and over-exposed" ("An Invisible Woman," 3). In Canada from 1966 to 1980, she adopted a voice of ironic detachment from homeland and host country. Citing V. S. Naipaul as her literary model at the time, she writes in Days and Nights in Calcutta, "it is he who has written most movingly about the pain and absurdity of art and exile, of 'Third World art' and exile among the former colonizers; the tolerant incomprehension of hosts, the absolute impossibility of ever having a home, a desh" (285). Irony serves as a defense in this expatriate aesthetic against despair, a signal of one's aloofness and difference. That difference, in turn, is predicated upon one's position outside the metropolitan center of, in Mukherjee's case, the Commonwealth, and it is articulated against the backdrop of nostalgia for a pre-colonial homeland. The stable identity of the writer necessitates continuation of an "other-ing" relationship to the colonial center because, as is all too obvious, one can never go home again. For Mukherjee, official, state-sponsored multiculturalism, itself full of unremarked upon irony, fosters this expatriate stance:

> Thanks to Canadian rhetoric on the highest level, I have learned several things about myself that I never suspected. The first is that I have no country of origin. In polite company, I'm an "East Indian" (the opposite, presumably, of "West Indian") [. . .] In impolite company, I'm a "Paki" [. . .] In an official Green Paper on Immigration and Population I learn that I'm something called a "visible minority"; from a "non-traditional area of immigration" who calls into question the "absorptive capacity" of Canada. And the big question (to which my contribution is really not invited) is, "What kind of society do we really want?" ("An Invisible Woman," 38)

The result of such rhetoric is a kind of psychic splitting as the social standing that permitted emigration to begin with suddenly fails to support a publicly sanctioned identity. Irony becomes a way of balancing dual demands for absorbable language and cultural specificity, while refusing to be claimed by either one.

Looking back on irony as a voice of privilege (signaling emigration by choice), Mukherjee refers to this aesthetic later as "the language of the supervictim, the language of the Commonwealth writer as the mimic man" ("Mimicry and Reinvention," 151). Mimicry reveals in this case a "deep sense of marginality" as a writer's experiences are forced into patterns dictated by the colonizer's language. It is only when experience shapes language that subversion becomes possible. In those instances, the "adopted language is so stretched and twisted in order to be true to the foreignness of the experience that the revisions become literally new vision or inventions" ("Mimicry," 148). Mukherjee's own aesthetic of engagement, which she characterizes as a direct response to the silences favored by Canadian multiculturalism, belies a facile division between mimicry and reinvention. Instead of speaking through characters of unalterable displacement as she did in early novels (e.g., Dimple in *Wife* and Tara in *The Tiger's Daughter*), Mukherjee has focused on "pioneers" and "hustlers," immigrants with "guts and energy and feistiness" since she moved to the United States. Immigration does not equal "melting pot" in this aesthetic; as she describes herself and her characters to Bill Moyers in a PBS interview, "We have come not to passively accommodate ourselves to someone else's dream of what we should be. We've come to America [. . .] to take over, to help build a new culture." The theme of immigration overrides nostalgia for any specific past, and it renders her "Indianness [. . .] a metaphor, a particular way of partially comprehending the world" (*Darkness*, xv).

Some critics have taken Mukherjee to task for this approach, citing her metaphoric deployment of "Indianness" as a way of maintaining a mark of difference while she appropriates European models of Ellis Island immigration in order to ensure her own acceptance into the American literary marketplace.[1] Anindyo Roy, writing about *Days and Nights in Calcutta* and *Jasmine* (in ways pertinent to *The Holder of the World*), argues that Mukherjee's aesthetic attempts to capitalize on an epic vision of immigration that elides the specificities of postcolonial experience. "By subsuming her postcoloniality in this Euro-centered aesthetic rite of passage," Roy maintains, "Mukherjee seeks to legitimize her own romantic 'epic' imagination, seamlessly weaving it into the archetypal European immigrant experience in the New World" (130). Mukherjee's aesthetic in this reading becomes little more than an extension of Orientalism, rendering India an exotic attribute comfortably contained by dominant forces of the Amercian literary marketplace. *The Holder of the World* is vulnerable to this charge in its parallel plot lines of three white women, their "Indian" (Native American and Indian) lovers, and British colonial expansion in America and the Indian subcontinent. Immigration is transcultural in the text and, as an overarching theme, spans four centuries. Reading the text solely along these lines, however, ignores the ways in which it explicitly interrogates the foundations of American national identity by focusing on female rather than male desire and desire that transgresses ethnic distinctions.

Mukherjee has also been faulted, most eloquently and convincingly by Kristin Carter-Sanborn writing about *Jasmine*, for failing to imbue her heroines with self-determining agency. Here it is Mukherjee's portrayal of "Indianness" which conflicts with precepts of American feminism. Carter-Sanborn critiques the text's appeal on the basis of "its simultaneous exoticism and domesticability" (575). Referring to a scene in which Jasmine, inspired by the goddess Kali, stabs her rapist instead of avenging her shame through suicide, Carter-Sanborn notes: "As Mukherjee represents her, the 'third world' woman cannot be violent without recourse to some original mythic, mystic 'presence' [. . .] that ironically blocks access to agency" (589). While this reading is, in its entirety, much more subtle than an accounting of the text according to white Western feminist standards, as Mukherjee charges such critics, it does raise the question of how to read gender across cultures. As with the argument concerning "epic" immigration, the criticism above may also apply to *The Holder of the World* in its treatment of the Indian servant, Bhagmati, who is subsumed by the narrative of white women's stories. *The Holder of the World*, like many of her previous works, also locates female agency in either maternity or fate.[2] Caught between these two camps (charging Eurocentric themes versus an "Orientalized" or passive feminine other), Mukherjee's fusion aesthetic seems destined for annihilation under fire from the critics.

What is most useful about these criticisms, however, is the way in which they work together, not to undermine the ethnic "authority" of the text, an authority Mukherjee herself would not claim, but to force us to read ethnic and gendered desire against the signifiers of national identity. It is by theorizing ethnicity and gender simultaneously, at the site of the competing histories structuring the text, that we wrest these categories from the control of the dominant fiction. *The Holder of the World* asks directly what it means to be American, though it does so under the familiar guise of the American Romance. Playing on the misnaming of Native Americans as Indians, Mukherjee rewrites the narrative of colonial expansion in America and India by rewriting *The Scarlet Letter*; by untangling the strands of language and law to reveal their naturalized foundations, she destabilizes the ethnic and gender divisions upon which our national identity rests. What have been repressed in this discourse of the dominant fiction are the conflated taboos of female desire and racial difference, the "I" for Indian lover masked by the "A" of Adultery. In place of what she terms a "morbid introspection into guilt and repression that many call our greatest work" (286), Mukherjee offers a national identity constructed around the liberation of female desire across ethnic and national borders.[3]

The Holder of the World calls upon *The Scarlet Letter* not only in the overt reference cited above, but also in its borrowing of names (from various Hawthorne texts: Hester, Legge, Pyncheon, Prynne), direct quotes ("Preach! Write! Act!"), historical details, and the link between the letter of the law and collective identity. In "Spaces In-Between," Judie Newman details the three-way relationship between Mukherjee, Hawthorne, and the characters of *The Holder of the World*. Arguing that the novel "deliberately brings the two 'spheres' together—postcolonial and American literature—upsetting institutional authorities in the process, crossing boundaries, and renegotiating the spaces of cultural authority" (81), Newman explores the multiple meanings implicit in the details: the parallels, nominally and personally, between Bharati Mukherjee and her narrator, Beigh Masters; the way in which the story of Asian trade is implicit in, yet absent from "The Custom House" chapter of *The Scarlet Letter*; the literary and economic significance of Yale University (Beigh's alma mater) as a symbol of cultural authority whose very existence derives from Elias Yale's trading in Madras. In its entirety, Newman concludes, the novel "celebrates imagination over fact" while simultaneously "restoring a history" (85).

Other critics largely agree that Mukherjee succeeds on both fictional and historical levels. As Claire Messud writes in her *Times Literary Supplement* review, "This is an alternative history which could revise forever the imaginative relations between immigrants and 'natives' in Mukherjee's America" (23). In *The New York Times Book Review*, K. Anthony Appiah similarly praises Mukherjee's revision: "And when, in the end, Bharati Mukherjee has the hubris, the chutzpah, the sheer unmitigated gall, to connect her book, in Beigh's voice, with Hawthorne's novel 'The Scarlet Letter' [. . .] it is, I think, a connection she has earned. Nathaniel Hawthorne is a relative of hers" (7). These reviews celebrate adding to the canon rather than fracturing it along the lines of ethnic content or authorship; and, that strategy is in keeping with Mukherjee's own aesthetic of fusion. At the same time, revising a text so thoroughly embedded in the textual foundation of national identity raises the following questions: What are the privileged signifiers that make possible a symbiotic relationship between the literary canon and national identity?[4] How does the revision alter, subvert, or reinforce the meaning and power of those signifiers? How do we as readers, teachers, and critics respond to revision as a strategy? Does it demand a reckoning with the violence and erasure implicit in colonial nation-building or simply make them more palatable?

The Holder of the World asks to be read as an (unhyphenated) American text in order to demonstrate the constitutive role of ethnicity in defining "American." Accompanying this strategy, as Shirley Geok-lin Lim points out, is the belief that separating out ethnically identified texts leads to an "appeal to 'authenticity' and the conflation of 'authenticity' with socially desirable and approved features of the community" (151). Incorporating ethnicity also guards against the possibility that it would devolve into an "otherness" that reinforces the centripetal force of the center–periphery model of nationhood. "Reading ethnic identity in Asian American texts as 'otherness' is a shifty paradox," Lim adds, "if a rejection of 'otherness' underlies the themes of ethnicity" (160). Replacing "otherness" with "difference" in this case would merely assuage the need to take responsibility for the unequal social valuing of differences and the social mechanisms that produce them; at least in the self/other configuration of identity, hierarchy is explicit and not glossed by the language of pluralism.[5] Lim warns just as strenuously, however, against automatic canonization of ethnic texts according to dominant literary standards, noting that the " 'problem' of ethnicity becomes 'resolved' in the writer's facility and ease with majority rhetoric and aesthetics, and the 'danger' posed by the unfamiliar and alien is thus defused" (160). The flip side of the argument for incorporation is that it subsumes all forms of difference within a Western aesthetic. The resulting canon may be "colored" slightly differently, but what counts as "literature" remains the same.

Mukherjee does not offer an easy escape from these dangers. In *The Holder of the World*, she adopts the voice of the contemporary white woman, Beigh, whose business interests (she is an "asset hunter") and family ancestry intersect in seventeenth-century colonial Massachusetts in Hannah Easton. The narrative is structured according to Beigh's search for the Emperor's Tear, the world's most perfect diamond, and runs along the parallel tracks of Beigh, Hannah, and Rebecca's (Hannah's mother's) lives. The text revises *The Scarlet Letter* according to the ambit of illicit desire as well as American Romance. When Hawthorne defines Romance in his preface to *The House of Seven Gables* he offers to the writer "a certain latitude, both as to its fashion and material, which he would not have felt himself entitled to assume had he professed to be writing a Novel." While he advises against using "the Marvellous" as more than just seasoning for "the dish offered to the Public," he also notes that disregarding such caution is not "a literary crime" ("Preface," 1). For Mukherjee, "the Marvellous" finds its most vivid expression in the Moghul miniature paintings she claims as her aesthetic model and in the virtual reality time travel which concludes Beigh's search. These two modes of representing and re-creating history vie for primacy: Beigh's readings of historical texts (from the paintings to shipping records to historical and literary accounts) compete with her partner Venn Iyer's virtual reality research at MIT. The incandescent letter of the law that marked the bodies of Hester Prynne and Arthur Dimmesdale circulates much more surreptitiously through the aesthetic structure of Mukherjee's revision.

Mukherjee's adoption of Moghul miniatures as an aesthetic standard coincides with her aesthetic of fusion and her move to the United States. *Darkness*, the short story collection in whose preface she specifies the difference between "the aloofness of expatriatism" and the "exuberance of immigration" (xv), ends with "Courtly Vision," a story drawn from an A.D. 1584 Moghul painting. In the final scene of the story, Mukherjee gives voice to the emperor as he rides away from his capital and into enemy territory. Looking back at the court painter, the emperor yearns for the combination of vision and pleasure only the painter can provide:

> Give me total vision, commands the emperor. His voice hisses above the
> hoarse calls of the camels. You, Basawan, who can paint my Begum on
> a grain of rice, see what you can do with the infinite vistas the size of my
> open hand. Hide nothing from me, my co-wanderer. Tell me how my

new capital will fail, will turn to dust and these marble terraces be home
to jackals and infidels. Tell me who to fear and who to kill but tell it to
me in a way that makes me smile. Transport me through dense fort walls
and stone grilles and into the hearts of men. (171)

Here total vision penetrates boundaries of time and space; the peripatetic
eye finds its own pleasure in looking into the future, through walls, and
within people. What Mukherjee is celebrating in the Moghul miniature
painting, as she explains in "A Four-Hundred-Year-Old Woman," is "its
crazy foreshortening of vanishing point, its insistence that everything
happens simultaneously, bound only by shape and color. In the miniature
paintings of India, there are a dozen separate foci, the most complicated
stories can be rendered on a grain of rice, the corners are as elaborate as
the centers. There is a sense of the interpenetration of all things" (28).

In *The Holder of the World*, Venn's programming becomes the contemporary perfection of this aesthetic; indeed, Beigh says, "[a]ttaining Nirvana,
for Venn, is attaining perfect design" (91). His goal is to create a reality of
the past through an amalgamation of bits of data which can interact with
personality. He "and all the other strategists at MIT are looking for an
information formula, an Einsteinian theory that will organize facts [. . .]
into some sort of pattern. He wants facts to grow like a crystal garden, he
wants to create a supersaturated medium, a data plasma, in which just
a sprinkle of data cues will precipitate a forest down below" (258). His
success will "enable any of us to insert ourselves anywhere and anytime on
the space–time continuum for as long as the grid can hold" (6), and, thus,
will give each user a glimpse of the power of total vision. Mukherjee enacts
the kind of fusion promised by the painting and computerized animation
of the past in her own modeling of *The Scarlet Letter* and American
Romance on Moghul Indian painting. As an aesthetic strategy, fusion
rejects authenticity as a value; as the emperor of "Courtly Visions"
commands, fusion must reveal what would otherwise be masked or elided,
but do so in the service of aesthetic pleasure. Searching for an "ethno-
aesthetics" here would mean demanding an essentialism that neither
author nor text supports. It is that refusal to claim "otherness" that makes
Mukherjee's writing so effective in disrupting neat literary categories.
Finding no content-based aesthetic to satisfy us, we are forced to address
the processes at work in her use of mimicry, revision, and reinvention.

* * *

These processes have both aesthetic and psychoanalytic connotations;
mimicry, revision, and reinvention denote ways of responding artistically

and psychically to a set of existing conditions. In *Four Fundamental Concepts of Psychoanalysis*, Lacan defines mimicry as a "camouflage." "It is not a question of harmonizing with the background," he states, "but, against a mottled background, of becoming mottled—exactly like the technique of camouflage practised in human warfare" (99). His metaphor implies that mimicry, while always a strategy of self-protection, may be used offensively or defensively. This image further suggests an opposition between warring factions, the stakes of whose conflict may be one's very life. Such an opposition is fractured in Mukherjee's aesthetic by the positing of multiple backgrounds against which to blend. Naming Moghul miniature painting, computerized time "retrieval," and American Romance as aesthetic standards generates a more complicated design on the cultural screen(s), without specifying whether there is more than one battle to be fought.

In order to discover what it takes to blend in, and thus to flourish, it is helpful to return to Lacan's foundational schemas of the subject, gaze, and screen. The viability of the subject, according to this model, depends upon self-recognition within the range of images made available by the cultural screen and illuminated by the gaze. Crucial to this process is the equating of the gaze with the point of light. It is that process of illumination, according to Lacan, that "determines me, at the most profound level, in the visible [. . .] It is through the gaze that I enter light and it is from the gaze that I receive its effects. Hence it comes about that the gaze is the instrument through which light is embodied and through which [. . .] I am photo-graphed" (106). Lacan specifies here that the gaze comes from "outside," an invisible position that naturalizes the power of the gaze even if we recognize it as culturally generated. Kaja Silverman, in *The Threshold of the Visible World*, insists upon a strict reading of this passage in order to show that while the gaze produces light needed for representation and recognition, it does not dictate the forms of identity and identification that result; those images depend upon the screen which mediates the identificatory process. The screen presents, she elsewhere explains, "that culturally generated image or repertoire of images through which subjects are not only constituted, but differentiated in relation to class, race, sexuality, age, and nationality" (*Male Subjectivity at the Margins*, 150). Those images glow with the wattage of their constitutive signifiers whose "obviousness" obscures the function of the gaze.

Silverman's analysis emphasizes the power of the screen to ensure ideological uniformity across multiple sites of identification, but it does not fully account for the visibility of the subject. We are left with the

r foundations of acquisition and control, they also seem
in a text modeled after the rhetoric of adventure and
those same rationales. The Moghul aesthetic Mukherjee
mes less a dispersal of a single gaze into multiple perspectives
ula for exoticizing the cultural "other" with its depiction of
des, the mysterious servant woman, jewels and finery, and
nsible rituals and religions. The mimicking and juxtaposi-
ltiple aesthetics, then, work to undermine the rationales of
wer even as they cooperate in legitimating the narrative plea-
power for a Western audience.
an is helpful in explaining the apparent ambivalence inherent
ultaneous use of multiple aesthetics. As she explains in
old of the Visible World, "In order to emerge within the field
he subject must not only align him- or herself identificatorily
reen, but must also be apprehended in that guise by the gaze"
statement implies the possibility that the subject could be
ized by the gaze, stand on the edge of its scope, or look
nd therefore distortingly, at the illuminated images of the
ce the gaze "has no power to constitute subjectivity except by
the screen on to the subject," as Silverman states in *Male*
y *at the Margins*, mis-recognition cannot account for failure to
hended" by the gaze. Such failure could only occur if the
re, so to speak, out of the spotlight. This means that while the
be "unlocalizable" (*TVW*, 18) it is not without direction;
s illuminating perspective with a vanishing point but no hori-
is schematic the subject and the look exist between the limits
tive, though not necessarily along a vanishing line. (Since the
rmines" the subject, one literally cannot speak of being outside
The transcendent position of the gaze "outside" the subject's
ision naturalizes the power of the gaze; it prohibits the viewer
ropriating "the epistemological authority in the perspectival
TVW, 132). The gaze seemingly comes from everywhere and
such that the subject becomes quite literally caught between
lights.
ugh the subject seems frozen here between the transfixing power
ze and the images available for reclamation, s/he nevertheless
ze limited potential to "play" with those images—a potential that
bly increases with the range of images available—within the
of mimicry itself as well as to move across the field of light.
, then, encompasses actions ranging from self-recognition to
on. Self-recognition refers to Lacan's broadest definition of

assumption of a singular cultural gaze and corresponding set of images. The question then becomes, in Mukherjee's case, whether the multiple cultural backgrounds she cites necessarily share privileged signifiers. On one hand, the subject's inevitable longing for coherence would seem to demand such uniformity, according to the logic that sustains the dominant fiction. On the other hand, if those signifiers emerge from culturally specific codifications of gendered desire, and the terms legitimating that desire (the petit objet *a*) are culturally variable, then multiplying cultural realms might yield loopholes in or "misreadings" of the dominant fiction.

In *The Holder of the World*, Beigh culls the story of Hannah Easton's transformation from Puritan daughter to Indian Raja's mistress to American patriot through the texts of different cultures: Beigh reads Hannah in the texts of colonial Massachusetts, in the Moghul miniature paintings that capture her life in South India, and through Venn's program. Through the combination of all three, Mukherjee presents Hannah as a woman "outside the pale of the two civilizations" (259) whose failure to be fully interpellated by one culture enables her to challenge the assumptions of both. Hannah's transformations—"her Christian-Hindu-Muslim self, her American-English-Indian self, her orphaned, abandoned, widowed, pregnant self, her *firangi* and bibi self" (268)—take place against the backdrop of British colonialism in America and India, making Hannah at once its agent and critic.

Orphaned as a child by her father's death and her mother Rebecca's abandoning her in favor of a Nipmuc Indian lover (staged as a murder before Hannah's eyes during a Nipmuc rebellion against the Puritans), Hannah is raised in Salem by pious relatives. Although she is dutiful and loyal (to her mother's secret and her adopted family's Puritan norms), the memories of her mother's transgression surface inadvertently through Hannah's fantastical embroidery and occasional "spells." She is, therefore, already, if subconsciously, marked by the conflict between her mother's passion and social strictures. When the Irish merchant sailor Gabriel Legge appears in Salem with stories of far-away exploits, Hannah succumbs—though she knows better than to believe all his tales, marries, and returns with him to England. His appetite for adventure eventually brings them, on behalf of a colonial trading company, to the outpost White Town in Moghul India.

As in Salem and England, Hannah is simultaneously a product of her surroundings and a detached observer. She performs the duties of a Company wife, but her growing friendship with her servant Bhagmati gradually breaks down the self/other opposition upon which colonial power rests. After Gabriel trades Company employment for piracy and takes an Indian mistress, Hannah finds herself literally unmoored from the social rules that had structured her world and dependent upon Bhagmati as guide in this now foreign land. Adrift in a flood and Indian rebellion against the colonial powers, she and Bhagmati are rescued by the Hindu Raja Singh who is fighting his own battle against the ruling Moghul emperor. The passion that Hannah could only release through embroidery as a child and in her medical skills in England finally reaches fruition with the Raja in the two weeks they spend in his fort. Their love affair is mutually empowering from a Western perspective. As an English traveler relates the story he heard from one of their maidservants, "The Lady pushed the Lion of Devgad down on the carpet alive with lion hunters grasping griffins with amber manes. The Lion trembled under her touch at first, and then, as though he too was under a spell, submitted to her slow deliberate caresses" (228). The Raja is also transfigured from feminized native—characterized initially as small, gentle, well-formed, and sensual, and whose military strategies include escape from danger and cunning over fortitude—to potent lover (as opposed to Gabriel). This passionate interlude, however, merely delays the inevitable war the Raja faces with the more powerful emperor. The first battle leaves the Raja near death and, although Hannah's medical prowess, developed out of Nipmuc herbal knowledge and her sewing skills, saves his life, it cannot restore the use of his arm. In retaliation for this symbolic loss of power and upon hearing of her pregnancy, he consigns her to the women's quarters "as a wife but no more than a wife" (259), a clearly less exalted position than that of foreign mistress as she is brought back into his domestic realm.

Outside her own domestic sphere, however, Hannah is "compelled" by her pregnancy to try to avert what will obviously be the Raja's last battle. Journeying to the Great Moghul's battlefield tent with Bhagmati, she lobbies him unsuccessfully; it is clear that her passion is no match for the driving force of religious and political conquest symbolized by his diamond, the Emperor's Tear. In response to Hannah's plea for peace and reconciliation, he defends his obligation to expand his empire by killing "the infidel": "I do not fight for treasure and glory in this life. The diamond is the tear I shed as I discharge my duty [. . .] The dutiful and the innocent, if they are pure and if they submit, will be judged by the all-seeing, all-merciful Allah. The sum of their lives will be weighed in the scales of judgment" (269), he says as he replaces the diamond in a golden sculpture of his hands.

After the battle, Hannah returns to Salem with her daughter, Pearl, who was born on the crossing: the new immigrant. Hannah locates her

mimicry as the "visual articulation," in Silverman's words, of the subject against the screen. Since subjectivity is formed in relation to the images on the screen, self-recognition can mean little more than "the passive duplication of a pre-existing image."[6] Both Silverman and Lacan also insist on the possibility of overt manipulation of the screen's images by the subject who "knows his or her necessary specularity." Lacan describes this manipulation on an individual level: "Man, in effect, knows how to play with the mask as that beyond which there is the gaze. The screen is here the locus of mediation" (*FFC*, 107).

Silverman takes the model of mimicry a step further with the possibility of conscious collective intervention; and, she does so by arguing for the efficacy of mimicry and its related strategies over alternatives such as defamiliarization (a display of cultural "otherness" designed and deployed to discomfort the dominant culture).[7] Since the subject only makes sense according to the images of the screen, manipulation of existing images ensures that the subject or collective may continue to be read. "Those attempts at a collective self-redefinition which rely upon masquerade, parody, inversion, and bricolage," Silverman argues, "will consequently be more successful than those aimed at the *ex nihilo* creation of new images, since they work upon the existing cultural imaginary" (*MSM*, 150).

It is important to note here, in further defense of the subversive potential of mimicry, that as a strategy it is both inevitable (on the level of self-recognition) and pragmatic (in that it must be done repeatedly, thereby presenting unending opportunities for subversion and/or perversion of normative images). The ability of privileged signifiers to function at a multitude of identificatory sites means that no one can step out of the dominant fiction that structures subjectivity, just as no one can step out of the gaze. If consciousness of one's own position between the gaze and the screen enables the subject to adopt images on the screen as a weapon through either exaggeration or denaturalization, we must ask where this self-conscious specularity originates. Such self-consciousness, Mukherjee's text suggests, might accrue to any subject needing to negotiate multiple spheres of cultural imagery. What Mukherjee's aesthetics of fusion forces us to do, then, is to examine continually the play of signification across the text and through its various aesthetic spheres.

* * *

By adopting a strategy of revision, she immediately identifies a set of privileged signifiers at work. The letter of the law remains the dominant symbol of the following overlapping themes: the "New World" with its echoes in and of America, South India, and the Garden of Eden; the covenant as collective glue; history as a Western story of progress, expansion, and knowledge. All are scripted within our dominant fiction in gendered terms as manifestations of masculinized desire for mastery and control of feminized objects of innocence or passivity. The dominant fiction that results is one of integration and moral superiority in the formation of the national collective. Redeploying the image of the law through revision denaturalizes its authority by making it the subject of investigation. Although the scarlet "A" no longer glows ominously throughout the text, its shadowy presence marks the boundaries of stages of Hannah's life, from her paradisical infancy to the Puritan piety of her childhood to the colonial separatism she finds in India. In each case, that surreptitious presence reminds us of the possibility of transgression rather than of the law's infallibility. As Lacan notes in his definition of mimicry, it "reveals something in so far as it is distinct from what might be called an itself that is behind" (99).

What remains behind is not something "original" or "authentic," as opposed to an imitation, but the effects of colonial power. Mimicry is less a mechanism for the unadulterated reproduction of that power, than an "ambivalent" process, to quote Bhabha in *The Location of Culture*, that "does not merely 'rupture' the discourse, but becomes transformed into an uncertainty which fixes the colonial subject as a 'partial' presence" (86). Inherent in the process of mimicry are slippages between the current representation and the projections of the screen. While mimicry acknowledges the priority of those projections, the fact that mimicry takes place at all indicates their limitations; that the mimic, by definition, is attempting to match the display of power traces the borders of power itself. In other words, as a process, mimicry underscores the distance between the screen and the subject. Maintaining a conceptual distinction between the "background" that Lacan describes and the screen assists here in explaining Bhabha's use of "uncertainty" and "partial presence." If the subject can only be said to exist as such in relation to and through idealization of images of the screen, then his/her conscious mimicry must occur in relation to just a subset of those images. The background depends upon the position of the subject vis à vis the gaze and screen. The mimicked identity is necessarily partial presence since the subject can turn the projection back toward its issuing power in an act of subversion. In neither the process of mimicry nor of mimicry as subversion does the subject ever disappear. As Bhabha argues, "The menace of mimicry is its double vision which in disclosing the ambivalence of colonial discourse also disrupts its authority" (88).

In *The Holder of the World*, introduction of an alternative cultural sphere to the Puritanism of *The Scarlet Letter* creates the opportunity for transformative, feminized, counter-colonial desire. It is Hannah's removal from spheres of cultural familiarity that serves as a catalyst for her sexual awakening and her various "translations." Through a reinvention of Hester Prynne as Hannah Easton-Fitch-Legge—'the Salem Bibi', Mukherjee creates a female heroine to alter the signifying terms of the romance she inhabits. In looking at ways in which the exercise of female desire calls into question the privileged signifiers of our national identity, we must ultimately ask: What in the text explains Hannah's (and with her, Rebecca and Beigh's) desire? What makes possible their idealization of unsanctioned identities? The thesis of *The Threshold of the Visible World* is that aesthetic works, functioning mnemonically, may facilitate conscious idealization of identities we would otherwise repudiate. One potentially subversive function of the aesthetic is its ability to intervene in the libidinal weighting of "new" memories (images created by the text that enter the unconscious and circulate in the chain of signification as memories) and emerging ones. The aesthetic text never escapes the gaze and screen that illuminate normative representations; however, as a product of the creative process, where "conscious and unconscious faculties 'lose their mutual exclusiveness' " (184), it does not necessarily adhere strictly to the dictates of the dominant fiction. By intervening in the stimulation and expression of both memory and desire, the aesthetic text may call forth as pleasurable images normally inadmissible. If desire, according to Silverman's model of inessential subjectivity, is predicated upon a psychic void that becomes socially inscribed in terms of privileged signifiers, then foregrounding those signifiers might enable us to denaturalize their libidinal power. This foregrounding, then, might constitute a first step in the conscious intervention into the representational field.

Moving beyond recognizing the constructedness of normative representations to, what Silverman terms, the productive look ("the active gift of love" which bestows ideality upon precisely what is "not me" after one consciously identifies with it) requires the dual mechanisms of distance and deferral. Together they ensure that the subject recognizes his/her own specularity within those cultural constructions (distance) and makes the conscious effort to look again at the formerly barred object of desire (deferral). We have already seen how mimicry as an aesthetic process works simultaneously to foreground those signifiers and to reveal their constructedness. Mimicry enacts its own forms of distanciation as follows: it makes explicit the position of the subject relative to the gaze and the screen, first by showing the idealization of certain images as a social process and, second, by showing that the power of those images is limited. In the case of multiple, potentially differing cultural signifiers, mimicry provides the conscious mimic with a choice of images, each of which may only partially represent him/her and the power at hand. In these ways, mimicry potentially enables an idealization outside of the confines of the valued familiar.

Deferral is also implicit in the process of mimicry in the lapse between what is "there" and the imitation. On the level of the psyche, deferral refers to the process by which a previously unassimilable or incomprehensible memory or experience becomes imbued with meaning within the subject's contemporary context. Laplanche and Pontalis define deferral according to the following characteristics:

    a. It is not lived experience in general that undergoes a deferred revision but, specifically, whatever has been impossible in the first instance to incorporate fully into a meaningful context. The traumatic event is the epitome of such unassimilated experience.

    b. Deferred revision is occasioned by events and situations, or by an organic maturation, which allow the subject to gain access to a new level of meaning and to rework his earlier experiences.

    c. Human sexuality, with the peculiar unevenness of its temporal development, provides an eminently suitable field for the phenomenon of deferred action.

Silverman builds upon this definition with the specification that deferral, as it functions in the productive look, must include a conscious revaluing of the mnemonic image into the contemporary field of meaning. In this way, deferral becomes a site of "conscious agency" and, therefore, of the ethical (173).

The transformation of Hester Prynne's guilt and shame into Hannah's pride takes place according to Silverman's process of deferral. While we never discover the trigger for Rebecca's decision to leave hearth and child for life with a Nipmuc warrior, that decision forms the basis of Hannah's first and only full memory of her mother. It is an image of the thresholds of desire:

> Rebecca by the window, her neck long and arched, her throat throbbing with song. A voice so strong and sweet that it softens the sternest spiritual phrases into voluptuous pleas [. . .] Rebecca singing each line by

herself first, then nodding to encourage Hannah; Hannah repeating the
line in a quavery, unformed voice. But, Hannah remembers, and this can
never be separated from the angelic choir pouring from her mother's
breast, there are faces at the window. (27)

The image melds social, religious, and political divisions which maintain Puritan legitimacy into a sensual and eroticized scene of transgression: the maternal duty to teach the psalms, symbol of the covenant and
the city on the hill, becomes a lesson in pleasure and possibility rather
than obligation; meanwhile, the protected domestic space both dissolves
and is reconstituted under the look from the "wilderness."[8] The phras-
ing of the passage provides two distinct, though related readings. One
possibility is that the faces at the window represent the unknown (and
unknowable) who, by definition, threaten the viability of the subject.
The other is that what actually constitutes the ideal domestic sphere in
Hannah's memory, and, therefore, her mother as an ideal subject, is
recognition by the Native Americans outside. This possibility depends
upon Hannah's view of the Nipmucs themselves as subjects (as capable
of bestowing an affirming look), a view that we learn later she had.

Although she witnesses the staging of her mother's murder—stab-
bing the dog and sullying with his blood Rebecca's Puritan garments,
her dressing in the Nipmuc clothes her lover had brought, the final
good-bye as the house is set on fire and Hannah is whisked away to
relatives' doorstep by a Nipmuc woman—Hannah "wills the memory
of this night away; she will orphan herself to that memory" (30).
Mukherjee describes this scene, and Hannah's sudden removal from the
pleasures of Rebecca's singing and their explorations in the forests, in
terms of a banishment from the Garden of Eden: "She has witnessed the
Fall, not Adam's Fall, Rebecca's Fall. Her mother's Fall, infinitely more
sinful than the fall of a man. She is the witness not merely of the occa-
sion of sin, but of the birth of sin itself" (30). Rebecca transgresses the
dictates of both ethnic separation and maternal "nature," and it is the
combination that most severely threatens the patriarchal structure of
colonial power. Not only does Rebecca act on her desires but she does
so at the expense of the sexual dominance of white men and the preservation of the covenant (by refusing not only to sustain its Puritan
rendering but also to pass it along). For Hannah, whose father died in
her infancy, Rebecca's decision confirmed what she already knew—that
the Nipmuc warrior was "her inadmissible father, the only man she'd
ever seen her mother with" (28)—and taught her the fragility of any
law, religious or social. Mukherjee's depiction of Rebecca's "fall" also

suggests, however, that Hannah's childhood with Rebecca and her lover before that night was, in fact, Edenic. Hannah's subsequent empowerment in India once she becomes pregnant and the reunion of mother and daughter that concludes the text further support this reading. The text sanctions female desire, then, to the extent that it engenders ethnic fusion and creates new immigrant-citizens.

The passion captured by Hannah's memory erupts in other guises throughout her childhood. Her extraordinary and exotic embroidery discloses an imaginative realm unauthorized by Puritan asceticism: "her needle spoke; it celebrated the trees, flowers, birds, fish of her infant days. Nostalgia, all the more forceful because it was unacknowledged, was augmented with fancy" (43). Hannah's embroidery is nothing less than "the embodiment of desire" (44) which remains, at this point, unintelligible and insatiable, though the very image of her hidden memory.[9] The sampler itself, a lushly embellished embroidery of the psalm Rebecca taught, echoes Hester Prynne's fanciful rendering of her scarlet letter. Hannah hangs the sampler by her bed where, "when she knelt by it to pray, it shot the familiar virtues she prayed for—humility, gratitude, meekness—with a pagan iridescence" (45). If we read the image of Rebecca's departure as an unassimilable sexual trauma, then we can trace the process of deferral through these attempted resurfacings. As Silverman notes, upon perception the image is embedded in a web of meanings and memories, even though it may not be available for comprehension or conscious expression. Moreover, those unconscious webs work "to permit the indirect and disguised expression of the desire for an object or scene which cannot be named directly" (*TVW*, 181). The subject's unconscious desire for a blocked object results in displacement of that desire on to another term or image. Since return is impossible, desire moves forward along the signifying chain, thereby performing a kind of unconscious psychic mimicry that, as Bhabha also remarks, functions metonymically (*LC*, 90). This succession of displacements, although it may attempt to follow the paths of normativity, nevertheless effectively introduces alterity into each movement in the space opened by the slippages between the subject's desire for a barred identity and its partial substitutions.

For Hannah, the forms of these unconscious displacements evolve as she matures. Living in the growing port of Salem, she becomes increasingly aware of the tensions within her own community, from growing commercialism and cosmopolitanism to uneasy relations with both the English and the Nipmucs. She finds the same elasticity of law and values in Fort St. Sebastian. By indicating a moral vacuum in British expansion in both America and India, Mukherjee creates a space for the realization of Hannah's desire. In colonial Salem and India, the letter of the law fails to engage and sustain collective identification and unity. The letters of sin and transgression—Adulterer, Blasphemer, Thief, Incest breeder, or Indian lover—displayed on the body in Salem "no longer excited the intended pity or fear; evidence of outrageous sin sometimes earned the wretch a farthing and a snicker" (41). In this realm of unstable authority, Hannah's memory yields other images long repressed that enable her to begin to write her own moral code. Her longest "spell," brought on by hearing Mrs. Rowlandson's account of her abduction by "Indians," ends when Hannah dreams herself as a child, pledging to follow Rebecca's "whispered, subversive alphabet" (54): act, boldness, character, dissent, ecstasy, forage, independence. In this instance, although the image of Rebecca's departure remains blocked, Mrs. Rowlandson's account, with its mixture of danger and adventure, unleashes Hannah's blissful memories of the forest and of Rebecca and her warrior. She responds scornfully to this account in which the "godless are invading the garden that the diligent have cleared from the forest primeval" (53). To her best friend, Hester, who asks for confirmation of Mrs. Rowlandson's story, Hannah replies, "[It] is such as the common press should wish of savages and gentlewomen alike" (54). Out of this articulation of narrative falsity, Rebecca and her alphabet surface in Hannah's consciousness, undermining both the moral lesson of Mrs. Rowlandson and the laws that support it.

In India, Hannah witnesses the same failure of the branded letter to be collectively and definitively read when Indians add their own marks to a victim's body in "promiscuous imitation of the English alphabet" (157). Her own desire first emerges out of this social and moral chaos, just after Gabriel has broken with the Company and is on his way to join a group of pirates. Beigh, narrating from scraps of recovered histories, writes, "We know that Hannah suddenly let go of her reins, that she twisted impulsively, violently, in her saddle, and kissed Gabriel" (160). Again, the link between colonial and sexual desire becomes explicit as a local boy watches this scene from behind a sand dune and sees, according to an account he later wrote in William III's court, "the beautiful white woman seize her man right there on the beach, *his* beach, and vent on him without coyness and without shame her wild *firangi* passions and selfish wants, and as he watched the woman greedily, shamelessly, he saw a vision of himself on another shore by another ocean, an adventurer without family, without caste, without country, cantering into worlds without rules" (161).[10] The awakening of Hannah's sexual desire is the story of her "becoming," though the narrative remains ambivalent as to whether desire can ever be anything other than colonizing; just so, the fisherman's boy attempts to appropriate the gaze of the colonizer.

The final stage in the psychic deferral of Hannah's memory depends on Bhagmati's intercession. Isolated from other denizens of White Town because of her husband's piracy, Hannah finds herself increasingly dependent upon Bhagmati for company and an understanding of the India across the bridge. Mukherjee creates a parallel here between the Hindu legend of Sita, the ideal wife, and Hannah in White Town. When Sita is lured out of the protective white circle around her in the forest, thereby disobeying the wishes of her husband, Prince Rama, she is kidnapped by the demon-king Ravanna. During a year's wait before her rescue, Sita refuses all of Ravanna's advances and gifts. Despite her faithfulness, Rama renounces her until she proves her innocence through a trial by fire, from which she emerges unscathed. From there, Mukherjee relates three different endings to the story. In Bhagmati's version, Sita's proof of innocence is the only relevant conclusion. According to Venn's mother (telling her version to Beigh), Sita throws herself back into the flames to spite her husband and "the hegemonic rules of Rama's kingdom." Venn's colleague, Jay, finally, believes his grandmother's version that Rama takes back his wife with great relief. Only that relief turns to doubt, not just as to whether Sita were violated (a shame he could forgive) but also as to her possible pleasure in violation. Unable to resolve these doubts, he banishes her once again to the forest, and once again asks her to undergo a trial by fire. She refuses, preferring instead to throw herself into the accepting embrace of "Mother Earth" (172–7). While Hannah imagines herself in Bhagmati's story, Beigh imagines all three endings and substitutes Hannah's account of her affair with the Raja for Sita's own silence about her captivity. This strategy of linking Mrs. Rowlandson, Rebecca, Sita, and Hannah's story of illicit desire shows how alterity is introduced through the process of displacement.

In order for deferral to lead to the productive look, the subject must learn not just to accept alterity but to identify with and idealize what is precisely "not me." Each resurgence of the catalytic memory is not a return, but a transferal of libidinal value to another term, which may not be culturally valorized. That process may end in a predilection for what is exotic, odd, or eccentric, rather than in idealization of a repudiated identity. It is not when that identity becomes valued libidinally in the unconscious, but only after the subject *consciously* recognizes that idealization that the ethical look is born. As Silverman explains, "The remembering look is not truly productive until it effects one final displacement—the displacement of the ego. It does not fully triumph over the forces that constrain it to see in predetermined ways until its appetite for alterity prevails, not only over sameness, but also over self-sameness" (183).

While Bhagmati's stories introduce Hannah to the world beyond the white circle, it is Bhagmati herself who effects the final displacement that turns Indians from objects into subjects in Hannah's eyes and makes possible her affair with the Raja. As they are held together in his fort after their capture/rescue (an ambivalence that echoes Sita's story), Bhagmati teaches Hannah how to wear a sari in a scene reminiscent of Rebecca's rebirth (like Sita's out of fire, no less) in Nipmuc clothes. Identifying herself in terms of another, Hannah suddenly thinks of her mother: "Perhaps Rebecca's embracing of the wilderness had started like this: a moment's sharp awareness, My God, they're alive! She remembered her mother, suddenly, wearing the beaded belt her lover had given her" (222). Sartorial transformation collapses the distance between Hannah and Bhagmati by erasing the parallel line Rebecca had trespassed. In an unfamiliar world where the letter of the law has no meaning, unleashed by the twin forces of memory and desire from the pre-assigned viewing position her colonial culture had dictated, Hannah consummates in both senses the power of the productive look: "she'd come to understand the aggressive satiety of total fulfillment" (237).

* * *

The Salem Bibi series of Moghul miniatures that document Hannah's affair, and which Beigh uses to construct her history, capture that moment from the same perspective Hannah had of her mother's final night. The erotic image Hannah recoups of Rebecca comes not from the socially prescribed viewing position; a spectator from that perspective could view her only as a sinful reminder of the perils of the New World and of women's sexuality, a threat to social and moral stability, or as victim of Satan's emissaries. Hannah appears in the miniatures not as a wanton whore or rape victim, but in the same sensualized light as the Rebecca of Hannah's memory, only removed from the domestic sphere and placed in the midst of political and religious struggle in India. In one painting, Hannah's arms are outstretched and "her chest is taut with audacious yearnings. Her neck, sinewy as a crane's, strains skyward" (16). In the next, which Beigh names "The Unravish'd Bride," Hannah stands on the fort, chanting "stubborn and curative myths to survive by" (18). Although these images of Hannah and Rebecca echo one another, it is important to see Hannah's desire as something other than a simple return to what is familiar if unmentionable. What makes the productive look—the idealization Hannah bestows on the Raja—ethical is that it is both conscious and excorporative. It is in this regard that Mukherjee's reinvention of transgressive desire becomes most useful: it acknowledges the radical otherness of the idealized body. This acknowledgement, moreover, constitutes the final link in the text between Hannah and Beigh's lovers. There were moments during Hannah and the Raja's two weeks in the fort that love and passion could not breach the gulf between their worlds, their respective identities and fictions. Describing the Raja's angered responses to Hannah's questioning of his motives and actions, Beigh comments:

> I know that reaction. It is the reaction [. . .] of Venn when I tell him about some new discovery I've made about the Coromandel, or Hannah, or even the diamond. In India, it takes a classic apprentice five years to learn how to sit at the sitar before he's allowed to play a note. It's not just the reaction that says How dare you know? It's something deeper: How dare you presume to know? (233)

"How dare you presume to know?" does more than point to distance and insist on deferral; it also asserts that knowledge and perspective are partial. As opposed to the illusion the gaze creates of all-encompassing, omniscient light, the productive look "means to confer ideality, not to find it" (*TVW*, 78). Hannah bestows this look from the intersection of two cultures where the letter of the law and the screen are unable to sustain a viable range of identificatory images. Her agency comes not out of nowhere, in imitation of the gaze, but from the series of displacements, cultural and mnemonic, launched by the image of Rebecca's passion and sexuality.

Hannah's productive look transforms mimicry—of Rebecca's "fall" and of exotic and adventurous romance—into a reinvention of the burgeoning nation's privileged signifiers. Instead of a national identity constructed in the wilderness upon a foundation of moral certainty (with its corollaries of innocence and purity and perseverance) and social cohesion maintained by gendered law, Mukherjee offers a vision of unrest, greed, and violence tempered by the possibility of "the active gift of love" (Silverman). This potential disrupts the authority of patriarchal power, as manifested in colonial expansion, by refiguring the gendered opposition upon which it rests. Whereas desire figures initially as a masculinized preserve inseparable from colonization, through Hannah it becomes a realm of love and procreation that fuses ethnicity with what it means to be American.

The subversive potential of the productive look is constrained in the text as a whole by the competing narratives of the past which reveal the story: Beigh's textual readings epitomized by the Moghul paintings versus Venn's programming. Hannah's encounter with the diamond just before the final battle prefigures a collision between these narratives, as Beigh's research is at an impasse. The last Moghul painting shows Hannah holding aloft the diamond in its golden orb on the edge of battle, and Beigh can find no further references to its whereabouts. She implores Venn to re-create seventeenth-century South India and promises him "the most perfect diamond in the world" for his efforts. When the program is ready, Beigh becomes Venn's subject as she dons helmet, goggles, and gloves for entry into the program. In this acting out of the fantasy of complete control over information and history, Beigh finds herself as Bhagmati (whom Hannah has renamed Hester in honor of her childhood friend), with Hannah, in the world of the final painting. Hannah grabs the diamond from the Moghul's hands and the two women rush out into the middle of the battle. "I scream with agony from the hot white flaming explosion in my shoulder that has spun me around and dropped me to the cool, wet soil," Beigh-as-Bhagmati narrates. "Hannah is on her knees, crying, Hester, Hester, Bhagmati, pray, pray, we must get back . . . I try to hold the diamond out, but it is slippery with my blood." Then, in the final moments of her "life," this virtual Bhagmati plunges a knife into her stomach and buries the diamond inside. When Beigh emerges from her "experience," pulse raging, shoulder and stomach throbbing, she recalls the grave marked Hester Hedges she saw in India and has reached the end of her search (282–3).

The dream such technology encompasses of perfect communication across cultures is transformed into a method of appropriation of the Indian woman's body, name, and history. Rather than a bridge across cultural divides that performs the function of the productive look, "time retrieval" here serves as an updated version of amusement park thrills. Instead of the conscious idealizing of what is unfamiliar and disavowed, the technology enables cultural sampling without commitment.[11] While the computer-generated interactions depend upon Beigh's personal engagement with the data, she remains in Venn's world and under his control (he wonders, e.g., when she screams and writhes whether he should pull her out of it). The identity of the Holder of the World, then, can only be Venn, the contemporary incarnation of the Moghul emperor, the court painter who can see through time and space, and the colonizer, whose golden globe has turned into a computer station. This conclusion elides any difference between the aesthetic designs of the painting and Venn's program. Beigh initially describes the final picture of Hannah as "an art that knows no limit, no perspective and vanishing point, no limit to extravagance, or to detail, that temperamentally cannot exclude, a miniature art forever expanding" (19), a description that could also apply to the gaze; and, Venn's design turns description into power driven by the familiar logic of seize and control. Both aesthetics serve as lenses for a common vision illuminated by a shared gaze.

Nevertheless, the text does not circle back to precisely the same place from which it began. That Mukherjee shows us the colonizing connections between past and present ways of seeing and knowing speaks not to a "failure" of the text, but to the entrenched power of the dominant fiction. Its strength comes from its elasticity, its ability to stretch to encompass the unfamiliar and then to squeeze it back into images already available (just as Mukherjee describes the process of mimicry); the dominant fiction absorbs the postcolonial subject, the "not quite/not white" subject into the images that already exist by foregrounding those signifiers the subject can recognize and which can recognize the subject. In *The Holder of the World*, the image of America as the land of opportunity remains true for immigrants like Venn who share the prevailing definitions of challenge and success. Mukherjee has accomplished more than strengthening that image of America by deploying it across four centuries in the text. If we return to her statement, "I am one of you now," which introduces this chapter, we find that she has shifted the focus of our reading from the alterity of "I" to that of "you," forcing an acknowledgment of ethnicity as constitutive of rather than assimilated into American identity. The difference is what enables Venn to ask Beigh, ironically a Boston Brahmin, "How dare you presume to know?"

CHAPTER 3

TRAUMATIC LEGACY AND THE PSYCHOANALYSIS OF RACE: AFRICAN AMERICAN MASCULINITY IN DARRYL PINCKNEY'S *HIGH COTTON*

> To know where you were going, you had to know where you'd come from, though the claims the past had on you were like cold hands in the dark.
>
> Darryl Pinckney, *High Cotton*

"No one sat me down and told me I was a Negro. That was something I figured out on the sly," begins the anonymous narrator of Darryl Pinckney's *High Cotton* (1992). The autobiographical novel traces the narrator's quest to recognize and define himself as an African American man from his middle-class, mid-western upbringing in Indianapolis in the 1960s and 1970s, through his travels in Europe, college years at Columbia, and finally employment in Manhattan. It is less a conventional *Bildungsroman*, however, than a serious parody of one. Rather than follow a narrator whose innate sensitivity propels both his loss of innocence and his burgeoning awareness, we find one who, at every juncture, wants to "hurry home, to sink back into that state where good news for modern Negroes couldn't find me" (25). The result is a novel that continually asks how blackness factors into the subject's yearning for coherence and recognition, how it might signify social value within rather than exclusion from the nation as family.

Against a historical backdrop—denoted by the nominative changes from Negro to black to African American—of racial awareness and social change, the narrator yearns for the social power awarded the nation's most valued subjects. He is continually torn between his Grandfather Eustace's vision of a black elite and the identities presented by the predominantly white communities the narrator inhabits. Trying desperately to escape the former and embrace the latter, he initially seeks recognition at the expense of his corporeal self, a manifestly doomed endeavor. The tension between corporeality and identification in the novel is reflected in a crisis in naming. By refusing to name himself while disavowing his obvious communal or corporeal identifications, he makes reconciling subjectivity, naming, and historical specificity into the central problem of the novel. If, as Judith Butler notes in *Excitable Speech*, one "'exists' not only by virtue of being recognized, but, in a prior sense, by being *recognizable*," then Pinckney asks how we can conceive of a subject who refuses to see himself in the terms in which he is most visible (17).

The narrator's own anonymity would seem to shift the weight of the subject's identification from family to race. By emphasizing the changing names of race and his reluctance to claim or be claimed by them, however, he destabilizes this potential community as foundational to his own subjectivity (as either explicitly empowered or oppressed). This insistence on "un-naming" himself, moreover, reminds us that the crisis in African American subjectivity historically takes place at the intersection of familial and racial identifications. The narrator's un-naming reiterates the question posed by Kimberly W. Benston in her essay "I yam what I yam" of "how [to] envision and name a people whose very existence was predicated upon expropriation of land, culture, and the binding imperatives and designations of what Ellison terms the 'familial past'" (152). The narrator refuses to call himself by the terms that bear with them a history of social negation; he ultimately strives, instead, to interrupt the positive versus negative, white versus black terms of identity.

Whereas Freudian and Hegelian models of subjectivity insist that the subject is constituted in relation to the Other, suggesting that both positions are somehow historically and hegemonically fixed, Pinckney renders them changeable and contingent. It is that instability that invokes the historical specificity these models of subjectivity seemingly elide. Since the novel revolves around a crisis in naming on familial and racial levels, it calls into question the efficacy of genealogy and national identity in structuring coherent subjectivity. The narrator reminds us that genealogy and full citizenship have been historically denied to African Americans, and thus constitute suspect foundations for African American subjectivity. One potential response would be for him to see himself as always and inevitably lacking these foundations, thereby reinforcing the fixity of this model of subjectivity. Instead, he works to re-signify his relationship to those markers that form ideological bridges through time and across identifications based on race, gender, and class. The relationship balances on a fulcrum of historical specificity, such that the narrator strives to understand his own and his family's historical contexts through markers that elide them. If, as Benston notes, "naming is inevitably genealogical revisionism" (152), then Pinckney's narrator seeks to revise the nation as family.

* * *

The relationship between historical specificity and African American racial identities, which both denote and deny that history, is inevitably one of trauma, as the identities must negotiate the very circumstances that devalue them. Defined as a "breach in the shield against stimuli" in Freud's most rudimentary formulation in *Beyond the Pleasure Principle*, traumatic experience is one unassimilable (particularly in a temporal sense) to the subject's understanding of him- or herself (608). Freud's definition resonates in Butler's recent description of the effects of injurious speech: "To be injured by speech is to suffer a loss of context, that is, not to know where you are. Indeed, it may be that what is *unanticipated* about injurious speech is what constitutes its injury, the sense of putting the addressee out of control" (*ES*, 4). Freud (in the example of his grandson's *fort-da* game) and Butler (through her theory of linguistic performativity) look to the subject's repetition of the trauma as a way to master the temporal and psychic disjunctions it occasioned.

Butler insists that the injurious power of a name lies in its historicity, its circulation within a given set of conventions and at a specific historical moment. She locates the power that names have to demean or injure in their ability to reiterate trauma, noting that such speech "works in part through an encoded memory or trauma, one that lives in language and is carried in language" (36). Thus, it is not the language in and of itself, but its reiteration that bears with it the force of trauma. Since trauma is, by definition, that which is somehow incomprehensible, its transmission is notable for its curious combination of effects: the muted, disguised, or confusing reiteration of an experience that both momentarily locates the subject and exceeds him or her, that brings the trauma back, so to speak, without bringing it to the fore: "The traumatic event is an extended experience that defies and propagates representation at once" (*ES*, 36).

While language carries with it the force of trauma, in the process of reiteration it also makes possible a response by interpellating the subject (who is defined as one whose entry into the Symbolic Order makes him or her capable of speech). Because the subject's discursive power exceeds the conditions of subject formation, as Butler notes, "[t]he subject of speech who is named becomes, potentially, one who might well name another in time" (29). In order to use its discursive power to blunt or even overcome the force of trauma, the subject must first achieve a critical and cognizant distance from the traumatic events the language conveys.

In citing Butler's recent work on hate speech, I do not wish to categorize names of black identities as derogatory, serving, at best, to constitute subjects who may one day "talk back." Nor do I want to reduce subjectivity to naming alone. Instead I want to look at the ways in which these identities incorporate traumatic experience and the ability to redefine that experience, as well as at how the psychoanalytic methods used to conceptualize these identities depend upon historical specificity.

Butler provides an understanding of how a given identity or discursive position simultaneously fixes, exceeds, and fails to account completely for the subject. Appellation and interpellation determine subject formation, bringing the subject into a social context governed by convention and normativity. As previously discussed with regard to the reiteration of subjectivity, Butler points out that this process of subject formation in language takes places repeatedly, that the Lacanian "bar" that denotes what may be spoken (and that signals subjectivity) "is reinvoked in political life when the question of being able to speak is once again a condition of the subject's survival" (ES, 135). She insists, and Pinckney evinces through the changing names and contexts of racial identity, that the constitution of the subject in language is an ongoing phenomenon in the subject's life rather than a one-time event in infancy.

While naming momentarily locates the subject within a given social context, and does so through the name's "sedimentary" history, it cannot completely control the subject's response nor the name's own future circulation. Similarly, the name cannot claim exclusive power over the subject's identity. As Butler asks rhetorically, "And what if one were to compile all the names that one has ever been called? Would they not present a quandary for identity?" (30). What Pinckney makes clear is that African American identities, whose definitions as such synthesize familial and national trauma in racial terms, do not denote a subject's static relationship to those traumas. By ensuring that the process of repetition is historically grounded, he underscores both the power of dominant forms of subjectivity and the limits of those forms in circumscribing all subjects. The narrator finds himself trying desperately to avoid the legacy of traumas that he did not experience yet cannot escape. They have become part of the fabric of social life and language, mutating to adapt to changing historical conditions; yet he refuses to submit to their forces of pejorative definition.

One possible interpretation of the narrator's "un-naming" is that it shows his desire to reject categorically the identities socially available in favor of radical self-determination. Benston describes a long history, beginning with Ancient Greek and Hebraic traditions, of "un-naming" which "invokes the power of the Sublime, a transcendent impulse to undo all categories, all metonymies and reifications, and thrust the self beyond received patterns and relationships into a stance of unchallenged authority [. . . it entails] passing from one mode of representation to another, of breaking the rhetoric and 'plot' of influence, of distinguishing the self from all else—including Eros, nature and community" (153). While "un-naming" in *High Cotton* reflects the narrator's awareness of and response to the limitations historically imposed on him through discourse, it stops short of the fantasy of social transcendence. Pinckney's narrator is neither a revolutionary nor a recluse; his thwarted desire is to achieve sanctioned social standing rather than dismantle it. Thus, his struggle for recognition within the prevailing social order necessitates the much more laborious process of redefining the process of identification within his historical context than attempting to escape history. In choosing this path, the narrator reinforces Butler and Silverman's argument that the subject can never undo the symbolic conditions of his or her own making.

The cloudy contiguity between historical experience and identification invites both literary and psychoanalytic readings. In *Unclaimed Experience*, Cathy Caruth, following Freud, finds at their intersection access to a theory of trauma: "If Freud turns to literature to describe traumatic experience, it is because literature, like psychoanalysis, is interested in the complex relationship between knowing and not knowing. And it is, indeed at the specific point at which knowing and not knowing intersect that the language of literature and the language of psychoanalytic theory of traumatic experience precisely meet" (3). *High Cotton* complicates Caruth's reading of literature's role in psychoanalytic understandings of trauma. The novel revolves around the problem of how to know oneself against and within the range of identities socially available. It not only "describes" the contemporary effects of a history of trauma; it also calls into question the efficacy of psychoanalytic methods for understanding race and racial trauma in a historical context. It is out of a dialogue between the literature and psychoanalytic theory that we may begin to theorize contemporary African American subjectivities marked by racial trauma. Literature and psychoanalysis ask of one another how we can understand the effects of trauma on subject formation in language that can only bear witness to the incomprehensibility of trauma.

The narrator of *High Cotton* plays on the relationship of literature and psychoanalysis by continually evoking the psychoanalytic models which cannot alone fully describe him. He uses the language of psychic splitting, for example, to characterize the struggle to see himself according to prevailing codes of identity:

> The ledger of how to be simultaneously yourself and everyone else who might observe you, the captain's log of travel in the dual consciousness, the white world as the deceptive sea and the black world as the armed galley, gave me the comic feeling that I was living alongside myself, that there was a me and a ventriloquist's replica of me on my lap, and that both of us awaited the intervention of a third me, the disembodied me, before we could begin the charade of dialogue. (220)

The image of the two selves, awaiting the intervention of a disembodied third, suggests the Lacanian, post-structuralist subject whose very formation depends upon psychic splitting through entry into language. The danger of this reading is the ease with which it may designate an abstract and ahistorical psychoanalytic theory as the third voice, employing the black body in the galley to traverse the white consciousness of the encompassing sea. Warning of such slippage into psychoanalytic universalism, Margaret Homans writes in " 'Women of Color' Writers and Feminist Theory" that too often black bodies "do the work of embodiment or identification" for white theorists who seek an "alibi" for anti-essentialist positions. Black bodies, in these cases, still figure as the all too familiar "other." Excluded from post-structuralism, they "define it by their difference from it" (87). A concomitant danger is the way in which the language of psychic splitting may appear to designate a subject forever separated by race from the ideal of masterful coherence.

Caruth cites an additional fear that post-structuralist readings similarly privilege their own aesthetic terms over those of historical context:

> In the wake of structuralist and poststructuralist developments in literary theory, a good deal of concern has arisen that these linguistically oriented theories of reading deny the possibility that language can give us access to history. The constant focus by poststructuralists on the linguistic devices by which meaning is produced, and by 'deconstruction' on the difficulties these devices create for our understanding of a text, seems to amount to a claim that language cannot refer adequately to the world and indeed may not truly refer to anything at all, leaving literature

and language, and even consciousness in general, cut off from historical reality. (73–4)

Instead of interpreting post-structuralist literary and psychoanalytic approaches as evasions of history, I want to follow Caruth in reading them as both demanding and revealing historical meaning. Post-structuralist accounts of subject formation and of the centrality of language in constructing meaning, because they locate meaning at the nexus of social forces, facilitate an awareness of the cultural and historical contexts of those forces. Such readings may enable us to understand the ideologies of gender, race, and class—those ideologies that have the greatest effect on our understanding of the subject—as changeable and contingent rather than universal, natural, and fixed. This means that we can read the relationship Pinckney invokes between black materiality and white consciousness as the product of an ideology dedicated to maintaining white social power.

Although *High Cotton* invokes the division between white consciousness and black corporeality, it does so subversively. Pinckney's narrator separates the conflation of the corporeal and the historical by remaining not only anonymous but virtually absent physically from his own story. We see the effects of race in various contexts, but rarely its embodiment. Except for brief glimpses he provides of his thick glasses or the various sartorial poses he adopts in childhood and adolescence, he is invisible throughout the novel. Describing his fantasy of joining the Vienna Choir Boys, for example, he makes this absence explicit: "The disturbing sign was that in my dream the uniform was visible, but I wasn't. Even when I pictured myself eating European style, with the knife in my right hand, the camera cut from the sailor's sleeve to the plate to get around the thorny problem of there having been no brown wrists in my prophetic film of the moment, *Almost Angels*" (75). This passage performs a double gesture: it introduces the terms of a psychoanalytic reading while asking if such a reading can have anything at all to say about subjectivity constituted, at least in part, by racial difference.

Pinckney's adoption of cinematic language and the camera's structuring gaze plays on film theory's psychoanalytic roots as the process of identification takes place within the frames of the camera's perspective. Initially assuming control of that perspective ("I pictured myself"), he seems to be the director, determining what can and cannot be shown. His authority vanishes in the next clause, however, when he distinguishes his own desire to see and be seen from what the camera reveals. The discrepancy between his and the camera's revelations raises the question of how psychoanalytic theories of identification (can) account for black identities. By presenting blackness only through the space of its absence, Pinckney warns against any universal application of a set psychoanalytic model and presents his own narrative voice as the mediator between the two halves of the self. It is that narrative voice, moreover, that simultaneously erases and constitutes the body in question. The "speech act itself," Butler maintains, "[is] a nexus of bodily and psychic forces" (141) in that both are governed by a shared set of rituals and conventions that determine normativity and recognition. The body, in other words, is only knowable through its circulation in the social context of the narrative and as "the site of an incorporated history" (152).

No application of psychoanalysis to a literary text devoted to racial identifications and subject formation can be innocent of the history of racial bias within psychoanalytic theories. Recent critical work has shown how the idea of coherent subjectivity is founded on an assumption of normative whiteness that leaves racial difference inevitably feminized and "other-ed" within the prevailing model of binary sexual opposition. Jean Walton's analysis of early feminist psychoanalytic work makes clear that "theorizations of gender and sexuality [. . .] depend upon an *un*theorized racial domain" (803). Through their readings of the foundations of psychoanalysis, Claudia Tate and Walton reveal both how models of subjectivity assume whiteness and how feminist revisions of these models, even as they undermine the restrictive logic of normative heterosexuality, often replicate the same racist biases.

It is through the intersection of selected feminist and postcolonial psychoanalytic approaches that we may begin to counter this trend, to broaden the range of subjectivities conceivable through psychoanalysis and attempt to keep them historically specific. This theoretical combination, which I would like to pursue initially through the work of Silverman and Frantz Fanon, enables an examination of psychic and social events crucial to conceiving contemporary African American subjectivities. Together these approaches contest the predominance of patriarchal ideology and its associative whiteness, as well as the notion of a universal, portable psychoanalytic method. They work in conjunction to illuminate how psychoanalysis may attend to the material realities of racial difference and account for inessential subjectivities masked by those realities.

Insisting on subjectivity as inessential, as defined in Silverman's model, means reading the lack that is constitutive of the subject (following Lacan) as culturally coded rather than inevitably, naturally phallic. This definition alters the aims of the psychoanalytic process, demanding that it address the social and historical contexts of subject formation and identification. In other words, psychoanalysis must be able to ask of itself the same questions regarding the criteria for valued identities that it asks of its subjects.

High Cotton does not simply provide a sample text for a psychoanalysis of contemporary African American subjectivity. It turns the terms of psychoanalytic identifications back on themselves, asking repeatedly how they can make sense of the narrator's own changing definitions of himself. To return to the language of split subjectivity, for instance, the narrator uses the same image of being separate from himself to characterize his place in black and white communities. Just as a visit to Aunt Clara in Alabama "demanded, like taking a vow, that a part of the self must die" (29), he says that entering the mostly white Westfield Junior High required that "what I was I set aside every morning at 7:45" (85). The repetition does not signify an inevitable failure in his bid for social recognition nor a static, if reiterated, fractured self. By repeating the image of the split subject in different contexts, the narrator denies the possibility of static subjectivity available for a psychoanalytic reading. Who he is and whom he sets apart from himself depends on the range of images made available by the historical and social moment. The role of psychoanalysis, then, is to investigate the connections between those moments, the forms of subjectivity they create, and the identities they promote.

* * *

High Cotton's narrator is continually torn between his desire to identify with dominant white images and to reconcile them with his family background. Whether he sees himself as a Vienna Choir Boy, a fully integrated Westfielder, or the true descendant of the British Romantics, he notes that the "old-timers boasted of their ability to bug you from the grave, saying one day you'd want to talk to them and they wouldn't be there anymore. They'd hint that they'd be watching you closely from wherever they went when they passed on. Your dearest reminded you every morning of the problem that you would never, never get away from" (6). Despite these persistent reminders, much of his childhood is spent rejecting, on grounds of irrelevance, the image of the "Also Chosen" promulgated by his Grandfather Eustace. With his "Holy Land" education at Brown and Harvard and family legacy of professionalism and "good marriages," Grandfather Eustace "took the high road, but because he made the journey in a black body he lived with the chronic dread that maybe he wasn't good enough" (6). To escape the need to be thankful for his opportunities and apologetic for his race, the narrator dismisses his grandfather's would-be lessons: "I spent much of my life running from him, centripetal fashion, because he was, to me, just a poor old darky" (6). At the same time, the narrator finds that running from his grandfather does not lead him to his idealized identities. As he describes his entry into Westfield, "Someone was always trying to interrupt, to get between me and the paradise of integration" (82). It is only later that he realizes the most he can be in that paradise is "a slave in heaven" (107).

The references to slavery that describe the characters' attempts to escape its lasting effects underscore the perpetuation of racist ideologies. Both the narrator and his grandfather strive for acceptance according to standards dictated by dominant, interrelated ideologies of gender, race, and class. For Grandfather Eustace this means gaining the degrees and social standing to prove himself acceptable to the white aristocracy he emulates, and then making sure the next generation does the same. As Uncle Castor, grandfather's brother, quotes, "Remember where you came from and send the elevator back down" (66). Whereas the older generation maintains a black version of a white social hierarchy, to provide the social movement forever off-limits in white communities, the narrator yearns to melt into the white world around him. With the family's move to the suburbs and his transfer to Westfield, he sees his chance: "I couldn't allow myself to look back, having presented myself to myself as one who had never been anywhere but where I was" (86).

Although the narrator characterizes his bid for social standing as oppositional to his grandfather's, he describes both in images of slaves' plantation life. The characters attempt to move up a social hierarchy modeled on the plantation in order to come as close as possible to achieving the now-symbolic white father's authority. This strategy necessitates a validation of the slave-owner's position that is irreconcilable with historical experiences of the family. Grandfather Eustace, for instance, keeps quiet "about the hardships that he had witnessed, just as his grandfather had thought it wise not to speak too truthfully about his years in bondage" (8); nevertheless, Grandfather Eustace insists that his grandfather had said of his owners, "The family was always kind and considerate of its slaves" (9).

The narrator uses the same plantation model to characterize his position in the white suburbs, as when he defines himself according to the "oft-cited genealogy of field niggers and house niggers," adding, "[w]hen I needed to blame a poor performance on something outside myself, I had only to hint that the field niggers were after me again" (107).

These reiterations of traumatic experience carry with them the multiple effects Butler describes. The continuation of this trope through five generations attests to the power of racist ideology to define the terms of identity. At the same time, since he uses this language to capture fluctuating rather than fixed identities, Pinckney insists that the images available to contemporary African Americans need not be restricted to those of black slaves. In the conscious intervention into these recurrent identities, he shows that the terms and the methods used to describe them are malleable. The aesthetic foregrounding of the terms, moreover, makes it impossible to take them for granted; we are asked to recognize their circulation within a given ideology and to reconsider the power dynamics they invoke.

Kaja Silverman and Frantz Fanon, in strikingly different contexts, call into question the dominant terms of subjectivity by focusing on the intersection of ideology and psychoanalysis. In her analysis of how aesthetic texts can disrupt the ideological process of identification, Silverman turns to Fanon: "*Black Skin, White Masks* helps us to understand, first of all, that our identifications must always be socially ratified. It also teaches us that only certain subjects have access to a flattering image of self, and that others have imposed upon them an image so deidealizing that no one would willingly identify with it" (*TVW*, 29). Social power (Butler's *pouvoir*), then, accrues to those subjects who can readily identify with dominant images of masculinity and whiteness. Fanon's thesis in *Black Skin, White Masks* is that ideology renders blackness the negative of whiteness, such that the black subject is most often predetermined as socially powerless. Reading Silverman and Fanon in tandem suggests that psychoanalysis can offer us a way of comprehending and altering those socially prescribed images, first by presenting the very real effects they have on structuring subjectivity and determining identity and second by outlining a process for recognizing that those same images are variable. It is only after recognizing that the terms of valued subjectivity are socially determined that we may consciously and collectively intervene in their circulation.

Silverman's psychoanalytic model, developed most thoroughly in *Male Subjectivity at the Margins*, divorces psychoanalysis from patriarchy and paternal law as ontological foundations of the subject. Central to her concept of inessential subjectivity (subjectivity predicated on an undefined lack which is outlined by the underlying ideologies of the Symbolic Order) is the cultural contingency of privileged signifiers—in our case, the phallus. Ideological consistency depends upon the "pivotal status of the phallus, [such that] more than sexual difference is sustained through the alignment of that signifier with the male sexual organ. Within every society, hegemony is keyed to certain privileged terms, around which there is a kind of doubling up of belief. Since everything that successfully passes for 'reality' within a given social formation is articulated in relation to these terms, they represent ideological stress points" (16). If, within the Symbolic Order, the Name-of-the-Father is the *local* articulation of kinship, the phallus is not the universal signifier of desire and the inevitable expression of the Law of Language in terms of the Law of Kinship; rather, the phallus functions as "the variable metaphor of an irreducible lack" (38). While the phallus alone is an expression of a privileged signifier, it is equated ideologically in the construction of our "reality" with the penis and the paternal family.[1] As a result, Silverman notes, "the continuation of our 'world' depends upon a collective belief in that equation" (65). This two-part model of the Symbolic Order, when writ large on the level of the dominant fiction, helps explain how the ideology of the paternal family becomes the prevailing metaphor for social life.

As the constitutive bond between subject and society, the dominant fiction maintains its hold by setting the terms for the articulation of concomitant ideologies of race and class. Ideological continuity is maintained by the expression of social groups such as community or nation in the language of the paternal family. By showing how the phallus functions as a privileged signifier on multiple ideological levels, Silverman emphasizes that subjectivity modeled on the Oedipus complex is a self-perpetuating *reflection* of how our culture works, rather than its "natural" expression. Her analysis forces us to become conscious of the terms of identity we are willing to recognize and idealize, even as we acknowledge our own dependence upon them. Thus we can see how the discourse of the plantation South sustains itself through generations of the subjects it oppresses. Since phallic power on the plantation included the economic and sexual control of families and property, it conflated masculinity and whiteness. As a continuing metaphor for social "reality," it insists upon that same conflation in setting the terms for contemporary valued identities.

Pinckney's narrator and Grandfather Eustace find themselves trapped by an unwished for identification with the only levels of social standing permitted by the dominant fiction (e.g., "the house niggers"). Pinckney intervenes in the identificatory process, however, by showing how the reiteration of traumatic experience contains within it the possibility of alternative identifications. The narrator tries on identities ranging from Vienna Choir Boy to black power activist to bohemian expatriate while keeping an ironic focus on the mirror in his mind's eye. Of his short-lived attempt to join the Heirs of Malcolm, for example, he notes that "[t]here was some unpleasantness between me and another revolutionary about what sort of grammar and spelling the sleeping masses could relate to" (114). Similarly in England, he tries to relieve his loneliness by joining another revolutionary group, this time hoping that "my blackness would be more prestigious than my politics" (130). These two examples illustrate the ways in which the narrator attempts willfully to deploy race rather than be defined by it in his ongoing bids for social acceptance.

* * *

High Cotton replicates the dominant nation as family metaphor by articulating the quest for a favored identity in terms of the relationship between the narrator and his grandfather and their strategies for social agency, as a question of genealogy as well as citizenship. Not only does the narrator ultimately try to reconcile his place within his family, African American masculinity, and dominant values, but the potential identities he may hold are themselves circumscribed by what is believable within the nation as family.

While Pinckney indicates the impossibility of stepping outside of the discursive constructs of subjectivity, he also shows that their layers of ideology do not necessarily cohere in their every reiteration. The narrator embarks on his journey of self-discovery after hearing ambivalence among those reiterations, particularly those taught him by Grandfather Eustace. Launching his journey is his inability to read the confusing markers of African American subjectivity:

> All men were created equal, but even so, lots of mixed messages with sharp teeth waited under my Roy Rogers pillow. You were just as good as anyone else out there, but they—whoever 'they' were—had rigged things so that you had to be close to perfect just to break even. You had nothing to fear, though every time you left the house for a Spelling Bee or a Music Memory Contest the future of the future hung in the balance. You were not an immigrant, there were no foreign accents, weird holidays, or funny foods to live down, but still you did not belong to the great beyond out there; yet though you did not belong it was your duty as the Also Chosen to get up and act as though you belonged, especially when no one wanted you to. (4)

The failure of the dominant fiction to interpellate him in a single voice—triggered by the incompatibility of a national and a racial "we"—initiates a process of psychic fragmentation. Splitting occurs in this example in two distinct ways: in the discourse of the dominant fiction as it perpetuates and, in its illegibility, subverts itself and in the subject who tries to see himself in the very terms that exclude him.

In *The Location of Culture*, Homi Bhabha notes that the splitting within colonial discourse "results in the production of multiple and contradictory belief. The enunciatory moment of multiple belief is both a defence against the anxiety of difference, and itself *productive* of differentiations" (132). Bhabha refers here to those moments in colonial texts when the discourse of authority becomes momentarily nonsensical or incomprehensible in its bid to encapsulate the "other" of the text, as, for example, when Forster's Marabar cave echoes in *A Passage to India* or Kurtz, in *The Heart of Darkness*, exclaims, "The horror! The horror!" Such indecipherable moments, like the barbed messages under the Roy Rogers pillow, hint, according to Bhabha, at ambivalence within colonial authority. They mark the anxiety that this authority may not be translatable across cultural boundaries, or, in Silverman's terms, that there is a weakness in the ideological fortifications of the dominant fiction. Through a reading of Foucault, Bhabha characterizes such moments as neither "symptomatic nor allegorical" indications of contradictions within hegemonic discourse but as performative moments whose subversive potential lies in enunciation. Their iterability, he argues, creates the possibility for the emergence of the uncanny, of what, in Foucault's words, "constantly eludes one."[2]

Bhabha draws his examples of incomprehensible discourse from colonial texts which, at these enunciatory moments, somehow fail to contain the colonized other. Adela Quested, Mrs. Moore, and Kurtz are confronted with experience that exceeds their capacity to describe it, so the iterability of the experience carries with it the fear felt by the colonizer that the unknown might actually be unknowable. By announcing a lack of complete control, these moments remind subject and reader of the trauma of colonialism itself (of the violence experienced by the colonized); however, they do so through the colonizer's perspective.

Pinckney reverses the terms of Bhabha's formulation by writing as the addressee of colonial discourse. Accordingly, the "mixed messages" in *High Cotton* whisper the impossibility of the narrator achieving the only identities deemed socially acceptable. At the same time, as interpellations in the Althusserian sense both Butler and Silverman cite, the messages confer subjectivity and make possible a response. For Pinckney's narrator, the unnameable fear he experiences provides him with multiple paths of identification as well as the caveat that some will be more perilous than others. Whereas in Bhabha's description "multiple and contradictory belief" is a liability in the quest for stable subjectivity, in *High Cotton* multiplicity (even if conflicted) produces options for the ever-changing subject. The only stable subject position in the novel is one of consistent oppression; therefore, it is in learning to accept that subjectivity is always in process and never fixed that the narrator can take an active role in overcoming his fear and subjugation.

The narrator responds initially to the symptoms rather than the causes of this splitting and, finding his grandfather's discourse confusing, disavows it by eliding racial and familial markers. In his desire to obtain the coherent subjectivity that the dominant fiction promises its most loyal adherents, he tries to divorce himself from any connections to subjugated subject positions defined by questionable or unstable identifications. Miscegenation, the denial of familial bonds during slavery, and the concomitant crisis of naming refute attempts at genealogical reconstruction. The narrator reproduces these hegemonic silences by rendering his parents and sisters anonymous and characterizing his own name as nothing more than a "contemporary Dixie-cup quality, and my surname, with its antebellum echo, only barely acceptable" (197). Familial relations are similarly ambiguous: he thinks his aunt's maid is a cousin, describes relatives in shades and percentages (such as his "beige stepgrandmother"), and notes that "[f]or all I knew as a child Grandfather Eustace came from an Oldsmobile" (17). In mimicking this disavowal of kinship the narrator is still "not quite . . . not white" (Bhabha); however, the self-consciousness and parodic treatment of these signifiers of paternity and legitimacy undermines their status as fixed markers of subjectivity.

Once we recognize the play of privileged signifiers, we may begin to heed Diana Fuss's reminder, in *Identification Papers*, to "focus attention on the ethnocentrism of the epistemological categories themselves— European identity categories that seem to me wholly inadequate to describe the many different consolidations, permutations, and transformations of what the West has come to understand, itself in myriad and contradictory fashion, under the sign 'sexuality' " (159). Not only does Fuss ward off the danger of universalizing, and thereby essentializing, psychoanalytic models, she also enhances the possibility of developing approaches that undermine the centrality of the Oedipal story. Although the passage cited above concludes rather than launches her text, it nonetheless underscores Fanon and Silverman's point that, in Fuss's words, *"the psychical operates precisely as a political formation"* (165, emphasis in original).

Silverman's approach explains subject formation within the context of our dominant fiction: subjectivity takes place at the nexus of discourse and ideology through privileging sexual and familial identifications over those of either race or class. Her chapter in *Male Subjectivity at the Margins* specifically devoted to race in its treatment of Lawrence of Arabia and colonizing discourses, for instance, is articulated in terms of Lawrence's homosexuality and his erotic identification with those involved in the cause of Arab nationalism. In this formulation, Arab nationalism and Lawrence's ambivalent position between colonizer and colonized are realized and described within the terms of the patriarchal family as a metaphor for the modern nation.

Silverman offers a much-needed analysis of how we are accommodated to the Symbolic Order and the dominant fiction through fantasy and desire; she emphasizes that even subversive subjectivities lack access to identifications founded on terms other than sexuality: "The dominant fiction neutralizes the contradictions which organize the social formation by fostering collective identifications and desires, identifications and desires which have a range of effects, but which are first and foremost constitutive of sexual difference" (54). This means that African American subjectivity, recognizable by and against the dominant fiction, must ultimately be read psychically in terms of sexual difference. This strategy corresponds to the centrality of the Name-of-the-Father and the incest taboo as fundamental units in the psychoanalytic approach describing our dominant culture, though it limits reading a palimpsest of racial and sexual effects.

In *The Threshold of the Visible World*, Silverman focuses explicitly on black masculinity in her analysis of the film, *Looking for Langston*. Here she takes the next step in the process of recognizing and then re-signifying dominant terms of identity by distinguishing between the images of the phallic order and their assigned meanings. Silverman looks specifically at the film's treatment of stereotypical attributes of black masculinity in order to see the black male character Beauty's nose, mouth, penis, dress, and language as images of an idealized rather than shunned identity. These attributes, which Fanon so clearly defines as symbols of the black male's paradoxical threat and inferiority to white male dominance, function in Silverman's reading of the film as markers of idealization for the desiring subject (white and black). The subject's agency comes from the dual process of being recognized as a desiring subject and in desiring what is consciously other than one's self. This process of conscious recognition of the terms of desire, a consciousness that facilitates control over those terms, underscores Butler's reminder that agency "is not a property of the subject, an inherent will or freedom, but an effect of power, it is constrained but not determined in advance" (139).

Fantasy and desire, according to Silverman, endow the object that stands in for the subject's initial sacrifice to language with a "psychic reality" (20); that reality, in turn, produces subjective identification in terms articulated by the dominant fiction. For Fanon, the black subject's fantasy is ultimately a desire for whiteness, a desire negotiated in relation to the national metaphor of the patriarchal family. That the metaphor of the dominant fiction is coded first by sexual difference and then by race again restricts potential avenues of subversive agency.[3] The problem this creates, as Walton writes in another context, is that "restoring to black men the patriarchal power that had been historically denied them" defines such power as "essential to masculine subjectivity" (783). Since accommodation to the dominant fiction, through the bar between what is speakable and unspeakable, determines subjectivity, that process necessarily constrains agency without predetermining it. The ongoing process of interpellation, through which the dominant fiction maintains its power, repeatedly constitutes a subject capable of response just as the desires foundational to subjectivity create one capable of desiring another.

The *contesting* subject would need to rewrite the metaphor of the family in both sexual and racial terms. Asking the subject, reader, or text to subvert or re-signify its relationship to the same dominant fiction that structures subject formation and our sense of "reality" is undoubtedly asking too much. Nevertheless, Silverman and Fanon suggest the possibility of withdrawing from—by becoming conscious of—the workings of the dominant fiction in ways that hold potential for alternative significations of subjectivity. Without imagining that we can step out of the gendered division that supports our own dominant fiction, we might learn to look again at its various manifestations within the signifying economy of the paternal family. It is in the conscious work of looking again, Silverman stresses in *The Threshold of the Visible World*, that we can locate an ethics of subjectivity.

* * *

According to Silverman, one potential site of opposition to the dominant fiction, for recognizing the variability of its metaphors, is historical trauma: "any historical event, whether socially engineered or of natural occurrence, which brings a large group of male subjects into such an intimate relation with lack that they are at least for the moment unable to sustain an imaginary relation with the phallus, and so withdraw their belief from the dominant fiction" (*MSM*, 55). As "a force capable of unbinding the male ego, and exposing the abyss that it conceals" (121), historical trauma reveals the structuring of ideological belief on the level of the psyche.

In order to address contemporary African American subjectivities, we need to expand Silverman's concept to account for the current legacies of past historical events. Whereas she uses historical trauma to describe events the subject experiences directly, we need to be able to read the contemporary effects of slavery's denial of familial bonds in kinship and naming.[4] What changes in the movement from historical trauma to traumatic legacy is the kind of memory forging (and damaging) the link between the subject and social ideology. Instead of the individual "reminisces" that haunt the subject of Freud's war trauma, we must read a complex narrative of communal memory and silences.[5] These narratives circulate within the dominant fiction to structure the process of identification—to determine what is normative, idealized, and shunned—as well as through African American communities formulating alternatives to the identifications made possible by the dominant fiction.

Summarizing Freud's work on trauma, Laplanche and Pontalis define it as "[a]n event in the subject's life defined by its intensity, by the subject's incapacity to respond adequately to it, and by the upheaval and long-lasting effects that it brings about in the psychic organisation" (465). Trauma constitutes a "breach" between the subject and his or her surroundings, an excess of energy that threatens the stability of the ego and the function of the pleasure principle. That breach, Freud states in *Beyond the Pleasure Principle*, is caused primarily by "the factor of surprise, of fright."[6] Although "trauma" comes from the Greek word for "wound," in Freud's formulation traumatic experience comes from psychic rather than physical violence and is contained by binding: according to Laplanche and Pontalis, "an operation tending to restrict the free flow of excitations, to link ideas to one another and to constitute and maintain relatively stable forms" (50). Physical "wound or injury inflicted simultaneously [to a psychic wound]," Freud adds, "works as a rule *against* the development of a neurosis" (*BPP*, 598).

With traumatic neurosis, the pleasure principle is suspended indefinitely as the subject repeatedly, if "unwittingly" (Caruth), re-imagines or re-enacts the original experience. These repetitions serve to transform the subject from passively suffering surprise or fright to actively controlling their mechanisms. It is in this active role, Freud argues, that the subject may begin to compensate for the temporal disjunction incurred by trauma.[7] Whether it occurs through a dream or through neurotic behavior, the unconscious repetition of trauma enables the psyche to "prepare" for what has already pierced its defenses. Freud seems to suggest that repetition alone cannot permanently repair the breach occasioned by the initial shock since it demands that the subject continually reopen the wound in order to close i: The analyst's role, then, is to help the subject move from unknowing repetition to remembering the event at a distance. According to Freud, the physician must encourage the subject "to re-experience some portion of his forgotten life, but must see to it, on the other hand, that the patient retains some degree of aloofness, which will enable him [. . .] to recognize that what appears to be reality is in fact only a reflection of a forgotten past" (602).

Freud's approach to overcoming traumatic neurosis shares with Butler and Bhabha's theories of perfomativity an emphasis on the enunciative moment. For Freud, each repetition of traumatic experience creates a fleeting sense of control over the initial irruption because it is the psyche rather than an outside force that brings the trauma back. In transforming the subject's relationship to that event from passivity to action, each repetition, as with Butler's reiteration, interpellates and, thus, constitutes the subject. Even as it defines the subject at that moment as the recipient of trauma, interpellation also makes possible a response, the parameters of which cannot be wholly constrained in advance.

For Bhabha, Freud, and Caruth, the iterative moment of trauma contains within it the unknown or the unassimilable. This would suggest that since the subject's coherent sense of self is evidently permeable (by the incomprehensible intrusion of the trauma itself), the dominant fiction upon which it rests must be, too. The effects of traumatic experience, then, present one method of identifying, in Butler's terms, the post-sovereign subject—the subject constituted by and acting within a network of social functions rather than one whose make-up is fixed and who acts solely upon others.

While Silverman teaches us that no response can completely free itself from the dominant fiction (since the dominant fiction helps determine what constitutes trauma to begin with), she also shows how trauma expands the range of possible responses. Whereas the initiating trauma may reveal the lack that underlies the dominant fiction, its repetitions may similarly make that unconscious lack more readily available for conscious revision. If the unconscious holds precisely what is inadmissible to the dominant fiction, what must be repressed, then access to it and a conscious reconsideration of its terms may yield a non-conforming response.[8] Confronting trauma and its legacies, in other words, may actually alter the dominant fiction.

* * *

High Cotton insists upon some alterations in trauma theory in order to account for the lasting legacy of trauma on African American masculinity as well as its changing historical contexts. To begin with, the founding trauma of the Middle Passage and slavery in the United States comprised both physical and psychic violence on individual and collective African Americans. The elements of fright and surprise were present in the wholesale elimination of the subject's control over his or her own corporeal, familial, and productive (in terms of both labor and procreation) integrity. By subordinating the subject's autonomy to a subjugated collective identification, slavery disempowered African Americans on a multitude of levels. (This is not to say, of course, that it effected complete domination. Every attempt to deny subjectivity was simultaneously an interpellation, conditions varied among slaves and slave owners, and slave resistance is well documented.)

Hortense Spillers refers to the trauma of slavery as an "American grammar" composed of "hieroglyphics of the flesh" passed down through generations of "various *symbolic substitutions* in an efficacy of meanings that repeat the initiating moments" (67). I do not mean to suggest that this grammar does or must consist of an alternative set of privileged signifiers, which exist outside the dominant fiction. Indeed, as discussed in chapter 2, since the subject only makes sense according to the images available on the cultural screen, manipulation of those images ensures that the subject or collective may continue to be read. Spillers's own terms reflect this strategy by demanding a rethinking of national identity according to the legacies of slavery (rather than ignoring the ideological consistency of the father–nation equation). Once again we are forced to acknowledge the way in which our concept of nationhood depends upon the multifaceted use of key signifiers.

When we move from a subject's direct experience of trauma to an individual or communal experience of its legacies, we are faced with a concurrent need to rethink the process of binding. Instead of the subject "taming" (Freud) traumatic memories through inhibition or repetition, communal binding might involve the creation of cultural stories that simultaneously define a community in relation to and protect it from the terms of the dominant fiction. Community might function as a mediator between subjective and national identities, if not an alternative to them. On the level of the subject, binding operates to repair that breach with the environment; on a communal level, it must then have the capacity to form a group in relation to the initial trauma and, through time, to allow that group to pass on culturally distinct memories that are not wholly bound by the images of the dominant fiction. If the response to trauma is a healing effort, then a community constituted in relation to trauma could only be sustained by re-working its terms of empowerment and integrity.

As a constituent of a marginalized community and the inescapable dominant fiction, an African American subject might re-appropriate existing privileged signifiers or recognize those operating alongside the phallus. The memories embodied in oral or literary discourses formed in response to oppressions of prevailing ideology may develop their own signifying practices as they are transferred and translated from one generation to the next. African American feminist criticism and literature has been particularly forthright in identifying this potential.

In Toni Morrison's fiction, for example, the namesakes of both *Sula* and *Beloved* function as signifiers of alternative identificatory economies. Mae Gwendolyn Henderson invokes *Sula* in explication of her theory of black women writers' heteroglossalia, or speaking in multiple (public) tongues. In this perceptive reading, Sula's birthmark is an initial sign of hollowness, which leaves her open to the identities ascribed to her by the community. Only through the "fusion" of her control over her own sexuality and language is she able to subvert dominant signifying practices: Sula's "poetic penetration of her lover [. . .] signals that her assumption of a 'masculine' role parallels the appropriation of the male voice, prerequisite for her entry into the symbolic order" (135). Henderson interprets Sula's self-definition as metaphor and model for black feminist literary criticism whose "function [. . .] is to interpret or interpenetrate the signifying structures of the dominant and subdominant discourse in order to formulate a critique and, ultimately, a transformation of the hegemonic white and male symbolic order" (135). Although this reading maintains the concept of coherent subjectivity predicated on a core self, phallic power, and linguistic control, it nonetheless suggests that these components may serve alternative ideological frameworks. For Sula, entry into the symbolic order enables her to counter the signifying practices of the black men around her.

In *Beloved*, Morrison effects an even greater transformation of the link between patriarchal and symbolic orders. Once again the female body becomes a site of inscription as Spillers's "American grammar" is whipped into Sethe's back. Instead of the family tree functioning as the "proof" of legitimacy and birthright, as the frequent symbol of both national and subjective "purity," it reads on Sethe as the mark of denial of sexual, familial, corporeal, and racial autonomy. Even as the tree symbolizes collective and individual trauma and deadens Sethe's sensations, its image circulates throughout the text as a harbinger of freedom and rebirth. Amy, the runaway who helps deliver Denver on Sethe's flight to freedom in Ohio, first names and tends the scars on

Sethe's back:

> It's a tree, Lu. A chokecherry tree. See, here's the trunk—it's red and split wide open, full of sap, and this here's the parting for the branches. You got a mighty lot of branches. Leaves, too, look like, and dern if these ain't blossoms. Tiny little cherry blossoms, just as white. Your back got a whole tree on it. In bloom. What God have in mind, I wonder. (79)

That flowering reappears in the novel to guide Paul D on his liberatory journey from prison north to the weaver lady and, finally, to Sethe. Following the instructions of a Cherokee, Paul D

> raced from dogwood to blossoming peach. When they thinned out he headed for cherry blossoms, then magnolia, chinaberry, pecan, walnut and prickly pear. At last he reached a field of apple trees whose flowers were just becoming tiny knots of fruit. Spring sauntered north, but he had to run like hell to keep it as his traveling companion. (113)

The flowering tree serves as the multivalent symbol of the violence of the past, its lasting scars, and the process of healing. Trauma and traumatic legacy are embedded in Sethe's tree not only in the pattern of the wound itself but also in the shadows of the tree's traditional imagery. Written on her with a violence that parallels Schoolteacher's ink-making and his listing of her characteristics, it signifies African Americans' forcible denial of family trees as well as Sethe's own murder of Beloved. The collective meaning is overlaid with the individual one of the price Sethe pays for wanting to legitimate, control, and protect her own family. The novel is, on one level, "about" what it means to want and to define a concept of family that has been historically denied; and, the image of the family tree reminds the reader that while the scars of trauma (of denial either by oneself or others) are permanent, they also indicate that healing can take place.

Although these two novels enact the process of re-appropriating and re-signifying privileged signifiers of the dominant fiction, remaining solely within a realm of black women's literature runs the risk of essentializing both race and gender in the very attempt to subvert colonizing essentialist gestures. If traumatic legacy, as passed down through ethnic stories and memories as well as the experience of lasting prejudice, may actually assist the formation of subjects not wholly circumscribed by the dominant fiction, then it should function to undermine privileged signifiers throughout its various communities.

In *High Cotton*, the narrator is, in his youth, unwilling to identify with socially marginalized communities, even when they constitute sources of support, preferring instead to dream about complete integration. On his way to his first Freedom Watch with his family, for instance, he notes that "when Grandfather said 'Negro' he described an abstraction"; and he adds, "Synaptic delay prevented my making the connection between Grandfather's parishioners and the offhand 'we' of my parents front-seat talk, talk that concerned the way 'we' were treated at lunch counters on the off-ramps to hell [. . .] My nerve endings finally passed on the news when I found myself walled in on all sides by Negroes about to define themselves" (23).

While these communities are sources of potential identification and strength for the narrator, they remain marked by the violence that spawned them, and those associations deter him. Even when he sees pictures of the race riots and attacks of the 1960s, he separates himself from their social and political meanings. When he finds that "[m]y friend the television set had begun to send awful pictures from the Old Country" (29), his feeling of betrayal by television is comforted by the thought that the pictures are of the "Old South" as opposed to his "New World." He thus remains loyal to the narrative of the nation as a story of progress and opportunity for all of its members, seeing in the Old Country that which must be forgotten rather than that which remains. At the same time, his invocation of this rhetoric brings it to the surface of the text and of his identifications, eventually enabling a reconsideration of its terms.

Despite his overwhelming desire to escape or forget the legacies of the past, echoes of slavery reverberate in *High Cotton* in both the language the narrator uses to describe himself and through his social interactions. The novel consistently indicates that traumatic legacy continues to impact on blacks and whites in their interactions and alone; it plays an integral role in the narrative of the dominant fiction on a multitude of social levels. We see, for example, how the narrator's attempts to divorce himself from racist biases and stereotypes are often futile or oddly degrading. "I carried props into the subway," he says, "— the latest *Semiotext(e)*, a hefty volume of the Frankfurt School—so that the employed would not get the wrong or, more to the point, the usual idea about me" (193). On a late night trip to a pharmacy, for the benefit of the "guys in the plexiglass cage," he similarly "switched automatically into the demeanor of reassurance: I was not one of the bad ones. They did not relent. One almost threw my change on the floor. It was insulting to hold out my hand and to have a clerk bang the money on the counter. I'd 'tommed' again for nothing" (274).

In these examples, the narrator struggles for acceptance via social codes that, by definition, punish him for trying. As color becomes conflated with economic and intellectual status, the most the narrator can hope for with this strategy is to separate himself from other blacks in hopes of assuaging the fears of the whites he encounters; it is a strategy, like the one he pursued in junior high school, of trying to approach rather than contest dominant standards. The fears the narrator wants to placate—of unemployed, violent, dishonest African American men—betray the ambivalences present in the white racist stereotyping: blacks are inferior yet threatening, lazy but aggressive.

In *The Location of Culture*, Bhabha points out that such stereotyping is a crucial component of colonial discourse. It insists on both " 'fixity' in the ideological construction of otherness" and its "anxious" repetition. Since otherness can never be fully known or proven, ambivalence, he argues, "gives the colonial stereotype its currency: ensures its repeatability in changing historical and discursive conjunctures; informs its strategies of individuation and marginalization; produces that effect of probabilistic truth and predictability which, for the stereotype, must always be in *excess* of what can be empirically proved or logically construed" (66). The anxiety of white subway riders or the pharmacy staff, then, may be read as both symptom and cause of traumatic legacy. In perpetuating the stereotype, these white characters maintain their own sense of coherent subjectivity through a differentiation from blackness (and its associative characteristics). Since that subject position is constitutive of and produces social power, it sustains the dominant fiction and its relegation of blackness to a subordinate otherness. As Bhabha notes in his reading of Fanon's discussion of stereotyping in *Black Skin, White Masks*, "the stereotype impedes the circulation and articulation of the signifier of 'race' as anything other than its *fixity* as racism" (75).

* * *

Race becomes "fixed" as racism to the extent that it can appear ahistorical and "natural," especially in relation to the narrative of the modern nation. On the one hand, racism is perpetuated through changing historical circumstances through the workings of the dominant fiction. Ideological consistency mandates a shared articulation of class, race, and gender hierarchies. In other words, these ideologies become naturalized through their ability to create a shared set of terms for the understanding of their historical contexts. On the other hand, racism is enacted through instances of historical violence, which the narrative of the modern nation must suture in order to sustain itself. As we have already seen in Benedict Anderson's reading of Ernest Renan's "What is a nation?", in order to maintain an ideology of cohesion and common purpose, the modern nation demands that its citizens remember what it is they must forget in the name of unity.[9]

Bhabha offers an insightful analysis of the ways in which Anderson's own conception of racism in the "homogeneous empty time" of the modern nation strengthens rather than contests the universalizing narrative of "modern cultural communities." In depicting the "People-as-one," Bhabha notes, that narrative (what Bhabha calls a "spatial fantasy") "deprives minorities of those marginal, liminal spaces from which they can intervene in the unifying and totalizing myths of the national culture" (LC, 249). To avoid replicating the ahistorical projection of the modern nation and timeless racism, Bhabha asks that "we see 'racism' not simply as a hangover from archaic conceptions of the aristocracy, but as part of the historical traditions of civic and liberal humanism that create ideological matrices of national aspiration, together with their concepts of a 'people' and its imagined community" (LC, 250).

Bhabha's argument, that we historicize racism and the modern nation together, demands that we remember instead of forget past traumas and their ongoing legacies in order to understand contemporary subjects and nations. Rather than the "homogeneous empty time" that Anderson characterizes as formative to the development of the modern nation, historical memory necessitates an accounting of the temporal disjunctions occasioned by trauma—the way trauma, by definition, disrupts the seamless narrative of subjective and national unity.[10] What we find in a consideration of traumatic legacy is that the dominant fiction cannot continually reproduce itself without simultaneously reproducing the very traumas it seeks to mask. This intersection of history and trauma within the narratives of identity challenges psychoanalytic theory to account for historical contexts and their relationship to the constitution of subjectivity.

High Cotton makes the same demand by showing how contemporary subjectivity depends upon the memories embedded in the dominant fiction and enacted in daily life. Cathy Caruth's recent work on trauma and history, *Unclaimed Experience*, explicitly addresses this need. Through a combined reading of Freud's *Beyond the Pleasure Principle* and *Moses and Monotheism*, she argues for an understanding of history as a "history of trauma," the ramifications of which "can be grasped only in the inaccessibility of its occurrence" (18). Literature and psychoanalysis working together, she argues, may bring trauma to the surface "in the attempt to tell us of a reality or truth that is otherwise not available" (4).

Caruth's work not only expands our conception of trauma to account for its individual and historical attributes, but it fulfills the vital function of insisting on the historicization of psychoanalysis itself. This dual purpose emerges from the central role she ascribes to the literary voice. Since trauma is that which both "defies and demands our witness," it can only be represented in "a language that is always somehow literary: a language that defies, even as it claims, our understanding" (5). She adds that the literary text may be "a parable of psychoanalytic theory itself as it listens to a voice that it cannot fully know but to which it nonetheless bears witness" (7). If subjectivity is achieved through entry into discursive normativity—an entrance that is performed repeatedly throughout the subject's life and that is marked by what must be repetitively excluded at the threshold, then Caruth is, in effect, saying that the literary may provide conscious access to that unconscious act of repeated foreclosure.

Silverman makes a parallel argument in *The Threshold of the Visible World*, situating the aesthetic, and its potential to alter the narrative of the dominant fiction, in the liminal space between consciousness and unconsciousness. As discussed previously, aesthetic texts may impact on the identifications we are willing to recognize by implanting " 'synthetic' memories—libidinally saturated associative clusters which act like those mnemic elements which, as a result of a psychic working over, have been made the vehicles for the expression of unconscious wishes" (185). While these " 'synthetic' memories" also exist within the scope of the dominant fiction, their libidinal charges, or aesthetic properties, enable them to bring "neglected or despised" images past the psychic censors and into consciousness. In their psychoanalytic readings of the aesthetic or literary, Caruth and Silverman share the belief that the transformative potential of these texts—their ability to bring to the fore what must otherwise be either repressed or unconsciously repeated—lies in their ability to show the culturally and historically specific terms of the dominant fiction at work.

Coming to terms with racial trauma and its legacies necessitates the same negotiation between the universal and the historically specific as does our belief in the value of psychoanalysis in understanding trauma. In order to countermand the obviousness of the dominant fiction and its associative ideologies of national unity, coherent subjectivity, and racial hierarchy, we must insist on historicizing the play of its privileged signifiers as well as our own methods of interpretation. The anxiety that underscores the need to reproduce a racist stereotype parallels the more general need to rearticulate constantly the terms of the dominant fiction and interpellate its subjects. These addresses and enunciations fulfill two interconnected functions: they enable the dominant fiction and its corresponding subjectivities to adapt to changing historical conditions while maintaining a consistent hierarchy and they keep producing subjects who threaten to disrupt the coherence promised by the dominant fiction. Just as Butler emphasizes the extent to which any interpellated subject simultaneously becomes one capable of speech, Bhabha in his reading of racial stereotypes points out that "[i]n the objectification of the scopic drive there is always the threat of the returned look" (81). Whether subjectivity emerges predominantly out of visual or verbal processes, it contains within it a power that exceeds those processes.

* * *

Pinckney incorporates both forms of subjectivity into the narrator whose search for identity takes place within and against colonial discourse.[11] *High Cotton* follows the narrator as he recognizes the impossibility of language and race as fixed components of subjectivity and accepts the slippages within them as his inevitable and only foundations. At the same time, he remains firmly rooted to the very models of race, gender, and national identity that launched his search. This duality, of contesting yet never erasing dominant terms of subjectivity, points to the potential uses and limitations of the psychoanalytic approaches that enable this reading.

The narrator's unstable identity fits within the process Fanon outlines of the "black psyche's" differentiation from whiteness. Desire, discourse, and fantasy for the black subject are structured according to valences of "whiteness," such that, "in order to achieve morality, it is essential that the black, the dark, the Negro vanish from consciousness" (*BSWM*, 194). For Fanon, the problem is one of transforming one's self from an object fixed by a white gaze to a subject no longer confined within the binary of "*turn white or disappear.*"

Invisibility, as discussed above, is the first strategy of survival adopted by Pinckney's narrator. At Westfield, to return to an earlier example, he tries literally to blend in, consciously to detach color, as a racial marker, from any content: "I behaved as though I had been among the

Westfielders all the while and was finally shedding the protective coloration that had kept me completely unseen [. . .] I lived entirely at my surface, passing without reflection from class to class, like someone out for a walk noting whether the clouds either darkened or dissipated" (85–6). As a ghost, the narrator's social agency is circumscribed by the definitions imposed by teachers and classmates. Refusing to acknowledge his own bodily specificity where others do leaves him prey to the ideologies of the dominant fiction that seek to perpetuate themselves at his expense. In this way, inessential subjectivity alone figures as a doomed escape from the corporeal, rather than as a means of reformulating its signification.

Although the narrator constantly invokes the traumatic legacy of slavery, he nonetheless strives for acceptance via the (white) nation as family model. He articulates this sense of belonging he both wants and repudiates on explicitly national terms—for example, he describes a conversation with his grandfather as one between Plessy v. Ferguson and Brown v. Board of Education. At the same time, Pinckney's invocations of the nation are frequently parodic, a gesture that opens them up for interrogation and raises the question of how African Americans may fit into, subvert, or redefine the nation as family. Re-signifying terms such as frontier, immigrant, Pilgrim, and Old Country, the narrator reminds us of the historical violence that they mask. The American narrative of white expansion, plenitude, and the American dream is suddenly imperiled by this reminder of the Middle Passage and its legacies.

Attempts to invoke the rhetoric of immigration and the melting pot in the novel repeatedly fail. "[Grandfather] come from the Old Country," the narrator says. "Not Lithuania, not Silesia. The Old Country, to us, meant Virginia, Georgia, the Carolinas, spectral mileposts of cane swamp and pine, remote tidewater countries swollen with menacing lore" (8). The Old Country as the plantation South excludes African Americans from the discourse of national identity as a voluntary communal enterprise, thereby calling that discourse itself into question. As the narrator reports a conversation he overheard in a restaurant, the city marshal "said with an eloquence I had not expected that all he knew was that he was not patriotic about any one country. He didn't know how to answer where he came from when he filled out a form. There were substitute countries, but prior to them his parents had been his homeland" (267). Once again we are reminded of how the discourse of national identity and national unity fails to interpellate all of its subjects. Pinckney's parodies, constructed in racial terms, force a re-reading of the nation as family metaphor; they demand another look at what the fantasy of national identity asks us to forget.

The parodies, ranging from the rhetoric of national identity to Farrakhan-style rallies, underscore the ambivalence and concurrent necessity of stereotypes in any form of colonial project. That racial and sexual stereotypes never completely cohere, however, suggests that parody may be an effective strategy of subverting them. In aestheticizing the language of the dominant fiction, parody makes it available for analysis and revision. The terms Pinckney chooses to reiterate are laden with the historical and cultural weight of the traumas foundational to contemporary African American subjectivity; so, by reproducing those terms in an explicitly aesthetic context, Pinckney calls attention to the traumas themselves. By appropriating such terms as "nigger" and "Old Country" in the voice of the black male narrator, Pinckney emphasizes how *inappropriate* they are as signifiers of his narrator's identity. Whereas Caruth emphasizes the subject's "unwitting" repetition of the language or voice of trauma, this literary strategy insists that conscious repetition can simultaneously acknowledge and invoke the continuation of trauma in order to negotiate with the dominant fiction.

Caruth sees the disjunction caused by trauma in terms of an epistemological and ethical relation with real (*UE*, 102). This disjunction may be so powerful that the immediate subject may lack the means to respond: "trauma already describes the individual experience as something that exceeds itself, that brings within individual experience as its most intense sense of isolation the very breaking of individual knowledge and mastery of events." Those who inherit traumatic legacy, on the other hand, may be more successful. As Caruth notes, "This notion of trauma also acknowledges that perhaps it is not possible for the witnessing of the trauma to occur within the individual at all, that it may only be in future generations that 'cure' or at least witnessing can take place."[12] As the parodies, *Bildungsroman* trope, and ironic voice in *High Cotton* make clear, traumatic legacy may also be repeated consciously and even strategically. Although the narrator initially tries to avoid the disjunctions caused by trauma by avoiding identifying himself as its target, those disjunctions are ultimately defined by the loss of control over one's own identity as much as by the loss of understanding. The narrator gains control over the terms of his own self-worth as he reconciles critically and consciously with his family and racial background.

* * *

Since the fantasy of national and individual cohesion is constructed racially and sexually, however, parodying the national genealogy from the standpoint of race alone fails to create an alternative national subject. Rather the combined articulation of racial *and* sexual difference "becomes crucial if it is held that the body is always simultaneously (if conflictually) inscribed in both the economy of pleasure and desire and the economy of discourse, domination and power" (Bhabha, *LC*, 67). One path from objectification by the dominant fiction to subjectivity is through the realization of desire. The desiring subject, Fanon writes, demands recognition and reciprocity (*BSWM*, 218), though that does not guarantee liberation from racist oppositions. Here the narrator's ability to undermine stereotypes of racist logic falters in his assertion of patriarchal and heterosexual tropes that structure the idealized identities he seeks. He adopts the standards of desirability and value set forth by the dominant fiction in terms of white patriarchal power.

Women in the novel receive seemingly unparodic, stereotypical treatment Pinckney otherwise contests. The narrator's quest for subjectivity takes place at the expense of women as he tries to realize a mode of subjectivity that will be recognized by the dominant fiction as outlined by Silverman and Fanon. Throughout much of the novel, his references to gender identity consist only of the repetition of stock formulas: he plays king–emperor while his sisters dress up; he wonders how his friend, Trip, deals with Ellen's "tendency to accumulate, that mysterious feminine ability to contrive a world of whispered things" (289). The women in the text are carefully contained within unthreatening stereotypes or appear as vocal and sexual challenges to masculine subjectivity. In addition to Ellen and the elderly Miss Djuna Barnes (for whom he works briefly), there is Bargetta, his college friend, whose striking independence vanishes with her boyfriend and for whom "going out with a white became like having a foreign car" (246). Jeanette, the only woman with whom the narrator has a sexual relationship, is positioned as a honey-colored proving ground for black masculinity, or, in Fanon's words, as a "ritual of initiation into 'authentic' manhood" (72). She emerges as a voracious conflation of orality and sexuality with her "bright red lip gloss," "her moist and out-of-breath entrance," and her "mouth grand and teeming in the pit of the door." "Men," the narrator adds, "had been through Jeanette like a canal" and he fears she may swallow him whole. Describing her with phrases such as "her hips said," the narrator strives to contain her sexually and vocally, though he is afraid of self-obliteration if he tries. Significantly the text is mute on how their relationship finally ends, leaving us with a vision only of his surviving masculinity.

The repetition of masculine/feminine stereotypes and normative heterosexuality illustrates the ways in which ideologies of race and gender work together to uphold the dominant fiction. Although the narrator remains within the paradigm of the patriarchal family, he acknowledges the ways in which that paradigm has caused the crisis in identification he seeks to overcome. Trying to escape racial identity by accepting a dominant model of sexual identity ultimately reproduces and reinforces the terms of the dominant fiction. Pinckney's narrator eventually recognizes this shortfall, and he sees the need to re-signify continually and historically what it means to be an American in racial terms.

This transformation begins as he leaves the cloistered worlds of family and school and enters the work force. There he sees Trip, the most assimilated and successful of his black friends, who, ironically, given his name, "developed a destination problem" (284) at his brokerage firm. The narrator subsequently encounters an employer who cannot distinguish between him and another black employee. The final change comes after a visit to the South where he finds that even though the "Old Country" has become the "New South," still "[p]eople who didn't know me at all opened their doors and hearts, just because I was family" (303). "The graveyards," he adds, "were the last remnants of the Old Country" (301). It is here that the "Gospel Choir sang 'I feel like going home,' with someone, somewhere, letting out a long, low, dry, 'Yes,' and the emotion I'd been looking for all those years finally came" (303). Instead of feeling the past as "cold hands in the dark," he at last recognizes it as a source of strength and direction.

Despite this seemingly romantic conclusion, Pinckney avoids conflating a return to family and community with a notion of static and coherent self. He concludes with an image of historical continuity and contingency with a vision of himself in his grandfather's role, a self-appointed "witness":

> One day—if it comes—I may be someone's old darky, exercising my ficti-
> tious cultural birthright to run off at the mouth, telling someone who
> may insist on being called a Senufo-American how in my day so many—
> black, white, and other—were afraid of black teenagers in big sneakers
> with the laces untied, and three o'clock, when the high schools let out,
> was considered the most perilous hour for subway riders. (309)

The quest comes full circle as the narrator imagines his assumption of Grandfather Eustace's familial standing and pedagogical imperative. While the narrator renders the category of race contingent, his primary identification with his grandfather as the embodiment of the hyphenated national identity maintains the image of the nation as family. At the same time, that image is no longer colored white.

According to Fanon, breaking out of the racial/racist model of self and other requires the subject's recognition of his "unconscious desire to change color." Fanon's goal is to foster the kind of critical distance necessary for conscious and ethical identifications: "my objective, once [the black man's] motivations have been brought into consciousness, will be to put him in a position to *choose* action (or passivity) with respect to the real source of the conflict—that is, toward the social structures" (*BSWM*, 100). Pinckney's hero follows this process, moving from recognizing racial difference to attempting invisibility to trying to master standards of whiteness to finally accepting the simultaneous need to contest social structures based upon racial ideologies and to accept the conditions of inessential subjectivity. In summarizing this journey, he says:

> I minded the strict rules of conduct and the tribal code that said that I, as a black, had a responsibility to help my people, to honor the race. Now I'm sorry that I went to such lengths not to be of much use to myself just so no one would be able to ask anything of me. To have nothing to offer was not, after all, the best way to have nothing to lose. (306)

What remains for the narrator is to act on the potential alliance between inessential identity and redefined, redeployed racial agency by inscribing the "tribal codes" for himself. As he begins to recognize race as both constructed and unerasable—a realization that transforms him from a passive to an active subject, he faces the challenge of enacting racial subjectivity in ways that support those codes.

Although the narrator holds on to patriarchal metaphors of social grouping and masculine subjectivity, he simultaneously challenges their power by recognizing the lack at the core of subjectivity and, therefore, the possibility of deciding upon the forms of compensation he seeks. In each renewed attempt for a stable and coherent identity, he discovers the instability of his would-be foundations. The novel is most effective here in its portrayal of the tension between the need for signification and the limits on subjectivity necessitated by the signifiers themselves. As the narrator negotiates the ambiguous space between corporeal and psychic markers, he reveals the way in which this ambiguity underlies the prevailing metaphors of the dominant fiction. The conscious awareness of lack that results forms the crucial first step in undermining the power of those metaphors without abandoning the communal memories that make his own subjectivity possible.

CHAPTER 4

POSTCOLONIAL LACK AND AESTHETIC PROMISE IN SALMAN RUSHDIE'S MIDNIGHT'S CHILDREN AND THE MOOR'S LAST SIGH

[M]y inheritance includes this gift, the gift of inventing new parents for myself whenever necessary.

Salman Rushdie, *Midnight's Children*

Just before midnight of August 15, 1947, Jawaharlal Nehru announced to the public and the Constituent Assembly that India's "tryst with destiny" was about to reach fruition: "At the stroke of the midnight hour, when the world sleeps, India will awake to life and freedom. A moment comes, which comes but rarely in history, when we step out from the old to the new, when an age ends and when the soul of a nation, long suppressed, finds utterance."[1] Nehru's landmark speech, which identifies India as a child of dubious parentage, opens Salman Rushdie's film, *The Riddle of Midnight* (1988), and supplies the central metaphor of the novel upon which it draws, *Midnight's Children* (1981), as well as the more recent *The Moor's Last Sigh* (1995). All three texts explore the question of how we can capture the nation's soul, how we can satisfy, in *Midnight's Children*'s terms, the "national longing for form."

In the film, the personification of the nation takes place through the ever-present crowd and the representative figure of Rushdie himself who returns to India 30 years after independence as a national investigator-cum-spokesman. The crowd greets him not with a narrative to record, however, but with a riddle to answer: "How can a country that never previously existed become independent? What does it mean to call this crowd of separate national histories, conflicting cultures, and warring faiths, a nation?" "It's by the lack of definition that you know it's you," he responds, though too late (and too little) to satisfy the pressing crowd. It soon surges onward and engulfs him in its wake.

If we jump from Nehru's speech and Rushdie's film to the books commemorating independent India's fiftieth anniversary, we find the riddle in new contexts. "[W]e are a land of belonging rather than blood," Shashi Tharoor writes in *India: From Midnight to the Millennium* (126). Addressing the same "tantalizing possibility of a principle of unity, but its evident empirical lack" (157), Sunil Khilnani in *The Idea of India* attempts to move beyond competing claims for a singular identity. In place of "the old opposition between the monochromy of the post-imperial imagination," "nationalist histories of a unified people," and "the pointillism of the new Indian historians, ever more ingeniously trawling and re-reading the archives for examples of 'resistance' (textual and practical) to the ideas of the nation and the state," he proposes "new routes, that do not altogether abandon the terrain of political history, but recount it in different terms" (3).

Midnight's Children and *The Moor's Last Sigh* work increasingly toward Khilnani's goal, though they remain tied to the most traditional trope of identity: the two novels depend upon an overt allegory between the familial and national epic. Through the identifications of the narrators, Saleem and the Moor, and their families with the nation, we are encouraged to see the ways in which the connective metaphor of the family links narratives of subjectivity and national identity in order to legitimate (repressive) authority. In the novels' postcolonial India, the family metaphor attempts to assuage differences in religion, caste, language, and ethnicity in the rush to modernize and to overcome the lasting legacy of the British. Nehru first presented that domestic ideal as a national objective when he exhorted the Assembly to "build the noble mansion of free India, where all her children may dwell." Rushdie, in literalizing the metaphor within the plots, details the demise of the dream through the disintegration of the narrators and their homes and families. Just as the film's narrator disappears into the crowd, Saleem ends in the "annihilating whirlpool of the multitudes" (552). Yet those bleak conclusions are partially offset by the regenerative potential of the multitudes themselves. Even the Moor, who dies alone, impotent, and outside India, rests with a faith that he will "awaken, renewed and joyful, into a better time" (434). While the novels assiduously critique the effects and efficacy of the nation as family metaphor, they, along with their narrators and, I suspect, most readers, remain tied to its foundational terms.

Saleem and the Moor are catalysts for identificatory relationships between reader, narrator, and nation. The meaning and narrative pleasure of the novels depend upon the alignment of the narrators with postcolonial India; and this allegory is constructed (and undone) through the family epic on the level of both content and structure. When Saleem announces at the beginning of the novel, "I must work fast, faster than Scheherazade, if I am to end up meaning—yes, meaning— something" (4), he makes us equally dependent on his progress. We must rely on the narrators' perspectives even when they are self-avowedly suspect—as when the Moor notes in one of his many addresses to the reader, "I don't know everything. I'm telling you what I know" (372). Saleem's birth corresponds with independence, and his narrative reflects an ongoing struggle to define himself in national terms, and vice versa, in the face of impending physical, social, and narrative dissolution (the novel ends with the Emergency years, 1975–77). In place of Saleem's bid, however faulty, to represent some form of national unity, the Moor (the son of a Christian mother and Jewish father) gives us an explicitly minority perspective. Born ten years after Saleem, the Moor brings India's political history up to date while also tracing it back, along genealogical lines, to the Moorish invaders. Although Rushdie draws attention to the narrators' self-serving invocation of the nation as family metaphor, the way the analogy adds importance to the details of their lives, he refuses to abandon it completely. Making sense of the novels depends to a large extent on one's willingness to read the metaphor and its gendered signifiers.

In choosing the family to capture the "soul" of the modern nation, Rushdie illuminates the metaphor's widespread circulation through discourses of national identity, asking us to rethink our easy acceptance of its terms. In a *New Yorker* essay, written for the fiftieth anniversary of independence, he notes that after writing *Midnight's Children*, he traveled around India only to find "the idea of a long saga-novel about a child born at the exact moment of independence [. . .] had occurred to other writers, too" (56). One of the sadly ironic aspects of the rising popularity of the metaphor in discourses from the height of British colonization onward, McClintock explains, is that the family "as *metaphor* offered a single genesis narrative for national history while, at the same time, the family as an *institution* became void of history and excluded from national power. The family became, at one and the same time, both the *organizing figure* for national history and its *antithesis*" (" 'No Longer a Future in Heaven'," 91). Rendering Saleem and the Moor's families as national allegory ascribes to them the very historical forces that exclude them, thereby masking the ways in which the nation appropriates other forms of social identification. By simultaneously constructing and deconstructing this metaphor as a literary device, Rushdie makes it available for the kind of critical revision suggested by this project. What he offers in place of a singular metaphor are the creative, regenerative possibilities of the aesthetic in multiple forms.

Perhaps unsurprisingly given its prominence in political and literary texts, the family metaphor has become a central trope in postcolonial criticism as well. Postcolonial criticism is beset by the question of aesthetic and material context: how to account for a text's relationship to colonial experience without subsuming all of its other attributes to a comparison with the West. This question frequently emerges in terms Fredric Jameson sets forth in his 1986 essay, "Third World Literature in the Era of Multinational Capitalism": "Third-world texts, even those which are seemingly private and invested with a properly libidinal dynamic—necessarily project a political dimension in the form of national allegory: *the story of the private individual destiny is always an allegory of the embattled situation of the public third-world culture and society*" (emphasis in original, 69). This model has been exhaustively critiqued for its homogenization of colonial experiences and its replication of colonialism's center–periphery organization.[2] As Revathi Krishnaswamy cautions in "Mythologies of Migrancy," Jameson's "paradigm of postcolonial literature as national allegory uniformly constitutes all 'Third World' intellectuals, regardless of their gender or class, as marginalized insurgents or as nationalists struggling against a monolithic Western imperialism. Difference is reduced to equivalence, interchangeability, syncretism, and diversity, while a levelling subversive subalternity is indiscriminately attributed to any and all" (129).

The most prevalent alternatives to Jameson's reading of postcolonial literature are those substituting class, gender, or racial identifications for national ones and those focusing on the local material–historical concerns of the text.[3] How, then, do we approach novels such as Rushdie's *Midnight's Children* and *The Moor's Last Sigh* that embody national allegory as organizing motifs? Rushdie invokes that allegory to question its underlying structures. In transposing terms from one story to another, allegory exposes the foundations of those stories and creates new systems of meaning. Rushdie's use of the family trope connects the texts, their narrators and readers with dominant narratives of the modern nation; in the process, it reveals the historical and psychic wounds those narratives try to mend.

* * *

The self-conscious invocation of the family in *Midnight's Children* and *The Moor's Last Sigh* is not a simple repetition of a formula or hegemonic application of a Western model to a postcolonial context, although it does bring that model to the forefront. I do not wish to suggest, for instance, that the family trope, in whatever form, is in and of itself an avowedly Western one; rather, the family as national allegory works, in the postcolonial contexts I discuss, through a series of metaphoric substitutions leading from a traditional division of gender roles to a definition of the modern nation based upon Western models of cultural, political, and economic progress.

Both novels draw unreservedly on a host of Western literary and historical sources in presenting what Rushdie intends as a specifically Indian tale.[4] In just one of countless examples, in a Joycean moment imitative of Stephen Dedalus's flight from Ireland "to forge in the smithy of my soul the uncreated conscience of my race" (*A Portrait of the Artist as a Young Man*, 253), Saleem predicts that Aadam, the infant he raises as his son, "was a member of a second generation of magical children who would grow up to be far tougher than the first, not looking for their fate in the prophecy of the stars, but forging it in the implacable furnaces of their wills" (534). Through a double gesture that seems either to confuse or to mute the question of cultural authenticity, Rushdie reinforces his own authority as chronicler of India by drawing on Joyce's image of the intellectual exile who hears the voice of his nation from outside of it. Such references serve less to condemn or celebrate Rushdie's far-reaching ear and voice than to reveal the overwhelming desire for coherent subjectivity and a national narrative. The circulation of the nation as family is not, then, a reflection of national identities but a particular response to the longing for self-definition, to the foundational lack we all share. In the case of Rushdie's postcolonial Indian fiction, that longing is complicated by the conflicted historical antecedents of the nation, by its complex indigenous and colonial lineages and the languages used to record them.

In *Mirrorwork*, Rushdie defends Indian writing in English and, implicitly, the kinds of cross-cultural references it bears, in terms that themselves invoke the family metaphor: "Like the Greek god Dionysos, who was dismembered and afterwards reassembled—and who, according to the myths, was one of India's earliest conquerors—Indian writing in English has been called 'twice-born' (by the critic Meenakshi Mukherjee) to suggest its double parentage" (x). Rushdie reads this image with a twist, insisting that English remains in India not as an alien but as the equivalent of a naturalized citizen: "English has become an Indian language" (xi).

Some critics have interpreted Rushdie's national allegory and its Western references as a clever transformation of expatriatism into marketability (these critiques were mostly written before the 1989 *fatwa* against him). Timothy Brennan, one of Rushdie's most astute critics, reads Rushdie's semantic and textual hybridity as a choice of cosmopolitanism over political action. Brennan cites Bharati Mukherjee and Rushdie as examples of his charge that, "[p]ropelled and defined by media and market, cosmopolitanism today involves not so much an elite *at home*, as it does spokespersons for a kind of perennial immigration, valorised by a rhetoric of wandering, and rife with allusions to the all-seeing eye of the nomadic sensibility." This sensibility denies "the old pattern of need to create a national *mythos* in the country of origin," and, he implies, to assume the political responsibility that would accompany it.[5] Michael Gorra points out that "to be cosmopolitan is, on this reading, to be inauthentic," and he goes on to argue that "Rushdie's work as a whole can perhaps best be seen as an attempt to contest the terms on which such judgments get made" (131).

In *Salman Rushdie and the Third World*, Brennan shows how Rushdie's fiction can cut both ways. Brennan's nuanced discussion of the neocolonial attributes of Rushdie's fiction reveals how Rushdie may be at once critical of neocolonial collaborators in postcolonial nationhood and complicit in their preference for European imagery. "Style is, of course, also social attitude," Brennan insists, "and for Rushdie the attitudes have not been formed in isolation [. . .] but as complementary poles in an imperial relationship" (84). Rushdie agrees that some of these effects are the product of a nation with a 51 percent illiteracy rate, whose authors most often come from a privileged class educated in English; though, he insists, "[i]t does not follow [. . .] that writers with the privilege of a good education will automatically write novels that seek only to portray the lives of the bourgeoisie" (*MW*, xii).

For me, Rushdie's polysemantics, while always playful and parodic, are testimony to the inevitability of hybridity rather than a preference for it over a stable and unitary identity. Hybridity, of language, form, and allusion, is what remains after the narratives of clear genealogies and authentic speech have unraveled. While politically void in and of itself, hybridity in Rushdie's hands is laden with self-conscious inferences of ongoing colonial relationships. Nowhere is this clearer than in *The Moor's Last Sigh*, in which the story of India is told by a descendant of the last Moorish sultan. The linguistic and aesthetic references to the decline of the Moorish empire do more than make an already fantastical tale more exotic. Rather, they demand a more complicated reading of postcolonialism in India beyond the departure of the British in 1947, insisting that colonial relationships and their effects be traced back far before the British and up through the present. It is this fraught history that makes the subject's desire for self-definition so difficult to satisfy.

* * *

In order to read Rushdie's use of the nation as family as a subversive strategy, we must account for the historical specificity of both the narrator-subject's sense of lack and yearning for completion as well as the nation as family metaphor that compensates for that yearning. In cinematic and psychoanalytic theories, the relationship of discourse to the subject who is constituted yet never completed by it emerges through the concept of suture. Medically, sutures bind flesh wounds to encourage healing growth of new tissue and to guard against infection. At the same time, black overhand stitches, dimpled edges of staples, or long tails of a running stitch trailing across the body draw attention to wounds as they heal and determine the shape of their scars. When suture binds psychic rather than physical wounds, according to Jacques-Alain Miller, it "names the relation of the subject to the chain of its discourse." Just as the medical suture compensates for torn tissue, psychoanalytic suture "figures there as the element which is lacking, in the form of a stand-in." Miller's analysis of suture, drawn from Lacan's model of subjectivity, emphasizes the underlying nature of the wound, the way suture defines lack. Suture describes, in other words, "the general relation of lack to the structure of which it is an element" (25–6). As suture becomes cinematic (and literary), it bridges the gulf between viewer and subject through the process of identification. That process offers the viewer the pleasure and fulfillment of narrative compensation for historical lack.

Condensing earlier theoretical work on suture, and building on her theory of lack at the center of all subjects, Silverman defines suture as "the name given to the procedures by means of which cinematic texts confer subjectivity upon their viewers" (SS, 193). Often, though not solely, enacted by the shot/reverse shot formation, where the "second shot shows the field from which the first shot is assumed to have been taken," suture aligns the viewer or reader's gaze with that of the speaking subject of the text in order to mask the role of the camera or author in structuring the shot.[6] This formation fosters "the illusion that what is shown has an autonomous existence, independent of any technological interference, or any coercive *gaze*" (201); "[i]n other words, the subject of the speech passes itself off as the speaking subject" (204). Through the blink of an eye, suture establishes the fictional subject as the removed site of plenitude, unity, and power, creating in the spectator or reader a desire to see more by adhering to the gaze.

The "other" of the text has, according to Silverman, "all the attributes of the mythical symbolic father: potency, knowledge, transcendental vision, self-sufficiency, and discursive power" (204). We see this mythic potency in Saleem as he explains his role, facilitated by his childhood omniscience and telepathy, as the mirror of the nation and father of the narrative: "[T]he feeling had come upon me that I was somehow creating a world; that the thoughts I jumped inside were *mine*, that the bodies I occupied acted at my command; which is to say, I had entered into the illusion of the artist, and thought of the multitudinous realities of the land as the raw unshaped material of my gift" (*MC*, 207). Adopting his perspective promises to reveal the nation, for as Nehru writes in his congratulatory letter to Baby Saleem as the first of midnight's children: "You are the newest bearer of that ancient face of India which is also eternally young. We shall be watching over your life with the closest attention; it will be, in a sense, the mirror of our own" (143).

In *Midnight's Children*, the self-determinant fantasy of nation creation and self-creation depends upon Saleem's pivotal roles as author, subject, and national spokesman. Yet our identifications with Saleem are repeatedly undermined by his unreliable narration with its partial truths and divergences, corporeal instability ("I am the bomb in Bombay"), and insecure family standing: he is the son of parents who are not his parents and the father of a son who is not his son. Despite this empirical attack on his authority, however, when the family discovers that Saleem, swapped at birth with his midnight rival, Shiva, is the child of a Hindu street singer and an Englishman, and not his wealthy Muslim parents, "it *made no difference!*" he exclaims. "In a kind of collective failure of imagination, we learned that we simply could not think our way out of our pasts" (137).

Saleem's parentage represents the inescapable, if idealized, plurality of the nation. Through the "literalization of metaphor," in Neil Ten Kortenaar's words, "[Rushdie] seeks to make readers aware again of the metaphorical nature of all bloodlines" (48). By maintaining his place in the family, his naturalized birthright, Saleem reminds us of the unavoidable British legacy in India without capitulating to the stigma of illegitimacy. Even as collective imagination secures his position, however, it is rendered suspect by this admitted fallacy. Saleem temporarily achieves family coherence at the expense of narrative purity and narrative coherence at the expense of family purity, thereby reminding us to be wary of genealogy as an ontological national myth. Any return to origins is suspect in these novels, even though such gestures are unavoidable in the search for meaning. The lesson is less in the unquenchable desire for self-knowledge than for purity itself; for as Rushdie remarked on "Talk of the Nation," "It has always been my view that purity has been one of the most dangerous ideas of the twentieth century."

While the text's dependence upon the nation as family metaphor reproduces Western modernity's hegemonic terms (conflating progress, paternity, and power), it also exposes the struts and rivets that uphold that ideology. Through the alignment of stable subjectivity and modern India, Rushdie illuminates the traumas underlying postcolonial Indian identities: the lasting influence of British culture, the inaccessibility of a purely "Indian" past, and the problem of defining modernity without acquiescing to the singular narrative of capital expansion. National allegory in the novel attempts to suture these traumas with rhetoric of familial and national purity. On the one hand, this structure reminds us of our inevitable yearning for stable meaning; on the other hand, it underscores the dangers of those yearnings.

* * *

The nation as family metaphor attempts to provide a common image for collective identification—"[n]ot that the fundamental matter of Indian selfhood has ever been settled," Khilnani reminds us (151)—through a conflation of gender roles, cultural motifs, and national history. In "Nationalism, Gender, and the Narrative of Identity," R. Radhakrishnan argues for a theoretical approach to gender and nationalism that does not subsume one to the other. He begins with Partha Chatterjee's model of nationalism and its opposition between Westernized nations and nativistic ones. This split—echoing in terms of public versus private, modernity versus timelessness, and male versus female—reduces gender to essentialized identities on the nation's linear path from feminine victim or goddess to masculine nation-state. Chatterjee traces this development through anticolonial to postcolonial Indian nationalism. In order to protect a sense of their own identity in the face of colonial power, he argues, indigenous colonized communities separate the material and spiritual: "The material is the domain of the 'outside,' of the economy and of statecraft, of science and technology, a domain where the West had proved its superiority and the East had succumbed [. . .] The spiritual, on the other hand, is an 'inner' domain bearing the 'essential' marks of cultural identity. The greater one's success in imitating Western skills in the material domain, therefore, the greater the need to preserve the distinctness of one's spiritual culture" (*The Nation and Its Fragments*, 6).

The model appears to create a trap for postcolonial nationalism. Internal identity, no matter how complicated or fraught with difference, becomes essential and mythic while external economic, political, and social identities are evaluated according to standards of modern liberal and capitalist ideology. As Radhakrishnan writes, "Woman becomes the allegorical name for a specific historical failure: the failure to coordinate the political or the ontological with the epistemological within an undivided agency" ("Nationalism, Gender, and the Narrative of Identity," 85). This failure is both essentially gendered and unavoidable as the model itself seemingly forecloses the possibility of alternative national identities.

Reading national identity in these gendered terms means that if the nation is an imagined community, then as Chatterjee notes, "[e]ven our imaginations remain forever colonized" (*NIF*, 5). Colonization occurs through the metaphor of the family and its gendered signifiers of the nation. The paternal family effectively fuses two narratives of national identity: legal-political and ethnic. Whereas the legal-political nation legitimates itself on the basis of history, territory, and, in modern liberal terms, the promise to protect private difference in return for public allegiance, the ethnic nation "is seen as a fictive 'super-family,' and it boasts pedigrees and genealogies to back up its claims [. . .] the nation can trace its roots to an imputed common ancestry and [. . .] therefore its members are brothers and sisters, or at least cousins, differentiated by family ties from outsiders."[7] In the case of India, that rhetoric anoints a state created by decree with a notion of national solidarity united more in opposition to the British than in ethnic, linguistic, or religious purity or cohesion.[8]

Rushdie's response to this model is to render it both literal and fantastic so that we are forced to see how it is constructed and to account for our own reliance on it. Saleem underscores this duality when he looks back on the eve of independent India:

> [T]here was an extra festival on the calendar, a new myth to celebrate, because a nation which had never previously existed was about to win its freedom, catapulting us into a world which, although it had five thousand years of history, although it had invented the game of chess and traded with Middle Kingdom Egypt, was nevertheless quite imaginary; into a mythical land, a country which would never exist except by the efforts of a phenomenal collective will—except in a dream we all agreed to dream [. . .]. (129–30)

Here Rushdie collapses the distinctions between postcolonial India's mythic and political formation. He intersperses passages such as the one above with official state rhetoric, making it easy to imagine Nehru or

Mohandas K. Gandhi as national fathers or Indira Gandhi's Emergency as a parental response to the nation's difficult adolescence (when, as she explained her suspension of civil and political rights during the Emergency, "there comes a time in the life of the nation when hard decisions have to be taken").[9]

While Rushdie's own ideal image of India corresponds more closely to Nehru's vision of a specifically Indian modernity based on pluralism than it does to Gandhi's rural vision, he does not condemn Gandhi's nationalist program. Instead, Rushdie warns of the dangers of conflating the political and the mythic through the figure of Indira Gandhi. When she appears in *Midnight's Children* as the Widow, she is both Prime Minister and the "Mother goddess," Kali (known for her destructive powers).[10] In his study of Hindu goddesses, David Kinsley describes Kali as a terrifying figure, her blackness bejeweled by children's corpses, serpents, and skulls and her long fingernails and teeth smeared with the blood of her victims (116). She is often pictured alone or with the God Shiva, the only one who can temper her excesses when she threatens to destroy the world she helped create. According to Joanna Liddle and Rama Joshi, she functions within rather than against a patriarchal religious structure: "The story of Kali—India's matriarchal myth—is that she was created to save the gods from their more powerful enemies, but having done so, she continued on a rampage of uncontrollable killing, which could only be stopped by her husband Shiva lying down in front of her" (55). Kinsley reads more flexibility in that image, noting that she often appears to be dancing on top of the prostrate or even corpse-like Shiva. In both cases, she remains the mythological embodiment of unrestrained feminine fury.

Kali's counterpart is Parvati, the goddess of domesticity who softens Shiva's destructiveness and who, in Kinsley's words, "persuaded or provoked him into creating a child, who was necessary for the preservation of the world" (41). Rushdie's Shiva and Parvati, the other two most important of midnight's children after Saleem, provide a parallel context for the figure of Kali in the novel. Shiva is Saleem's enemy, rival, and midnight twin, and Parvati is Saleem's one true ally, whose liaison with Shiva produces Aadam (Saleem's surrogate son and the representative of the next generation of Indian independence).

Indira Gandhi as Kali first appears to Saleem in a dream. Dressed in the colors of the national flag and foreshadowing the future she has in store for midnight's children, the Widow

sits on a high chair the chair is green the seat is black the Widow's hair has a centre-parting it is green on the left and on the right black. High as the sky the chair is green the seat is black the Widow's arm is long as death its skin is green the fingernails are long and sharp and black. Between the walls the children green the walls are green the Widow's arm comes snaking down the snake is green the children scream the fingernails are black they scratch the Widow's arm is hunting see the children run and scream the Widow's hand curls round them green and black. (249)

With this malevolent image, Rushdie denounces Indira Gandhi's attempts to legitimate her power—as captured in the slogan "Indira is India"— through mythic references that place her own harsh measures within the context of Hinduism and what Stanley Wolpert calls its "reconciliation of extremes: erotic passion and ascetic renunciation, frenzied motion and unmoving calm, violence and passivity" (*A New History of India*, 82). By referring to her only as the Widow, Rushdie insists such reconciliation is impossible: her usurpation of traditionally masculinized state power and sexual power goes unchecked in the absence of a husband. Shiva in the novel serves not as her husband but as her son—perhaps the true child of midnight as well as the Widow's henchman. When Rushdie replicates the Hindu dualities of the Widow or Kali (destruction) and Parvati (benevolence), he does so to warn of these rhetorical and metaphorical ploys; at the same time, by scripting these religious figures according to marital status, he reinforces a patriarchal critique of Indira Gandhi's authority.[11] While Parvati does give birth to the next generation of midnight's children, she is nonetheless destroyed in one of the Widow's campaigns. Wifely obedience and loyalty are no match for unrestrained, insatiable feminine appetite for power. Rather than serve to define and protect some form of inclusive Indian community, these references ultimately mythologize authoritarian rule and the suppression of difference while reinforcing a patriarchal political ideology.

What we see in this example—both in the role Gandhi defines for herself and Rushdie's characterization of it—is an attempt to bridge precolonial and postcolonial identities through the metaphor of the family tree. By representing herself as simultaneously timeless and modern, Indira Gandhi legitimates her power through a seamless construction of Indian identity, one that connects, in Chatterjee's terms, spiritual and material domains. She is "Mother India" in its mythic and modern form. As both the daughter of Nehru and, through her marriage, the namesake (though not a relative) of Gandhi, figures who have themselves gained near mythic status, Indira represents the contemporary scion of a lineage of nationalist power. In encouraging her image as "Mother India" (Indira-Mata), she hopes to capitalize on the beneficent associations with the image.

Whereas the language of the family should describe a national community that is continuous and united, in *Midnight's Children* it reveals the desire for those attributes and their costs. The Widow uses her power to suppress figurative and literal challenges to her authority: she dismisses parliament, suspends civil rights, and, true to Rushdie's metaphor, sterilizes the children of midnight to drain them of their magic and fertility. Saleem, like Rushdie, wavers between this hopeless view of modern India, where the only "purpose of Midnight's Children might be annihilation" (274), and the endless possibilities for alternative stories permeating the narrative form itself.

We see another example of the centrality and failure of the family metaphor at the highpoint of Saleem's powers: when he nightly convenes the Midnight Children's Conference (MCC), acting as translator, parliamentarian, president, and D.J. for all the voices in his head of the children born at the moment of India's independence. Upon recognizing his power to tune into and connect all the thought communications of midnight's children, Saleem conceives of himself as the foundation for an ideal bourgeois public sphere: "I had in mind [. . .] a sort of loose confederation of equals, all points of view given equal expression" (263). For Habermas, defining the liberal bourgeois model which informs the MCC, the ideal public sphere is a space, between the private domain of the home and the official public domain of the state and courts, in which individuals converse as generic citizens on the common good. Communication itself is disinterested and undistorted so that identity remains non-corporeal and discourse alone constitutes the group. Although Habermas recognizes this as ideal, he nonetheless sees it as a crucial component of completing the heretofore incomplete project of modernity.

Rushdie illustrates the inherent failures of the model: the impossibility of erasing identity (Saleem transmits visual and oral communications; the children are motivated by self-interest), of delineating this sphere from others, and of creating a neutral, equal space (although "ungrounded" in many respects, the conference takes place in Saleem's mind).[12] Almost as soon as this microcosm of a secular and participatory public sphere commences, it is fractured by power struggles, conflicts of belief, and an inability to transform discourse into concerted action.

The first to speak out is Shiva, Saleem's rival in magic powers (as opposed to Saleem's telepathy, Shiva has the gift of physical prowess, used to destroy enemies and to father an untold number of illegitimate children), whose denied birthright has condemned him to life on the streets. In response to Saleem's idea for the MCC, Shiva demands,

"What we ever goin' to do with a gang like that? Gangs gotta have gang bosses." While Saleem tries to maintain order through his role as "big brother" over the family of magically gifted children who together symbolize the birth of the new nation, Shiva disrupts it with ridicule and contempt. In response to Saleem's search for the common good, his rival thunders, "Rich kid, you don't know one damn thing! What *purpose*, man? What thing in the whole sister-sleeping world got *reason*, yara? [. . . You] got to get what you can, do what you can with it, and then you got to die. That's reason, rich boy. Everything else is only mother-sleeping *wind*!" (263–4). Saleem eventually fails at maintaining the allegiance of his "siblings" in this national family and the conference, as reflected in Saleem's own body, gradually disintegrates. In an ironic twist on the family metaphor and its capacity for "mother-sleeping" and "sister-sleeping" corruption, Shiva becomes the Widow's enforcer, leading the sterilization program (as did Indira Gandhi's son, Rajiv) and thereby escaping its ultimate effects. His lasting legacy is the horde of children he fathers (before voluntarily undergoing sterilization), including Aadam, his son with Parvati (his figurative sister in the family of midnight's children).

Once again the mythic allusions to Shiva and Parvati and to the "reconciliation of extremes" are domesticated through the nation as family metaphor. It is no surprise then that Shiva and Aadam survive while Parvati dies in the Widow's destruction of the magicians' ghetto. By juxtaposing the Widow and the MCC, Rushdie shows how the nation as family serves multiple political agendas. It is at once a critique of the metaphor used to legitimate political power and an acknowledgment of the necessity of metaphor in creating a sense of belonging. The novel stops short of providing alternatives to the model it criticizes, although it offers the imaginative space for such an alternative to exist.

* * *

Radhakrishnan and Chatterjee call for a recognition of communal identities outside the spectrum defined by the Enlightenment subject and his [sic] nation, identities that may form the basis for alternative constructions of national identity. Chatterjee's historiographic project illuminates examples of specifically Indian modernity to unravel "an inelegant braiding of an idea of community with the concept of capital" (*NIF*, 237). Instead of beginning to read modern postcolonial nationalism according to Western standards of political organization, he looks at formations of nationalism within the "spiritual domain" during the colonial era (6). Thus, in a reformulation of the traditional gender roles used to substantiate national identity, the inner or spiritual domain becomes the foundation for alternative modernities.

This approach, combined with Radhakrishnan's insistence on reading nation and gender simultaneously, suggests a way out of the dilemma posed by Jameson's approach to national allegory as well as the dualistic model Chatterjee describes. Here the connections between the libidinal or private and the national are neither refuted nor evaluated solely in terms of their relationship to the imperial center; rather, alternative historiographies expand and critique the category of the modern nation "from within itself," to include non-Western examples drawn from community identifications (Chatterjee, *NIF*, 237). Despite his attempts to theorize community as foundational to Indian modernity, however, Chatterjee ends on a note of disappointment:

> The irony is, of course, that this other narrative is again violently interrupted once the postcolonial nation state attempts to resume its journey along the trajectory of world-historical development. The modern state, embedded as it is within the universal narrative of capital, cannot recognize within its jurisdiction any form of community except the single, determinate, demographically enumerable form of the nation. It must therefore subjugate, if necessary by the use of state violence, all such aspirations of community identity. These other aspirations, in turn, can give to themselves a historically valid justification only by claiming an alternative nationhood with rights to an alternative state. (238)

He concludes that efforts to decolonize the imagination of the modern postcolonial national subject are ultimately thwarted by an inability to theorize nation and community simultaneously.[13] Modernity itself in this reading becomes synonymous with subject-nation identifications defined by essentialized genders and capital expansion.

Rushdie does not offer successful mediating communities in the subject-nation relationship; he makes the relationship itself suspect through its literalization. As Chatterjee predicts, communities like the magicians' ghetto—home of "conjurers and contortionists and jugglers and fakirs" (*MC*, 461) who "disbelieved, with the absolute certainty of illusionists-by-trade, in the possibility of magic" (*MC*, 462)—which challenge the Widow's mythic stature are destroyed; those that flourish, such as the pickle factory, support the prevailing ideology of economic growth and historical progress.

The transformation of Saleem's childhood home, Methwold's Estate, into the pickle factory, site of his current literary and culinary endeavors, illustrates how that ideology is domesticated and maintained. When William Methwold sold his estate of four villas to Indian families he stipulated that "the houses be bought complete with every last thing in them, that the entire contents be retained by the new owners; and that the actual transfer should not take place until midnight on August 15th" (109). As Methwold intended, his estate (in addition to his unacknowledged fathering of Saleem) exerts his influence long after independence, determining much of the flavor of Saleem's childhood "kingdom":

> the Estate, Methwold's Estate, is changing them. Every evening at six they are out in their gardens, celebrating the cocktail hour, and when William Methwold comes to call they slip effortlessly into their imitation Oxford drawls [. . .] and Methwold, supervising their transformation, is mumbling under his breath. Listen carefully: what is he saying? Yes, that's it. 'Sabkuch ticktock hai,' mumbles William Methwold. All is well. (113)

When family fortunes decline in political, religious, and economic turmoil, a group of enterprising, industrializing women inherit the estate and transform it first into a land reclamation project (a miniaturized version of the British construction of Bombay) and later the pickle factory. Thus, Saleem ends his story back "home" where he began it, as manager of the factory under his old nurse Mary Pereira by day and writer by night. Although geographically circular, Saleem's path traces the linear development of the modernizing nation-state, the legacy of Methwold and his estate. What has changed in the process, however, is the gendering of public and private worlds, rather than the phallic power that prevails, as the women control the process of capitalization Methwold began.

The transformation of the domestic into the commercial has a re-visionary potential in terms of the gendered signifiers of the nation as family metaphor. That potential is limited, however, by the depiction of the "formidable" and "strong armed" women who took over Methwold's Estate, marking their endeavor with a pink obelisk, and by Saleem's own insistence at remaining at the center of the story as the preserver of history.[14]

* * *

As bridges between readers, subjects, and nations, the narrators are successful to the extent that they can define themselves as spokesmen for the nation in order to naturalize the nation as family metaphor. Challenges to that metaphor appear simultaneously as challenges to the narrators' authority and, thus, to our own reading pleasure such that we work with them to preserve the illusion of narrative authority. When we identify with the narrators in this role, they function as cinematic sutures, roles that seem particularly appropriate for an author who honors the Bombay film industry with cinematic images, language, and processes of identification.[15] In *Midnight's Children*, time passes through images such as "a calendar ruffled by a breeze, its pages flying off in rapid succession to denote the passing of the years" (414), and chapters "fade out." Rushdie creates a relationship between text and reader that is both constructed and real when he invites readers to approach the screen until the images dissolve and "the illusion itself is reality" (197). We are urged to surrender ourselves temporarily to the text as we might to a film in a darkened theater.

Rushdie makes this relationship seductive through magic realism with its destabilizing conflation of the fantastical, historical, and quotidian; we enter a world where meaning depends on our willingness to accede to the interdependence of the fantastic and the "real." Since the novel refuses any return to secure epistemological or ontological foundations, we must rely on the terms the narrative provides for our identifications. At the same time, *Midnight's Children* and *The Moor's Last Sigh* are historically grounded and motivated. Magic realism forces us to recognize, however, that we conceptualize our histories through ideologically scripted metaphors, that identification takes place in the (Lacanian) Imaginary. While we can never step outside the beliefs that structure our realities, we can learn to recognize our complicity with those signifying systems.

Rushdie's novels can seem at once profoundly misogynist and self-critical. They present the authoritative masculine mind as constituting and constructing the narrative of the modern nation against as well as for a sensual, material, feminine ground. Saleem and the Moor are literally writing for their lives and their texts substitute for children they cannot father. While Saleem writes for Padma, his female audience and caretaker, the "lotus-goddess of the present," the Moor writes to keep alive himself and Aoi Uë, his fellow prisoner, comforter, and conscience who "dragged him down to earth." The reader is feminized through the perspective of these female audiences for the narrators. As Jonathan Greenberg points out with respect to *The Moor's Last Sigh*, "the reader is put in the position of Aoi Uë [a painting restorer], peeling away one work of art to uncover another" (104).

In *Midnight's Children*, the relationship between author and audience replicates the gendered divisions of national identity described by Radhakrishnan and Chatterjee: Saleem has agency to write the nation while Padma maintains his literally essential foundation of rural, feminine national spirit. Without Padma, her "ignorance and superstition" and her "paradoxical earthiness of spirit," Saleem loses his inspiration. It is only when she returns to care for him that he says, "I am balanced once more—the base of my isosceles triangle is secure. I hover at the apex, above past and present, and feel fluency returning to my pen" (232). At the same time, his faulty memories, labyrinthine discourse, impotence, and impending disintegration mock the dominant ideology of the modern nation.

Saleem's authority becomes suspect when he separates it from historical "truth." In its chronicle of Indian independence, for example, the story jumps from the Amritsar massacre of 1919 (when General Dyer ordered Indian troops to open fire on unarmed civilians gathered for a Hindu festival) to 1942 (the year of Gandhi's "Quit India" campaign). Brennan points out that in the historical gap, with its virtual excision of Gandhi's role in the independence movement, "the story of Indian nationalism is erased from the book that documents its sad outcome, and the most dramatic illustration of Rushdie's argument is an absence" (SRTW, 84).

This erasure is not the same critique of nationalism Rushdie makes through the character of the Widow; there authoritarian nationalism, rationalized in mythic terms, works in the name of purity to suppress difference. In the forementioned example, eliding Gandhian political forces of nationalism (while noting the religious factionalism among Indians) has two distinct effects: it privileges Jawaharlal Nehru's vision of Indian nationhood over Gandhi's and it leaves a void Saleem fills with his own claims to power. Even as Saleem's telepathy brings him into the minds of the Prime Minister and his cabinet, however, he reminds us of his own fallibility:

> Re-reading my work, I discovered an error in chronology. The assassination of Mahatma Gandhi occurs, in these pages, on the wrong date. But I cannot say, now, what the actual sequence of events might have been; in my India, Gandhi will continue to die at the wrong time.
>
> Does one error invalidate the entire fabric? Am I so far gone, in my desperate need for meaning, that I am prepared to distort everything— to rewrite the whole history of my times purely in order to place myself in a central role? (198)

Although he is quite willing to keep himself at the center of the story at all costs, Saleem's questions serve as a reminder that other sources of knowledge (as well as other kinds of political nationalism, such as

Nehru's) exist, though within the text only he can provide access to them. These lies, faults, or failures, however, do not invalidate his narrative in favor of another; he emphasizes in his parodies of "official" histories as well as by interweaving historical and his own fictional renderings of events that "[n]obody, no country, has a monopoly of untruth" (389). As David Lipscomb makes clear, Rushdie's amalgamation of perspectives, "denies the reader the comfort of settled 'truths,' 'truths' that some claim to find in univocal political or disciplinary discourses" ("Caught in a Strange Middle Ground," 164).[16] Rushdie himself suggests in " 'Errata'," "The reading of Saleem's unreliable narration might be [. . .] a useful analogy for the way in which we all, every day, attempt to 'read' the world" (*IH*, 25).

By continually asserting and subverting the narrator's power, Rushdie employs two literary suturing techniques defined by Brian Finney: point-of-view narration and meta-fiction. In point-of-view narration, the protagonist gives us an unfettered view of events, thereby masking the presence of the author: "[W]e oscillate between anxiety at the threatened intrusion of the narrator's voice and pleasure (*jouissance*) once we have sutured over this intrusion by occupying a similar locus to that of the protagonist" (138). While the idea that point-of-view narration could succeed in fully masking the author's presence only makes more sense theoretically than practically, Rushdie presents an egregious example of this perspective to call its effects into question. Saleem, for example, asks the reader to "imagine yourself inside me somehow, looking out through my eyes, hearing the noise, the voices" (202). The reader's pleasure and satisfaction necessitate a willingness to trust the process of signification, even as the suture itself (by addressing the reader directly) hints at the fissures underlying our desire for narrative cohesion.

Point-of-view narration in the novels promotes the identification between narrator and reader in the paternalistic terms Silverman outlines. By contrasting the feminine audiences' desire for simple linearity with the narrators' convoluted and metaphorical texts, readers may mark their own sophistication at the expense of that fictional, feminine audience with whom they have been encouraged to identify.[17] When Saleem, frustrated by Padma's demands for a more straightforward tale, wishes for "a more discerning audience, someone who would understand the need for rhythm, pacing, the subtle introduction of minor chords which will later rise" (116), he is, of course, invoking and flattering the contemporary reader.

The second narrative technique, meta-fiction, works in opposition to point-of-view narration to align the reader with the author at the expense of the fictional subject. Rushdie does this by regularly addressing the reader in a voice that does not quite match that of the ostensible narrator. In *The Moor's Last Sigh*, Rushdie writes: "And so for the yarn of the Moor: if I were forced to choose between logic and childhood memory, between head and heart, then sure; in spite of all the foregoing, I'd go along with the tale" (85-6). The passage reads contextually as the Moor's musing on what to believe about his past, though it may also read as an authorial reminder to the reader that he or she is also *choosing* to "go along with the tale." At other times, the novel addresses the reader directly in anticipation of questions he or she is probably asking: "Control, please, your horses," the meta-narrator insists to ward off impatience and retain the reader's allegiance.

In an example from *Midnight's Children*, Rushdie and/as Saleem seem to speak in tandem when the narrator describes the metaphorical possibilities of midnight's children:

> Reality can have a metaphorical content; that does not make it less real. A thousand and one children were born; there were a thousand and one possibilities which had never been present in one place at one time before; and there were a thousand and one dead ends. Midnight's children can be made to represent many things, according to your point of view; they can be seen as the last throw of everything antiquated and retrogressive in our myth-ridden nation, whose defeat was entirely desirable in the context of a modernizing, twentieth-century economy; or as the true hope of freedom, which is now forever extinguished; but what they must not become is the bizarre creation of a rambling, diseased mind. (240)

Rather than enabling the reader to experience the pleasure of identification with the protagonist, meta-fiction, according to Finney, "constitutes its readers as intellectual problem solvers," as "participants in" rather than "consumers of" the text (140); the resulting pleasure masks its origins in the meta-textual strategy itself. In the quote above, we can indulge with Saleem in a philosophical moment that defends his own narrative or we can separate ourselves from Saleem and join with Rushdie in deciphering the puzzles of Indian independence. What we must not do, however, is dismiss them both.

Rushdie also disrupts the authority of point-of-view narration with his diverse literary allusions, which emphasize narrative construction. Such references, drawn often from canonical Western texts, presumably resonate loudest with Western readers. At the same time, since the premise of the novels is the relationship between the protagonists and modern India, readers may find themselves trying to solve the "riddle of midnight"—of independent India—with "external" clues. In the name of hybridity, this cross-cultural puzzle underscores the interpenetrability of cultures which Rushdie self-consciously represents: "I did not have to make a synthesis. I was merely the echo of a culture which is really plural."[18] Read critically, the puzzle reproduces the terms of Jameson's model of postcolonial literature in that what counts as a modern nation is measured by Western standards. Aijaz Ahmad, for example, cites Rushdie's cosmopolitan literary tastes, as Brennan does, as an evasion of political responsibility for counteracting imperialism, a self-indulgent reflection of Rushdie's own privileged migrancy. While Rushdie's allusions stem no doubt in large part from British schooling and expatriate life, they do not reconstruct a homogeneous Western tradition; rather, much like Saleem's own mixed legacy, they emphasize the lack of epistemological purity in narrating the nation, a lack that corresponds to a nation's own history.

In a final example of the variety of meta-fictional effects at work, in *The Moor's Last Sigh*, Rushdie's own recent political predicament (in which he was writing the novel) sometimes leaps out of the narrative: "[H]ad I slipped accidentally from one page, one book of life on to another,—in my wretched, disoriented state, had my reading finger perhaps slipped from the sentence of my own story on to this other, outlandish, incomprehensible text that had been lying, by chance, just underneath?" (285). These diverse strategies challenge the reader's complacent assumption of a stable perspective vis à vis the text, yet all work simultaneously to involve the reader in the stakes defined by the narrative.

Point-of-view narration and meta-fiction compete for the reader's loyalty. As we shift from the narrator to the author's perspective(s) and back again, we are reminded again and again of how our "national longing for form" supersedes our, and the text's, ability to meet it. The tension or play of perspectives merely reproduces our desire for allegorical purity and narrative cohesion on more than one level. We look for Saleem and the Moor to show us what India "looks like" in the familial terms both we and they understand, and we turn to Rushdie for an invitation to help "solve" the riddle of midnight as posed by the characters. In this way, we rely on the division of material and spiritual, masculine and feminine national identities because our own perspectives align with those of the empowered and modern "authors." Despite the allegorical frameworks of the novels, Rushdie insists that "they don't work in any kind of exact formal sense; you cannot translate the structure of

[*Midnight's Children*] into the secret meaning, the book is not a code" ("*Midnight's Children* and *Shame*," 3). The conflicting paths of identification disrupt any pat formulas; the two kinds of suture continually draw attention to the very wounds they seek to bind.

* * *

Revisiting the wound reminds the reader of the historical crises in the nation's history, moments when the nation as family failed to hold its members together: its colonial past, interreligious strife, the Emergency, the rise of the neocolonial elite, and the secessionist wars. It reminds us of the impossible task of definitively solving the riddle of midnight. In moving from point-of-view narration to meta-fiction, we recognize the spatial difference between our own corporeal coordinates and those of the subject of the text and of the temporal lapses implicit in these shifting identifications. In other words, although identification is necessarily unconscious, we become aware of its processes and their dependence upon the text's mnemonic structure.

Memory, Saleem and Rushdie's, forms the connective tissue of *Midnight's Children*: "Morality, judgment, character . . . it all starts with memory," Saleem writes, "and I am keeping the carbons" (253). The story is "[m]emory's truth, because memory has its own special kind. It selects, eliminates, alters, exaggerates, minimizes, glorifies, and vilifies also; but in the end it creates its own reality, its heterogeneous but usually coherent version of events; and no sane human being ever trusts someone else's version more than his own" (253). Caught between Saleem and Rushdie's memory, the coherence we seek continually unravels from the instigatory mnemic traces driving the narrative itself.

In *Midnight's Children*, memory is neither trustworthy nor nostalgic, but it is productive, even as it calls forth ruptures in coherent subjectivity and national identity. Memory's implicit heterogeneity holds the promise for pluralism that the text itself attempts to deliver. As Joseph Swann argues, memory in the text spurs "the reproductive cycle of art," the only reproductive capacity Saleem retains and Rushdie can offer (260). Just as Silverman outlines in her aesthetic theory how the aesthetic works through the stimulation of "new" and barred memories to displace the subject from normative identifications, in *Midnight's Children* we see how memory's productive capacity—creating its own truths, stimulating the narrative itself, presenting other ways of seeing as well as the terms of its own critique—serves as an antidote to national purity.

Rushdie recognizes the danger implicit in such a reading of turning his aesthetic (with its selective memories) into an escape from history rather than an entry into it. He notes in *Imaginary Homelands*, for instance, that "imaginative truth is simultaneously honourable and suspect" (10), though he defends his "broken mirror" of memory as a useful reflection of the "provisional nature of all truths" (12). Gorra raises the question more pointedly in his discussion of Rushdie's aesthetic principle: "to bend Indian life this way or that, to make us believe in the illusions of telepathy or in metaphors that seem to come literally true—and always to remember what reality is. The illusion becomes not an aspect of the country's corruption but a comment on it" (146). While this strategy aims to make us "think critically not only about Indian politics and identity but also about the terrible seductive force of Saleem's—of [Rushdie's] own—desire to encapsulate the whole of reality" (146), Gorra remains "troubled that a book about the nightmare of history cannot make me care about the individual characters to whom that history happens" (147).

Gorra's definition of Rushdie's aesthetic principle is a useful one, particularly in its characterization of the ways in which illusion and metaphor refocus our attention on the nature of reality. His definition elucidates how meta-fictional perspectives eventually surpass Saleem's point of view in garnering our attention. I am not convinced, however, that the privileging of intellect over emotion necessarily limits the aesthetic value or the historical commitment of the text. Rushdie's aesthetic insists that ideological beliefs work in collaboration with rather than despite libidinal stimulation to create pleasure, that both aesthetics and history share a set of signifiers and images through which we see the world. Indeed, his project seems less about separating aesthetics and history than about showing how we can understand one through the other. The memories that fuel Saleem's overflowing story may replicate the images provided by the dominant fiction; but it is Rushdie's aesthetic focus on those images, and his manipulation of them through illusion and metaphor, that allows us to achieve the critical distance necessary to see how they are deployed historically and ideologically.

Unsurprisingly, then, Saleem's amnesia, suffered between the two wars with Pakistan (he was "only wiped clean whilst others, less fortunate, were wiped out," 413), is both purifying and nearly lethal. While the blow that makes him "empty and free, because all the Saleems go pouring out [. . .] restored to innocence and purity" (419–20) initially provides relief from his weighty inheritance, it turns into a "seceding from history" and, with it, political responsibility. "But how convenient this amnesia is, how much it excuses!" Saleem later exclaims looking back on his shifting political allegiances and his wartime activities (426). Amnesia facilitates his ultimate political submission (he becomes a citizen and "soldier" of Pakistan) and reduces him to his most basic desires. His extraordinary sense of smell the only vestige of his former self, he is used as a tracking dog by Pakistani forces during the second war (resulting in the independence of Bangladesh) with India.

When he finally leads his three companions astray from their wartime mission in the jungle, without hope of being found and divorced from all ties to their former lives and from "the type of memories which give men a firm hold on reality" (417), all four fall prey to the immediacy of their own fantasies. Instead of trying to rescue themselves by remembering who they are and what their responsibilities might be, they worship at Kali's jungle temple for the illusory rewards of nightly visits from four "soft women." It is only when they suddenly recognize their growing transparence that "they understood that this was the last and worst of the jungle's tricks, that by giving them their heart's desire it was fooling them into using up their dreams, so that as their dreamlife seeped out of them they became as hollow and translucent as glass" (439). Kali's dissipation of their dreams parallels the Widow's sterilization campaign, which Saleem terms, "Sperectomy: the draining out of hope" (521). Both seek to eliminate heterogeneous beliefs, memories, and histories in the name of ideological purity and to channel the subject's desires into forms easily satisfied or contained by the state.

These ectomies initiate the spreading of invisible cracks that threaten to turn Saleem into "specks of voiceless dust" (552): "Because in drainage lie the origins of the cracks: my hapless, pulverized body, drained above and below, began to crack because it was dried out" (550). To forestall the surfacing of lack that threatens both his and the nation's unity, he spins memories into a national and personal narrative of unity. During Padma's temporary absence, for example, he complains, "A balance has been upset; I feel cracks widening down the length of my body; because suddenly I am alone, without my necessary ear, and it isn't enough" (177). While the narrative process can only delay Saleem's inevitable break-up, Rushdie intends its form, modeled on the oral narrative, to capture "the Indian talent for non-stop self-regeneration [. . .] The form—multitudinous, hinting at the infinite possibilities of the country—is the optimistic counterweight to Saleem's personal tragedy" (*IH*, 16).

* * *

In "Post-Colonial Literary Studies: A Neo-Orientalism?" Elleke Boehmer warns strenuously against critics', and perhaps Rushdie's own, celebrations of multiplicity as a new form of orientalism. Using the critical reception to *The Moor's Last Sigh* as his primary example, Boehmer sees it as "very much like another Western way of scrutinizing the loud, rich, wild and various manifestations of the Other, the effect of which is to reify a view of other worlds as exotic, chaotic, teeming, crowded with noise and fury" (240). Such a position, he argues, creates its own "hegemon[y]," its own "objectification of difference" (240). Like Brennan, he maintains that this is particularly true when we consider that cultural hybridity is often the result of gross global economic inequity and is celebrated by those "migrant writers" who are economically privileged. Yet the argument holds its own dangers when it seems to suggest that fiction and criticism must never venture beyond their most local contexts.

As discussed earlier in this chapter, hybridity in and of itself does not have political value. Automatically equating postcolonial multiplicity with subversion of a colonizing aesthetic makes no more sense than saying all free verse is necessarily (politically) liberating and rhyme and meter reactionary. Such "dichotomies," Alan Shapiro cautions, "blind us [. . .] to the theory-defying richness of the work itself" (*In Praise of the Impure*, 38). Boehmer is right to insist on the partiality of all knowledge and the need for closer attention to a work's social and historical contexts ("Post-Colonial Literary Studies," 244); and those are precisely the kinds of critical perspectives Rushdie's novels demand. In *Midnight's Children*, the diverse cultural borrowings that frame Saleem's cracks, his failed attempts at genealogical and narrative consistency, and his traumatic embodiment of Indian national history do less to exoticize the "other" (whomever that might be to the reader) than the familiar. In this way, the novel portrays and provokes what Shapiro defines as an "ethical imagination": one that shows us "what our picture of the world excludes" (10) as well as turns "what we know best into something strange and puzzling, thereby enabling us to see our lives, the apparent givenness and stability of our arrangements, as only a way of living, as a contingent set of possibilities always open to reform or corruption" (26).

While *Midnight's Children* represents such contingency in Saleem's narrative and bodily fissures, *The Moor's Last Sigh* does so through the palimpsest.[19] This takes us beyond the lack that founds subjectivity and the concomitant traumas that found the nation, both of which we see so clearly in *Midnight's Children*, to the various images used to bind subject and nation. To create a composite national image in *The Idea of India*, Khilnani begins with the vastly different but ultimately collaboratory visions of Jawaharlal Nehru and Mahatma Gandhi for an independent India and proceeds through key cities—Delhi,

Bombay, Bangalore—which each represent a different "veneer [. . .] to the contradictory life of its society" (149). *The Moor's Last Sigh* charts a similar journey through the workings of a national imagination, invoking both geographic spaces and ideological metaphors. Rather than see the veneers Khilnani describes as distinct, partial views of the nation, Rushdie overlays them in aesthetic approaches competing to express that "national longing for form" as well as its inevitable dissatisfaction.

This approach has a historical basis as well. Nehru pictured Indian history as a palimpsest of successful intercultural exchanges which themselves constituted a unified history that the new nation would constitutionally extend and guarantee. In *The Discovery of India*, Nehru described India "with all her infinite charm and variety" as

> some ancient palimpsest on which layer upon layer of thought and reverie had been inscribed, yet no succeeding layer had completely hidden or erased what had been written previously. All of these existed in our conscious and subconscious selves, though we may not have been aware of them, and they had gone on to build up the complex and mysterious personality of India. (60)

His historical research and, thus, "discovery" took place "through[out] India in the company of mighty travellers from China and Western and Central Asia" (51), over the Himalayas and down to the banks of the Ganges, and then from the Khyber Pass to the southern tip of the subcontinent. Whether among Pathans or Tamils, Nehru finds that "a dream of unity has occupied the mind of India since the dawn of civilization" (63). He personifies the dream in the figure of *Bharat Mata*, Mother India. Facing a crowd parallel to the one Rushdie portrays in *The Riddle of Midnight*, Nehru responds to their desire for a common identity. Rather than the riddle Rushdie offers ("It's by the lack of a definition that you know it's you"), Nehru invokes *Bharat Mata*: "You are the parts of this *Bharat Mata*, [. . .] you are in a manner yourselves *Bharat Mata*, and as this idea slowly soaked into their brains, their eyes would light up as if they had made a great discovery" (62).

Like Nehru, Gandhi was adept at fusing conflicting symbols of the nation into those of a supposedly essential Indian identity to legitimate and bolster the cause of nationalism. Although he launched his political movement from the city of Ahmedabad and was himself educated abroad, as was Nehru, he crafted his political identity as oppositional to Western modernization (represented by urbanization and industry). Khilnani lauds the skill with which Gandhi "reversed priorities, and embraced the very values the colonial imagination rejected" by promoting an image of rural life: "He composed his own pastorale, and used it both to disrupt the order and regularities of the colonial city and to ridicule the hollow mimicry of the Indian elites and middle classes. He brought the nationalist idea from the city to the villages, and through the long foot marches he took across the countryside [. . .] he constructed a new topography of India, defined not by the railway tracks that linked cities but by the routes that connected villages" (125). This strategy does not detract from the sincerity of Gandhi's commitment to political self-determination through rural life; rather, it exemplifies the way in which the gendered model of the nation (here figured as the opposition between feminized rural life and pacification on the one hand and masculinized urban colonial violence on the other) may create a foundation for political resistance.

The Moor's Last Sigh details the failure of those unified visions through an expanded metaphor of the nation as family. Playing off the rich associative traditions of the Western paternal family and Mother India, Rushdie shows their conflicted attempts to forge unity out of historical, ethnic, religious, caste, and linguistic difference. We find in the narrator, the Moor, a representative of India's complicated colonial past, encompassing not just British colonization but stretching from the Moorish invaders to the present. Counterbalancing this paternal genealogy of conquest and modernization, which is itself rendered suspect and fallible in the novel, is Nehru's dream of Indian unity. Rushdie shows that even that ideal, however, is fractured by competing images of Mother India. Representatives of Mother India in the novel range from the Moor's rebellious, artistic mother, Aurora, to Hindu goddesses to Indira Gandhi to icons of popular culture; it is an inconsistent and unwieldy mix of religious, political, and aesthetic figures of unification across historical periods. Rushdie works from both matriarchal and patriarchal traditions, striving to fuse national identity out of multiple images while exposing the cracks and slippages between them. The novel ultimately argues that nation and family cannot satisfy the subject's desire with a singular image, though the artist might offer alternative sites of meaning and pleasure.

* * *

As in Midnight's Children, though now for different reasons, Rushdie rejects the possibility of a mediating communal identity, along the lines proposed by Radhakrishnan and Chatterjee in their theorizing of national identity. In The Moor's Last Sigh, community is not beneficent, but violently and authoritatively exclusionary. The strongest community in the novel is that of the Hindu Nationalists, led by Raman "Mainduck" Fielding, a caricature of the leader Bal Thackeray, and Rushdie holds them responsible for the transformation of his beloved cosmopolitan Bombay into sectarian Mumbai. Rushdie therefore turns back to the image of the nation as family, both paternal and maternal, to try to resurrect an inclusive image of Indian plurality.

Carrying this immense burden of reconciliation and resurrection in the novel is the Moor, born in 1957 a descendant of Vasco de Gama, the ancient Jewish community of Cochin, the last Moorish sultan, and possibly even Prime Minister Nehru (the Moor's mother and Nehru are possible lovers). As the only son of this illustrious or infamous family whose wealth stems from the spice trade, the Moor is expected to fulfill familial, social, and aesthetic goals: to extend the family name and wealth into the next generation, to embody Indian pluralism in his own right and in his mother Aurora's paintings, and to capture the reader's imagination. In each of these areas, however, the Moor struggles against his failings: the taint of his own possible illegitimacy and, later, disinheritance; his impotence and disfigurement; and his inability to find a singular truth behind each peeled back layer of the familial and national palimpsest.

Once again the text depends upon the paternal family to reproduce Western modernity's hegemonic terms and upon the image of Mother India for unifying social plurality; at the same time, it underscores the impossibility of either image producing a stable subject or nation. The theme of paternal power addresses the resulting traumas with the rhetoric of familial and national purity. It finds its current expression in the novel in the undeclared war between the Hindu fundamentalist "Mumbai Axis" of the Moor's employer and the corrupt capitalist "Scar-Zogoiby Axis" of his father. The competition underscores the dangers of those yearnings for stable meaning by portraying them as authoritarian, intolerant, and corrupt.

The maternal image, by contrast, works horizontally to bind disparate beliefs and cultures into a singular national tableau. This strategy too fails, as its promise is undone by competition for the contemporary role of Mother India between Indira Gandhi, Aurora, and the Moor's girlfriend, Uma. Aurora's artistic vision charts historical change and offers the most inclusive view of modern India, yet it cannot help but document the decline of India's idealistic pluralism. Her painting career begins with a huge fantastical mural of historical, religious, and cultural imagery and "progresses" to paintings of fractured worlds to diptychs and triptychs to a final sinister palimpsest.

The Moor, as son, artist's model, and narrator, mediates between these images of the nation and the reader. He maintains ideological consistency for both when he can define himself as national spokesman, animating the nation as family metaphor. By continually asserting and subverting the narrator's power, Rushdie once again employs the two literary suturing techniques discussed earlier. In this way, we rely on the division of material and spiritual, masculine and feminine national identities in order to align our perspectives with that of the should-be empowered and modern "author." Yet that author/narrator fails to offer a singular history or pure lineage to impose order on historical trauma, and we founder among the two narratives claiming our allegiance.

The Moor's Last Sigh investigates impurity in all its forms: it details how love of country eroticizes the nation as family metaphor, resulting in a seemingly endless array of sexual, economic, political, and religious corruptions. At the same time, the novel is a paean to the revelatory potential of the aesthetic. With the image of the palimpsest, which runs throughout the novel to characterize Bombay, markets, paintings, politics, characters, and the story itself, Rushdie suggests that aesthetic texts can reveal what usually remains hidden, that within their impurities lie other truths.

The Moor is our guide through a series of false Edens in which the "romantic myth of the plural, hybrid nation" (227) gives way to "debauchery and crime" (303). He defines himself as a "jewholic-anonymous, a cathjew nut, a stewpot, a mongrel cur. I was—what's the word these days?—*atomised.* Yessir: a real Bombay mix" (104). Born a decade after independence, he represents the city itself, his own fantastical growth rate (he ages at twice the average speed) a mirror of urban sprawl: "I grew in all directions, willy-nilly. My father was a big man but by the age of ten my shoulders had grown wider than his coats. I was a skyscraper freed of all legal restraints, a one-man population explosion, a megalopolis, a shirt-ripping, button-popping Hulk" (188).

In addition to his accelerated development, the Moor is distinguished by his deformed right hand. This deformity symbolizes and substitutes for the phallic power the narrator wants yet can never wholly achieve, particularly after his impotence. As Silverman notes in *Male Subjectivity at the Margins,* ideological consistency depends upon the alignment of phallic power with the male sexual organ. In making that metaphorical connection literal in the novel, Rushdie makes it available for conscious scrutiny. The Moor is unable to assume his legacy as the only son of Aurora and Abraham.

Once again the image of Mother India determines the contemporary terms of that legacy. The Moor, who unwittingly insults his mother and trades an eroticized relationship with her for a doomed affair with multi-personality Uma, is disinherited for his disloyalty and cast into the underworld from the Eden of his mother's artistic salon. The cost of losing his mother's love, or of forsaking it, is his familiar identity. Finding himself in the hidden bowels of the central jail, beneath the city he thought he knew in its entirety, he imagined "that my skin was indeed coming away from my body, as I had dreamed so long ago that it would. But in this version of the dream, my peeling skin took with it all the elements of my personality. I was becoming nobody, nothing; or, rather, I was becoming what had been made of me. I was what the Warder saw, what my nose smelled on my body, what the rats were beginning, with growing enthusiasm, to approach. I was scum" (288). Without the protective and unifying image of Aurora, the Moor finds himself at the disposal of competing ideological factions led by his father and the Hindu Nationalist, Raman Fielding.

This tension, between the eroticization of the nation as family and the need for the metaphor in maintaining a sense of self, is replayed throughout the novel. What varies is the image of Mother India herself. In one scene, Aurora, whose paintings present her son against an express-sionistic national backdrop, presides over one of her famous soirees. Within the novel as whole she represents an irreverent and urban alter-native to Indira Gandhi's "Indira is India" and the hit film *Mother India*'s feminine symbolics (which rely on images of Hindu mythology and rural spirit). At the party, Aurora addresses the leading lady of *Mother India*, who plays Radha, and the actress's husband Sunil who plays the wayward son Birju:

> The first time I saw that picture, I took one look at your Bad Son, Birju, and I thought, O boy, what a handsome guy—too much sizzle, too much chilli, bring water. He may be a thief and a bounder, but that is some A-class loverboy goods. And now look—you have gone and marry-o'ed him! What sexy lives you movie people leadofy: to marry your own son, I swear, wowie. (137)

Despite the guests' shocked protestations regarding the difference between "fictions" and "flesh and blood," Aurora insists on conflating them. Another painter—Aurora's devotee and, later, the Moor's captor—Vasco Miranda, encourages the analogy at the guests' expense: "Sublimation, of mutual parent–child longings, is deep-rooted in the national psyche [. . .] *Mother India* is the dark side of the Radha-Krishna story, with the subsidiary theme of forbidden love added on. But what the hell; Oedipus-schmoedipus!" (138). Rushdie intertwines the actual film (arguably the most widely recognized national icon produced by Bollywood) and its actors with a fictitious storyline (made, in the case of *Aurora and the Moor*, to suggest the film version), in order to make literal the metaphors of national identity as well as to ask if any of these incarnations of Mother India has a greater claim on "reality" than the others.

This strategy forces readers to reconsider readings of the film itself, its importance as an image of national identity, and the wider validity of the nation as family image as embodied by the maternal figure. The film, actually made in 1957, the year of the Moor's birth, achieves its success through the displacement of minority identities in favor of Hindu nationalism. According to Nalini Natarajan in her analysis of the film, the lead actress's Muslim identity is co-opted and forgotten in her marriage to her Hindu co-star and in the film's Hindu "cultural message [. . .] with its echoes of Radha, Parvati, Sita with all of the traditional self-sacrificing virtues ascribed to these women. We have, then, a nationalist articulation of Hindu religion and culture focusing on the figure of a Muslim actress" (85). In Rushdie's hands, the film's image of Mother India is complicit with rather than oppositional to the patriarchal model of the nation as family. While Mother India might seem to provide the basis for alternative national identifications, based on the split between feminized tradition and masculinized modernity, as suggested by R. Radhakrishnan, in fact that image works to promote both majoritarian politics and the normative identifications of the Oedipal complex.

In the novel, Rushdie plays off and subverts the familiarity of the image of Mother India by revealing the layers of conflicting meanings it contains. On one level of the plot he contrasts Indira Gandhi's authoritarianism with the vision of pluralism in Aurora's paintings, noting that these two perspectives are mutually exclusive ideologically and public favor wavers from one to the other. Through the incompatibility of Aurora and Indira's visions of the nation (Aurora's paintings are panned by the public when Indira's authority heightens), Rushdie shows how aesthetic value remains tied to political context. Further confusing the imagery of the age, while the public rejects Aurora's exhibit, it embraces Uma's abstract sculptures on the themes of religion and motherhood. Thus, the dichotomy between the domestic, benevolent Parvati and violent, all-consuming Kali, as female goddesses competing to represent the nation, surfaces in the fortunes of Uma and the Prime Minister.

Despite her artistic success and ability to insinuate herself into positions of power, Uma fails to maintain a stable alternative identity, even as Parvati. Her aesthetic depiction of religion and motherhood is just one of many veneers she dons to get what she wants. Those veneers mask a dangerous and hollow core dedicated, much like Kali herself, to consuming and destroying everything in her path in an insatiable bid for control. It is only after she has contrived to destroy the Moor's relationship with his family and finally kills herself that the Moor sees her as a warning against facile multiplicity: "what had happened was, in a way, a defeat for the pluralist philosophy on which we had all been raised. For in the matter of Uma Sarasvati it had been the pluralist Uma, with her multiple selves, her highly inventive commitment to the infinite malleability of the real, her modernistically provisional sense of truth, who had turned out to be the bad egg" (272). When difference is reduced to equivalence, or multiculturalism becomes a matter of style and not belief, Rushdie warns, it loses its historical and political foundations. Uma easily exchanges one identity for another, depending on political expediency, thereby emptying them all of real significance.

Despite her political irrelevance during Indira Gandhi's rule, Aurora remains the most important alternative to the rural matriarch of the film and to Gandhi's own maternal image. Whereas *Mother India* realizes "the Indian peasant woman [. . .] as bride, mother, and producer of sons; as long-suffering, stoical, loving, redemptive, and conservatively wedded to the maintenance of the status quo," Aurora, the Moor says, "was a city girl, perhaps *the* city girl, as much the incarnation of the smartyboots metropolis as Mother India was village earth made flesh" (139). The ironic comparison is between the cosmopolitan Bombay film industry and its most popular product. Wealthy, headstrong, and visionary, Aurora refuses to bend her artistic and personal attitudes to prevailing tastes. Although she flouts tradition as a matter of course—from her marriage to the Jewish duty manager in her father's vast export company to her artistic flamboyance to her many lovers, she remains committed to the ideal image, promulgated by Nehru, of a secular India dedicated to protecting its diverse community interests. That same commitment to political communion distinguishes Aurora's aesthetic of pluralism from Uma's.

As a member of an (elite) economic, religious, and ethnic minority, Aurora tries to incorporate her family history into a national aesthetic vision. Uma, and Adam as we shall see, two representatives of the next generation of Indians, define themselves through a seemingly ahistorical internationalization of languages and images rather than their plural or hybrid forms. The familial and cultural contexts of both Uma and Adam are either wholly fabricated (on Uma's part) or elided (Adam's quasi-mythic parentage by Shiva and Parvati and his rearing by Saleem and the pickle factory women remain the concerns of *Midnight's Children*).

In contrast, Aurora's paintings reflect the changing fortunes of her family and the nation, within and against images of Mother India. Her "career" begins with the mural she paints across her room after her mother Belle's death dispels the idyllic trance of childhood. The mural incorporates stories of her childhood without their sanitizing gloss: Vasco de Gama, her ancestor, arriving in India, smelling spices and money; the Last Supper with her family members attending their feasting servants; the masons of the Taj Mahal losing their hands to prevent any finer constructions; the approaching war for independence; erotic temple imagery through a child's eye and her own fanciful gods. Like the crowd that swallows Saleem at the end of *Midnight's Children* and Rushdie himself in *The Riddle of Midnight*, the mural draws Aurora's father "onward" into "the crowd without boundaries." It was Mother India in all her manifestations—"Mother India with her garishness and her inexhaustible motion, Mother India who loved and betrayed and ate and destroyed and again loved her children, and with whom the children's passionate conjoining and eternal quarrel stretched long beyond the grave" (61)—presided over from the center and height of the ceiling by Belle's face. Personal and national longing unite in recognition of the lack that can never be made good, the melancholia that can never be resolved; Aurora's overabundant, imaginative depictions of histories and identities offer the only possible compensation.

Aurora's aesthetic aims are communal rather than comprehensive: the paintings explore the problem of imagining the nation rather than present a singular, definitive perspective of it. After independence, for example, Aurora finds herself in creative conundrum, caught between "Vasco Miranda's playful influence, his fondness for imaginary worlds whose only natural law was his own sovereign whimsicality, and Abraham's dogmatic insistence on the importance, at that historical juncture, of a clear-sighted naturalism that would help India describe herself to herself" (173). Aurora's use of layers, mirrors, diptychs and triptychs emphasizes the multifaceted dimensions of the real and the need to look beyond the surface to find it.

Aurora's subsequent artistic periods loosely mark the Moor's development alongside the political fortunes of Indira Gandhi and her family. These paintings, divided into her early period (1957–77, from the Moor's birth to the ousting of Gandhi after the Emergency), high period (1977–81, until Gandhi regained power), and dark period (1981–87, from the Moor's disinheritance through the assassinations of Indira and Rajiv, marking the end of the Gandhi "dynasty"), all focus on the Moor. He functions not only as a representative of the nation and as a window into his own family's affairs, but also, in his depiction as Sultan Boabdil (the last sultan of Granada) from whom he is descended on his father's side, as a symbol of the nation's long history.

In the early period, as if to record the hopefulness of India and her only son as well as of the dawn she personifies, Aurora paints eroticized portraits of herself and the Moor in which his deformed hand, otherwise a sign of colonialism's disfigurement of the national body, "was transformed into a series of miracles" (224). As torches of light and symbols of power and fertility, these depictions of the Moor's hand make vestiges of the colonial past into a new source of strength. That strength lasts as long as he remains loyal to his mother as his one love. In these paintings, his deformity, which marks him, as does his heritage, as marginal and possibly even cursed (the family name, Zogoiby, translates as "unlucky"), transforms the world around him into his kingdom. Aurora's masterpieces of the period portray their affluent Malabar Hill home as the Moor's fantastical palace, a vestige of the Moorish invaders' sister forts in Delhi and Alhambra. The fantastical worlds of Palimpstine and Mooristan that Aurora creates encapsulate the romantic myth of Indian pluralism, and throughout her life Aurora urges her son to search for them. Even after the Emergency forever ends that period of hopefulness, and her paintings turn from palimpsests to apocalyptic images of division, she gives him a passport with a Spanish visa and a one-way ticket: "Always keep it valid [. . .] Only don't go to the English. We have had enough of them. Go find Palimpstine; go see Mooristan" (234–5).

Aurora invokes the symbol of the Moorish invaders' power, Delhi's Red Fort, to represent Nehru's "noble mansion of free India where all her children may dwell." Rushdie himself creates a historical palimpsest, layering, as it were, architectural references to India's political history stretching from the Moorish invasion to the Moghul empire to British colonialism to the current seat of the central state government. He circulates the image of the Red Fort in an attempt to accomplish aesthetically what Nehru tried politically: to forge symbols of a united India that simultaneously reflect its complicated past. Aware of the need for symbolic identification to compensate for the lack of historical unity, Nehru inaugurated the state ritual of raising the national flag from the fort on each anniversary of independence. The image of the Red Fort thus forces readers into the conflicted realm of memory and forgetting, making identification with the unified nation a matter of suspended disbelief.

Despite the transformative potential of these reworked images of national identity, Rushdie never completely abandons the paternal nation as family model. He encourages us to read the Moor's disfigurement as a similar conflation of personal and national disaster: "Banished from the natural, what choice did I have but to embrace its opposite? Which is to say, *unnaturalism*, the only real ism of these back-to-front and jabberwocky days. Placed beyond the Pale, would you not seek to make light of the Dark? Just so. Moraes Zogoiby, expelled from his story, tumbled towards history" (5). Rushdie's criticism of the effects of history on the subject-nation derive not from a desire to separate aesthetics and history, but from the historical and political events themselves. When the Moor transfers his devotion from his mother to Uma (coinciding with the Emergency), Aurora's paintings turn dark and threatening. In place of multiple worlds fading in and out of one another, she paints jagged fissures swallowing up her fantastical creatures and shows the fort crumbling into rubble. Gradually her style becomes mores naturalistic as she shows herself watching the Moor watching Uma. It reveals Aurora's self-conscious awareness of her ebbing power to hold his love and allegiance.

After Uma engineers the Moor's expulsion from his family, Aurora's aesthetic eye trails him into the underworld where she watches his decline with increasing horror. He later sees himself in these last paintings as "[m]otherless [. . .] his previous metaphorical role as a unifier of opposites, a standard-bearer of pluralism, ceasing to stand as a symbol—however approximate—of the new nation, and being transformed, instead, into a semi-allegorical figure of decay" (302). To survive in the underworld beneath cosmopolitan Bombay, he learns to use his deformed hand as a club, enforcing the will of Raman Fielding. Here we find what Norman Rush calls in his review of the novel, "a mordant reflection on the final outlook for religious nationalism in India, whose most cheering conclusion is that any hope for the downfall of that institution lies in the infinite mercenary corruptibility of the human species" (7). The only escape from the underworld is, paradoxically, up through its ranks of corruption. At the top the Moor finds his father, Abraham, presiding over a corporate empire that stretches from land development to drug smuggling to weapons production.

Rushdie presents religious nationalism and economic corruption as the tides that fill the void left by the modern plurality of Aurora's vision and Bombay's cosmopolitanism. The Moor's downfall mirrors the changing fortunes of the city itself, as Khilnani describes them; his underworld experiences find political expression in the rise of Bombay's Shiv Sena (Army of Shivaji) party. In the vacuum left by the organizational collapse of the Congress Party, begun by Indira Gandhi's restructuring of the central party's regional alliances after Nehru's death in 1964, and by the increasing disparity in Bombay between the political power of the rich and poor, the Shiv Sena movement provides a source of communal identification and political will.

Khilnani charts Shiv Sena's rise from the 1960s to the present as the triumph of religious sectarianism over pluralism. What began as an "anti-immigrant party, dedicated to protecting employment and educational opportunities for Bombay's Marathi-speakers" has, with a keen sense of political opportunity, increased its power by targeting Tamils, other English-speaking migrants, and, most recently, Muslims (142). It has increased its political might by providing basic services to its constituents and, in the 1980s, by fostering sectarianism through violent riots against Muslims and their property. The alliance the Shiv Sena forged with the BJP in 1984 provides a further example of the way in which, at least for Rushdie, the transformation of Bombay into Mumbai reflects the wider political climate of the nation. Khilnani supports this comparison, as he cites Rushdie's vision of Indian plurality in his analysis of Shiv Sena:

> "In Bombay all Indias met and merged. In Bombay, too, all-India met what-was-not India . . . what was beautiful in Bombay was that it belonged to nobody and to all"—that old nationalist dream of Bombay, and the sense of its end, suffuses Salman Rushdie's lament for the city . . . The Shiv Sena visualizes India not as a land of cosmopolitan miscegenation, but as a hierarchical grid that contains internally homogenous communities, each insulated from the others. This idea seeks to efface Bombay's cosmopolitanism, to annex its modernity and distribute its benefits to one closed, community. (143–4)

Just as Rushdie represents the differences between Nehru and Indira Gandhi's national visions through Aurora and Uma, he shows the more recent conflict between national and international identifications through Aurora and Vasco Miranda's paintings. Aurora's final painting, which the Moor sees only after his death and whose title he appropriates for his own story, shows mother and son reunited in one panel but not reconciled. While she holds out her hand in forgiveness, a sign of India's infinite capacity for inclusion, he is in the foreground, "lost in limbo like a wandering shade" (315). *The Moor's Last Sigh* is also the title of Miranda's homage to Aurora's palimpsests. Initially commissioned by Abraham in 1947 to do a portrait of Aurora and their first child, Miranda painted a bare-breasted Aurora cradling air. Abraham, incensed by the apparent insult, rejects the portrait and sends Miranda back to the studio where be paints a self-portrait as the last sultan—*The Artist* as *Boadbil, the Unlucky (el-Zogoiby), Last Sultan of Granada, Seen Departing from the Alhambra. Or, The Moor's Last Sigh*—over the rejected Madonna tableau. The self-portrait quickly confirms his commercial potential, launching his career as an internationally renowned muralist of airports and corporate headquarters. In the aesthetic comparisons Rushdie makes between Aurora, Uma, and Miranda, he represents the dual challenge to pluralism by rising communitarianism and globalization of culture and capital. Both drain an aesthetic of difference of its historical and cultural substance.

The multiple meanings of the title converge at the end of the novel when, seeking to escape the collapse of his family empire and the city he loves, the Moor travels to Spain, hoping to find in Miranda's "Little Alhambra" Aurora's four stolen paintings. He locates Miranda ensconced in what at first appears to be a fantastical tribute to Aurora's imagination, but gradually is revealed to be "no New Moorusalem, but an ugly, pretentious house" (409). This realization comes too late to save the Moor from imprisonment in a garish tower with a Japanese painting restorer, Aoi Uë. While she must work each day to uncover the Madonna composition beneath Miranda's self-portrait, the Moor is forced to record his family history as his own "last sigh." The Moor's pilgrimage ends in failure because he finds "an anti-Jerusalem: not a home, but an away. A place that did not bind, but dissolved" (388). Ultimately only Aurora's aesthetic vision, with its melding of history, myth, and imagination, can mend his physical and psychological wounds. His narrative imitates the potential of the palimpsest as an aesthetic form. After Aurora's death, Miranda's destruction of his portrait of her (he fires a shot through it), and the theft and loss of her own paintings, only the text itself re-creates her images.

Rushdie presents alternatives to secular pluralism bound by the maternal image as nothing more than false Edens. In addition to the religious singularity Rushdie countermands for obvious reasons, he presents unscrupulous and unrestrained capitalization as yet another national affliction. Adam and Abraham epitomize this most recent corruption. Last seen as an infant in *Midnight's Children*, Adam reappears here as the symbol of the global market. At only 17, he has amassed a private fortune with his business savvy founded, like Uma's success, on his linguistic flexibility. As the Moor says, "[t]here was a generation waiting to inherit the earth, caring nothing for old-timers' concerns: dedicated to the pursuit of the new, speaking the future's strange, binary, affectless speech—quite a change from our melodramatic garam-masala exclamations" (343). That language, which Abraham recognizes for its potential, works hand in hand with his own ability to lose his "humble origins" in becoming a corporate legend, his shady economic interests, and a compliant political climate. When the government declares, for instance, that city dwellers not listed on the recent census (the homeless) do not exist, Abraham sees opportunity, "hiring as many phantoms as they could to work on the huge construction sites springing up on every inch of the new land, and even going so far—O philanthropists!—as to pay them small amounts of cash for their work. 'Nobody ever heard of paying spooks until we began the practice,' said ancient Abraham, cackling wheezily. 'But naturally we accepted no responsibility in case of ill-health or injury. It would have been, if you follow my line, illogical' " (187). Only after the corrupt foundations of his wealth begin to emerge does Abraham feel regret at the loss of one more Eden: "The magic stops working when people start seeing the strings," he tells the Moor. "To hell! I had a damn fine run. Have a bloody apple" (187).

Adam and Abraham represent the threat corporate colonialism poses to national identity. As opposed to religious nationalism, we find economic post-nationalism. Similarly, we might find in Khilnani's analysis of India's cities an urban counterpart to Adam and Abraham in Bangalore. Populated by a relatively new entrepreneurial, industrial, and technical professional class, Bangalore is home to many of the largest multinationals operating in India. While India provides highly trained, relatively inexpensive labor for corporations such as IBM and Hewlett-Packard, they in turn offer workers salaries unmatchable in other parts of the country or sectors of the economy. These corporations wield an economic power that both carries with it and produces international identifications, such that, Khilnani writes, the city itself "has become the capital of Non-Resident India [. . . and] this new class too has a secessionist understanding of the idea of India" (148).

The image of false Edens, economic, political, and aesthetic, whose idyllic veils are eventually stripped away, apportions blame for corruption on Indians themselves rather than on outside forces. Those "sequestered, serpented, Edenic-infernal private universes" (15) that enclose the Moor's family history are sites of privilege and opportunity squandered by greed and corruption. As both elite minority and national spokesman, the Moor insists that there are no pure lineages and that all bear responsibility for the nation's fate. His Moorish lineage does not absolve the majority from political responsibility; instead it draws attention to the spread of neocolonialism in business and politics.

The Moor with whom he is continually compared, Boadbil, last sultan of Granada, effectively ended his empire by betraying his father and then capitulating to the Spanish. Rushdie is clearly aware of the ironies of colonialism intersecting in the Sultan's story. Boadbil is the last trace of Arab power in Europe, power that once competed with Vasco de Gama for trade routes to Asia and which stretched from the Iberian Peninsula to the Sultanate of Delhi, and his decline makes way for the aggrandizement of Spanish and Portuguese global reach. These two imperial narratives intersect in Christopher Columbus, who, in Spain to seek Isabella's patronage for his intended voyage to India, attends the ceremony marking Boadbil's abdication to Catholic rule over Granada in 1491, thus marking the beginning of a whole other colonial narrative.[20] John Clement Ball, J.M. Coetzee, and Paul A. Castor read Rushdie's invocation of Moorish Spain as, Cantor writes, "a model of a multicultural society [. . .]—a world in which the tolerance of the Muslim rulers for Christian and Jewish citizens [the Moor's parentage, we must remember] led to the flourishing of a highly complex and productive culture" (324). Aurora's celebrations of Mooristan and Palimpstine also lend themselves to this reading. Thus, the rise of Shiv Sena parallels Christian Spain's victory over the Moors, at which point "Ferdinand and Isabella identified the interests of the nation-state with those of a single religious group" (Ball, "Acid in the Nation's Bloodstream," 42).

Rushdie's analogy between Moorish Spain and pluralist India is not, however, completely celebratory. The Moor bears the weight of colonial history (it constitutes another part of his inheritance), yet insists upon taking responsibility for national affairs rather than attributing them to the failures of the past. As he departs with his stuffed dog Jawaharlal (a sad commentary on the Prime Minister's legacy) from Bombay to Spain, for example, he ruminates on Macaulay's 1835 "Minute on Education" with its encapsulation of British colonial mentality, concluding "a class of Macaulay's Minutemen [Indians educated by the British to facilitate colonization] would hate the best of India [. . .] We [his family] were not, had never been, that class. The best, and worst, were in us, and fought in us, as they fought in the land at large. In some of us, the worst triumphed; but we could still say—and say truthfully—that we had loved the best" (376). The love that perseveres at the end of the novel is for Aurora's hybrid Mother India, despite its colonial antecedents. Just as Aoi Uë painstakingly unveils her from beneath the Sultan's image, the Moor tries to reconstruct her in his narrative. Yet Aurora has already died, the painting will be destroyed before it is restored, and, just as in Aurora's childhood mural, the emphasis is on the lack that can never be filled and, therefore, on the aesthetic processes that attempt to suture it. *The Moor's Last Sigh* retains hope in the aesthetic's capacity for imaginative renewal and penetrating vision, powers that depend upon an acknowledgment of the lack they try to overcome.

* * *

The continual reminder of lack has a productive function in the creation of the distance and deferral, between reader and text, necessary for re-vision of the nation (as in Mukherjee's *The Holder of the World*). In *The Moor's Last Sigh*, distance and deferral come from the shifting narrative perspectives and the trope of the palimpsest that always hints at another vision lying just below the surface. According to Silverman, the re-visionary potential of distance and deferral stems from the way memory functions in aesthetic texts. Whether by uncovering otherwise repressed memories or instilling "new" memories in the unconscious, Silverman argues, aesthetic texts open up paths of identification that are normally foreclosed by the dominant fiction. In the novel, Rushdie constructs the living presence of India's hybrid history out of word plays, parodies, and images; that history refuses to conform to a nostalgic vision of a unified past. As aesthetic value depends upon pleasure and desire, when a text stimulates these memories it potentially expands our libidinal range. Rushdie makes this possible through the nation as family metaphor whose familiarity invites our identification with it. Although that metaphor attempts to domesticate difference in order to create a singular national identity, by showing the processes of domestication at work, both its successes and failures, he calls attention to its expanded range of identifications. In becoming conscious of that expanded range, we may learn to idealize what is outside ourselves. Distance and deferral are the conditions necessary for this "ex-corporative idealization" (Silverman) and, therefore, identification. The aesthetic intervenes in these normative processes by simultaneously allowing conscious "scrutiny" of their terms and unconscious libidinal stimulation necessary for identification.

Silverman describes the process of ex-corporative identification in terms of sublimation. Following Lacan, she defines sublimation as the "shift away from the impossible non-object of desire that is produced with entry into language and the 'fading' of the real to a nameable and specific object." That new object becomes laden with the responsibility of "making good the subject's lack." Narrative or aesthetic compensation, then, offers the subject images with which to assuage his or her foundational desires: "When one treats an object this way, one of course idealizes it. To sublimate is thus to confer ideality on that someone or something through which the subject articulates his or her ineffable desire" (*TVW*, 75).

We see this process at work in the novel through the transformation of the character Nadia Wadia.[21] She is at first the reigning Miss India and Miss World, who "after her victory became an emblem of the nation" (314). Betrothed to the Moor, she is adored by Fielding, who wants her to validate his Hindu Nationalist politics, and his bodyguard, who merely falls in love. As beauty queen and national spokeswoman, Nadia's fortunes rise upon Aurora's death, such that Nadia clearly represents a pan-Indian aesthetic; yet she is described, like the famous actress after whom she is named, as "tall, Valkyrean Nadia" (311). The original ("real") Nadia Wadia was the English and Greek Mary Evans who married producer Homi Wadia, changed her first name, and performed as the stunt queen "Fearless Nadia" in the early days of Bollywood (1930s and 1940s). The films shared a common theme: the princess-turned-stunt-woman must conquer evil power in the kingdom and set free good subjects and rulers. Sumita S. Chakravarty writes in *National Identity in Indian Popular Cinema, 1947–1987*, "To a people still under colonial rule, such fantasies of power and action must have provided intense psychological satisfaction, particularly since the stunts were performed by a woman" (60). By revising an early female image of national independence, Rushdie insists upon a radically open definition of "Indian."

Nadia Wadia of the novel clinches her claim to represent the nation by having the last word in India before the story shifts in the last section to the Moor's final decline in Spain. The catalyst for his departure is the explosion of Bombay, a narrative event that suggests the destruction of the sixteenth-century mosque, Babri Masjid by the Hindu Nationalists in Ayodhya in order to build a Hindu temple on the site (the controversy and subsequent violence also ended the rule of the Congress Party and helped to bring the BJP to power). On the day of the city's explosion in the novel, the lovestruck bodyguard slashes Nadia Wadia's face, unable to bear the unattainable status of his ideal. Soon after, she reappears in the public eye "when the scars across her face were still livid, the permanence of the disfigurement all too evident" (376). Rather than become a symbol of the failure of what could have been, she insists on representing the hope of the future. As she says to her television viewers:

> So I asked myself, Nadia Wadia, is it the end for you? Is it curtains? And for some time I thought, achha, yes, it's all over, khalaas. But then I was asking myself, what are you talking, men? At twenty-three to say that

whole of life is funtoosh? What pagalpan, what nonsense, Nadia Wadia!
Girl, get a grip, OK? The city will survive. New towers will rise. Better
days will come. Now I am saying it every day. Nadia Wadia, the future
beckons. Hearken to its call. (376–7)

This final female face of India is scarred but still beautiful and her
language, unlike that of Uma or Adam, reflects her local rather than
global context. Her stitches, much like the theoretical and aesthetic
sutures running through the book, ensure that violence girding the
nation will not be forgotten and that idealization can only take place
through a conscious coming to terms with her altered image. Whereas
the Moor's concluding wish is that he might "hope to awaken, renewed
and joyful, into a better time" (434), Nadia forces her audience to face
the present. Both the nation as family metaphor and the aesthetic
undergo a revision in this conclusion. Rushdie divorces the feminine
from the maternal, suggesting, along with decline of the Moor, Aurora
and Indira Gandhi, the ultimate failure of the nation as family
metaphor. In its place, and in the place of the political realm and the
world of high art in which aesthetics previously operated, he offers
popular culture as the site of aesthetic and national renewal. That
renewal must take place through the unveiling of memories and histories, of the horrific alongside the beautiful. Such a conclusion can be
read optimistically or parodically (or both, suggests Laura Moss), as we
are forced to wonder if our imaginations are up to the task of reconsti-
tuting our worlds.

* * *

Despite the concluding hope (and, indeed, echo) of *The Moor's Last
Sigh*, that we might "hope to awaken, renewed and joyful, into a better
time," when Rushdie invites us into the aesthetic realm to escape from
the political present, he simultaneously insists that we take responsibility for the aesthetic images of ourselves we sanction and condemn. This
requires a step beyond the ethical imagination Shapiro describes to the
active, critical judgment ethical imagination should spawn. The enormous challenge of this charge manifests itself in the political (in the
sense of the actualization of state power) and aesthetic limitations of
Rushdie's pluralist ideal.

Nehru's tremendous gift as a statesman, particularly as India's first
Prime Minister, was his recognition of the need to create both an idea
of India available for collective identification and a state apparatus and
agenda capable of rewarding subjects for that identification in their daily

lives (through political and economic opportunity, education and health care, and so forth). As previously described, Nehru, working in the realm of the imaginary like Rushdie, adopted the image of the palimpsest as a metaphor for Indian heterogeneity and unity.[22] It would be unfair to read the decline of the Congress Party and the rise of religious nationalism and global capitalism, or even of the lapsing fortunes of Nehru's pluralism more generally, as the product solely of a failure of imagination. Whether attributed to the immense task of governing close to a billion people or to specific political failures, the fact that India retains inequalities of wealth, education, and opportunity provides an impetus for political unrest. In other words, disparities between the ideal of the nation and the actual compensation the state offers facilitate subjects' withdrawal from the nation's founding ideology. Moreover, although the examples from *The Moor's Last Sigh* discussed above focus on the relationship between Rushdie's aesthetic and Nehru's urban modernity, it is important to remember that the idea of India was founded on the collaborative visions of Nehru and Gandhi and, thus, on urban and rural identifications.

In drawing attention to these two constitutive tenets of modern India—the idea of unity awaiting political (national) expression and the joint set of identifications proffered by the "founding fathers," Nehru and Gandhi—I want to emphasize the access they give us to the nature of the nation's lack. Both Judith Butler and William Connolly, in their psychoanalytic and political analyses of how the state exercises power to maintain the allegiance of its citizens, stress the problem inherent in the legitimation of that power. While the nation, as an ideal, inaugurates the subject's desire for and, thus identification with it, the state (the actuality of that ideal) will always fall short and substitute coercive power for voluntary identification. The relationship between the nation's ideal and coercive powers creates a parallel set of powers within its citizen-subjects. As Butler explains (and as discussed in chapter 1), an ideal such as nation sets the terms for subjection (*assujetissement*) to the Symbolic Order that makes possible the subject's (self-) expression; at the same time, it constitutes a subject capable of wielding power (*pouvoir*). The state, Butler argues, at once promotes its status as an ideal and "cultivates melancholia among its citizenry" in order to exercise its power. Citizens, meanwhile, constituted in terms of the ideal forever try to satisfy the desires spurred by its inaugural and inevitable loss.

The exact nature of lack remains inarticulable and unthinkable, precisely because it is foundational to subjectivity. Yet we may approach it through analysis of the cultural narratives that attempt to compensate for the melancholia as well as through the desires such loss generates. In Rushdie's celebration of plurality (through Saleem's narrative superfluity, Aurora's imaginative abundance, and the Moor's embodiment of cosmopolitan Bombay) we see the yearning for a unity constructed out of the combined visions of Nehru and Gandhi, a reconciliation of the competing familial images. This yearning points to two "unassimilable" (Caruth) traumas, which both found and undermine the nation. The first, and perhaps most wrenching, is Partition, which Khilnani terms, "the unspeakable sadness at the heart of the idea of India: a *memento mori* that what made India possible also profoundly diminished the integral value of the idea" (201–2). The second and related event is Gandhi's assassination by a Hindu militant, who thought Gandhi too pro-Muslim, five months after independence. Both traumas point to the impossibility of the ideal of unity and tolerance.

* * *

Both Partition and Gandhi's assassination suggest that the centrality of struggles over identification might be located in accommodating religion and secular plurality. We see these struggles in Rushdie's novels in numerous ways: the virtual elision of Gandhi from the story of Indian independence (as Brennan remarks); the privileging of an urban modernity that simultaneously neglects the conditions of rural Indians (although it shows the negative effects of modernization and capitalism, particularly on the urban poor); and the critique of the rise of sectarianism in pluralism's wake. The sad irony of the novels, however, is that their social critiques—of capitalism, militant religious fundamentalism, and narratives of purity—sometimes appear in the all-too-familiar terms of ethnic and religious stereotyping, in the divisive terms the novels otherwise contest.

Rushdie's hope, like Nehru's, is for an Indian pluralism that will provide a viable alternative vision of the modern nation. He outlined this hope in an NPR interview on *The Moor's Last Sigh*: "What India at its best represents is a wonderful demonstration of multiplicity; it's a wonderful demonstration of how people of completely different backgrounds and faiths and ideas can live together and form a composite culture which is greater than the sum of its parts." His writing attempts to capture that multiplicity through excess and flamboyance which strains against, yet ultimately produces, a sense of coherence. The narrative pleasures of his aesthetic provide compensation for and identification with the terms of the ideal nation. More importantly, it is that aesthetic excess that fosters the kind of critical distance necessary for conscious, and therefore possibly ethical, identifications.

While these teeming narratives work stylistically, and I maintain that they are rooted in historical context, their political effects are more ambiguous. The difference underscores the limitations of the aesthetic in challenging the prevailing social order. In the case of *The Satanic Verses*, of course, imaginative license led to retrenched political and religious strictures and to a state's ultimate expression of its terrorizing potential. To return to Connolly's discussion of how the state maintains ideological power by targeting internal and external enemies, the *fatwa* illustrates this complicated relationship between state power and identification. As John Ball succinctly states, the *fatwa* "imposed a state of paradoxical inclusion and exclusion: 'yes, you are one of us,' it said, and then: 'but we reject you' " (47). What began as, in Rushdie's words, a "lovesong to our mongrel selves" (*IH*, 394), turned into a vehicle for defining cultural animosity between Islam and not India (which banned the novel) but the West; and that animosity echoes the sectarianism of Partition and Gandhi's death. In Britain and America, the "Rushdie affair," helped define Islam as the West's new bugaboo, replacing the "evil empire" of the Soviet Union with a new supposed threat to freedom and prosperity. Current political rhetoric in the United States barely distinguishes between the Ayatollah Khomeini, President Khatami, Saddam Hussein, Osama bin Laden, the World Trade Center bombing, and the embassy bombings: all are evidence of an insidious attack on "our values" and, in the first George Bush's rallying wartime words, on "the family of nations."

Rushdie is only too aware of how political reaction detracts from his literary intentions, how it provides a lens through which to read the book that obscures its larger aesthetic aims. It is worth quoting his interview with James Fenton in 1991 (two years after the *fatwa* began) at length:

> What I feel most of all, and really this is not bullshit, is a sense of overwhelming failure. [. . . W]hat I tried to do was to bring [. . .] India, Islam, the West—these three worlds, all of which are present inside me in a very vivid way—I tried to bring them together. I tried to describe each in terms of the other. Well, it didn't work. Whatever one may feel about *The Satanic Verses* as a novel, if you look at the event of *The Satanic Verses* it pushed those worlds further apart [. . .]
>
> There were many times in the months after this began that I said to myself that I no longer wished to be a writer. I felt that everything I had put into the act of being a writer had failed, had simply been invalidated

by what had happened. You write out of what you think of as your best self, the best there is in you. If the upshot of that is that the whole planet thinks of you as a complete bastard, you wonder what it's about, what it was for, and why do it.

His attempt to describe different worlds "in terms of each other" is undoubtedly a difficult strategy but perhaps an unavoidable one in a "mongrel" world, plural nation, or textual palimpsest. Much of the time, his overt metaphors bring our prejudices and otherwise naturalized ideologies to the fore, enabling us to look anew at them. Thus, the gradual cracking of Saleem in *Midnight's Children* or the Oedipal jokes in *The Moor's Last Sigh* promote humor and understanding, rather than outrage. In the case of religion, however, as *The Satanic Verses* "event" makes clear, it is more difficult to theorize the effects of the texts' central images. There we see that the pleasure and compensation promised by the aesthetic is thwarted by the very losses it seeks to assuage. The problem, as Anouar Majid frames it in *Unveiling Traditions: Postcolonial Islam in a Polycentric World*, is that while the "global furor over the Rushdie affair did more than any recent event to bring postcolonial fiction into the mainstream, [. . .] with very few exceptions, postcolonial criticism never seriously examined the place of Islam in debates of multiculturalism" (vii).

I would extend Majid's argument about postcolonial theory's inadequacy in examining Islam in multicultural societies to religious communities in general. Whereas Rushdie's condemnation of fundamentalist religious nationalism is clear, other religious references are more ambiguous. For example, many critics, myself included, wonder why Rushdie would turn in *The Moor's Last Sigh* to the figure of Abraham as the father of capitalist corruption. Even though Rushdie's metaphors are always suggestive rather than prescriptive, using the Jewish patriarch to epitomize the inherent dangers of rampant, corrupt capitalism seems too conveniently to exacerbate anti-Semitic stereotypes. Rushdie's critique of capitalism is based in part on its homogenizing effects on cultural difference, its devaluing of the historical and material components of identity. It is unfortunate, then, that his gambit to celebrate impurity of subject, nation and language reinforces ethnic and religious animosities and expands the realms in which they operate.

This sensitivity to the depiction of Abraham, and the anger expressed by some critics, seems *not quite* to correspond to the vocal defense of *The Satanic Verses* on the basis of artistic freedom. I am certainly not attempting to argue here against artistic freedom, for anti-Semitism stereotypes, or for the *fatwa*; rather, the different reception of the two novels along religious lines points to another shortcoming of these theoretical paradigms. It is the problem Radhakrishnan and Chatterjee define of theorizing a specific kind of community, in this case one whose profound effect on belief may either compete with the (secular) dominant fiction for the subject's allegiance or work with it.

For Majid, this failure to theorize religion's role in a pluralist society raises the much larger question: "At what price postcoloniality?" (27). "For while the Western academic conscience is readily assuaged by the symbolic representation of the Other," or, we might say, Others, that comfort (or ethical engagement) stops well short of advocating "genuine political sovereignty" (27), particularly for Islamic nations. The problem faced by critics for whom secularity is an accepted, fundamental good is that the "cultural rights of Others must be presented even if they are radically at odds with secular premises. Such a thing is not always easy to do, for the line between capitalist ethics and cultural ones has become so blurred as to render any criticism of capitalism into an attack on Western values" (30). The ways of understanding subjectivity and national identity that I have put in play here cannot address those instances when "absolute differences cannot be accommodated without substantially altering one's very identity" (31).

Midnight's Children, The Satanic Verses, and *The Moor's Last Sigh* bring the problem of religious coexistence, if not reconciliation, in a pluralist nation to the forefront both of national identity and postcolonial theory. Perhaps the problem of imagining alternative images of subject and nation marks the limit, both my own and Rushdie's, of coming to terms with our foundational loss. For how can we conceptualize some form of liberatory political sovereignty when we call ourselves, in Butler's words, "post-sovereign" subjects? And, can we theorize any kind of liberatory religious political sovereignty, given our current models? It seems that our political goals are at odds. As Saleem says, all too easily, "New myths are needed; but that's none of my business" (*MC,* 546).

CHAPTER 5

FAMILY MATTERS IN JAMAICA KINCAID'S *THE AUTOBIOGRAPHY OF MY MOTHER*: THE DECLINE OF THE NATION AS FAMILY AND THE REGENERATION OF THE AESTHETIC

> That could be you. A sense of identification . . . if it's lost in human communication, that's where the trouble begins . . .
>
> Jamaica Kincaid, in an interview with Diane Simmons

Amit S. Rai begins his essay, " 'Thus Spake the Subaltern . . . ' Postcolonial Criticism and the Scene of Desire," with the following question: "If we are sure today that the subaltern cannot speak, can we be as sure that her ghost does not, especially when postcolonial criticism seems to re-present the discourse of that ghost?" (91). In *The Autobiography of My Mother*, that ghost speaks in multiple voices that blur the lines between fiction, biography, autobiography, and criticism. I adopt Rai's figure of the ghost here not to detract from the powerful subjectivity of Kincaid's narrator, Xuela, whom Kincaid calls "more godlike" than her previous protagonists, but to emphasize her ability to transcend traditional literary and political realms (Ferguson, "A Lot of Memory," 187). Xuela tells of her life on postcolonial Dominica, and while her story is ostensibly private, avoiding mention of the island's political affairs in favor of her thoughts and relationships, it is imbrued with the history of colonialism and slavery. The story also draws on Kincaid's own life (as does all of her fiction) and that of her grandmother, such that, as Alison Donnell writes in "When Writing the Other is Being True to the Self," "we cannot be certain who the auto-biographer is [of] this text, or if there is more than one, for if this is Kincaid's mother's auto/biography, then Kincaid is still present as the 'ghost' writer/biographer" (127). The layered voices of the female narrator disrupt familiar patterns of subjectivity and nationhood as well as of the autobiographical form. Those voices disavow the dominant metaphor of the family and, simultaneously, begin to articulate an alternative aesthetic.

In a passage from her essay, "In History," which could well be spoken by Xuela or Derek Walcott's Shabine, Kincaid writes:

> What to call the thing that happened to me and all who look like me?
> Should I call it history?
> If so, what should history mean to someone like me?
> Should it be an idea, should it be an open wound and each breath I take in and expel healing and opening the wound again and again, over and over, or is it a moment that began in 1492 and has come to no end yet? Is it a collection of facts, all true and precise details, and, if so, when I come across these true and precise details, what should I do, how should I feel, where should I place myself? (1)

In *The Autobiography of My Mother*, Kincaid addresses these questions where they intersect: in the metaphor of the paternal family that dominates social organization on Dominica. Xuela asks repeatedly, "Who was I? My mother died at the moment I was born." But her turn for answers to the family tableau subverts rather than reinforces its power to subjugate her as a woman and as one of the Carib and African peoples (she is the daughter of a Carib mother and a Scot African father). Xuela's story exemplifies self-production rather than negation, though both remain tied to the image of the family that structures her understanding of herself and her historical context.

By both invoking and critiquing the metaphor of the paternal family on multiple levels, Kincaid asks us to reconsider its efficacy, even when it leads to sympathetic readings of postcolonial female voices. She heeds Sara Suleri's warning in "Woman Skin Deep" that the "coupling of *postcolonial* with *woman* [. . .] almost inevitably leads to the simplicities that underlie unthinking celebrations of oppression, elevating the racially female voice into a metaphor for the 'good' " (273). Xuela is socially denigrated and mentally strong, but not necessarily good; her story is not one of triumph over adversity or of unremitting oppression, but of building subjectivity out of lack and historical trauma. Kincaid thus effects the kind of "space-clearing" that Kwame Anthony Appiah advocates between postmodernism and postcolonialism: the book's inconclusivity is not merely a stylistic gesture, but an opening up of the identifications made possible by a historically specific postcolonial condition.

The questions raised by Kincaid's use of the nation as family metaphor parallel those raised by Pinckney and Rushdie. What can psychoanalysis, with its history of privileging gender over race and its focus on phallic power, say about a Carib African Scot woman of Dominica who identifies herself as one of the defeated, yet who demands to be heard? What can postcolonial studies, which often vacillates between nostalgia for a pre-colonial past and yearning for a postcolonial modernity, say about Xuela's refusal to countenance any time except her own painful present? For as Xuela states, "history was not only the past: it was the past and it was also the present [. . .] I did not see the future" (139). Together such theoretical discourses might silence even the ghost of the subaltern subject, particularly if she refuses to represent, in Susheila Nasta's words, "motherlands, mothercultures, mothertongues" (211). But Xuela does speak, using her father's language, appropriated from the colonizers, but against the full force of the symbolic order it conveys. Thus, I once again bring strands of these two discourses together because they are inextricably linked to one another, to Xuela's oppression, and to her determination to write her own story.

* * *

This apparent paradox, between the methods and the objects of theory, reflects what McClintock calls "the paradox of the family." It finds its most egregious form in past slave-holding colonies, such as the Antigua of Kincaid's birth and the Dominica of the novel. There the metaphor of the de facto white paternal family, translated into colonial authority, served to abrogate the familial ties of the slaves themselves. In the neo-colonial world of the novel, the imaginary superiority of the white slaveholder survives through a contemporary hierarchy of skin color, race, language, religion, and class. The most lasting division of all is that of gender: paternal power determines social standing, and that power legitimates itself in the slave-holding tradition of control over (black and white) women's bodies.

Female black characters are doubly displaced by such dynamics. Nasta identifies two primary stereotypes that male writers present of their Caribbean female characters: they appear "either as the rural folk matriarch figure, representing the doer, the repository for the oral tradition, the perpetuator of myths and stories, the communicator of fibres and feelings, or, alternatively, woman, as a sexy mulatto figure, a luscious fruit living on and off the edges of urban communities belonging to no settled culture or tradition" (214). Nasta suggests women's articulation of their experiences as mothers as an alternative to these stereotypes, one that reverses the gendered terms of social value by positing the figure of the mother as the antidote to paternal power. The value of this strategy is the power it ascribes to historically devalued subjects; the danger is the way it limits female sexuality and identity to procreation, thereby re-inscribing the metaphor of the family.

Xuela rejects all of these paths. Instead, Kincaid chooses the kind of subtle, shifting subject position that contemporary postcolonial critics often search for in their own work. Xuela at once recognizes her place within the historical circumstances that have created a continuum of female experience in the Dominica of the novel and rejects the options it presents to her: she refuses sexual subjugation, motherhood, and the role of the liminal temptress, choosing instead to validate her own sexual pleasure within the gendered and racial oppressions that govern her life. Similarly, she yearns for identification with the missing mother, yet constructs herself through her father's language. In this way, she chooses absence and lack (both genealogically and linguistically) over stable, if devalued, identifications. As Xuela writes at the end of the novel,

> This account of my life has been an account of my mother's life as much as it has been an account of mine, and even so, again it is an account of the life of the children I did not have, as it is their account of me. In me is the voice I never heard, the face I never saw, the being I came from. In me are the voices that should have come out of me, the faces I never allowed to form, the eyes I never allowed to see me. This account is an account of the person who was never allowed to be and an account of the person I did not allow myself to become. (228)

The passage clearly celebrates the ability of the narrative itself to extend beyond the confines of existing history in the hope of altering the course of the future.

The choice of such radical instability suggests both the promises and limits of psychoanalysis in this context. Xuela initially appears to be an exemplary Lacanian subject, defined in Kaja Silverman's words "almost entirely [. . .] by lack" (SS, 151). Yearning for that "oceanic" (Lacan) oneness with the maternal body, she desires compensation for the initial separation of birth that also took her mother's life. At the same time, as an infant and throughout her maturation, Xuela rejects attempting to satisfy her desire with either substitute or symbolic maternal objects. When her father gives the motherless infant to his laundress for nursing and care, Xuela refuses the woman's milk and with it an imaginary identification with her maternal role. Thus Xuela's mirror stage recognition of her ideal image takes place without the mediating and approving third term of the mother's gaze: "No one observed and beheld me, I observed and beheld myself; the invisible current went out and it came back to me" (56).

* * *

The question remains of how a literary subject, her author and readers may achieve this kind of radical critical distance from the very terms that define their worlds. Even if we see critical self-consciousness as a faculty that subjects may develop in time, we need to account for the way that faculty may challenge the subject's situated identifications rather than subjectivity itself. This problem is both political and methodological. If, on a political level, subjectivity only makes sense in the ideologically coded terms of the dominant fiction, then how can a subject transform or even reject that which renders her own consciousness possible? We must ask the same question of the psychoanalytic methods that define this problem, methods themselves embedded in the cultural contexts they critique. In understanding Xuela through psychoanalysis, we need again to be able to invoke psychoanalysis in a sense against itself, to examine the subversive potential of the very subjects the methodology itself produces. I want to return briefly to the different yet complementary ways in which Kaja Silverman and Judith Butler's readings of Freud and Lacan help us to achieve the kind of critical distance from psychoanalysis that Xuela evinces of her own subjectivity.

Lacan specifies that although the mirror stage precedes entry into the Symbolic Order, it only makes sense retrospectively to the subject. This suggests that both the idealized image of the mirror stage and the subsequent identifications made possible by the symbolic order are culturally mediated. For Xuela, these conditions produce an unusual combination of self-mastery and idealization on the one hand and recognition of her cultural denigration as black, Carib, and female on the other. Without that validating parental gaze to affirm her infant view of herself, Xuela recognizes herself only as the self-same and not as other; adopting an outside perspective but only to see herself as herself, she notes that "there was never a moment that I can remember when I did not know myself completely" (225). Even as she insists on her autonomy, however, she recognizes her liminal social status. Of her father's decision to bring her along with his laundry to Eunice Paul, for example, Xuela notes: "He would have handled one more gently than the other, he would have given more careful instructions for the care of one over the other, he would have expected better care for one than the other, but which one I don't know, because he was a very vain man, his clothes were very important to him" (4).

Xuela's glance of self-recognition, as well as her perception that for some she is little more than a bundle of laundry, draws attention to her corporeality. As discussed in chapter 1, Silverman insists that we understand that glance, and the experience of the body accompanying it, as culturally informed. Since the mirror stage and entry into the Symbolic Order together produce the lack at the core of subjectivity (the recognition that the coherent image is identification "at a distance"), lack itself is culturally determined according to the laws of the Symbolic Order; lack describes what the child forever abandons at the constitutive moment of subjectivity within the Symbolic Order. This makes it clear that the subject's body and the experiences it perceives are "always already" social. It also creates a role for racial identifications as well as gendered ones in the foundation of subjectivity. By insisting that her own ideal image is not at a distance, however, Xuela rewrites the terms of lack. Rather than that socially scripted lack being what forever relegates her to devalued subject positions, lack appears in the disjunction between the ideal image and her social context.

For Xuela, the ideal image she has of her own totality competes with one presented to her—through the absence of her mother, her father's rejection, the loveless care she receives from Eunice Paul (the laundress)—of her worthlessness. Out of this ambivalent social status comes her ability to claim instruments of power for herself. While her own social value versus the laundry remains a question, that of her father by comparison is clear. His red hair (inherited from his Scottish father), his skin "the color of corruption" (181), his ability to drop off and pick up his laundry, to come and go every two weeks from the house that limits her world, all signify his power. Without a maternal image to internalize, however, Xuela remains just outside the Oedipal identifications that "should" inculcate her subordinate role in this structure. Thus in staging her dramatic entry into the Symbolic Order, she takes advantage of the breakdown in genealogical destiny to claim the colonial language, appropriated by her father, as her own. At age four she utters her first words: " 'Where is my father?' I said it in English—not French patois or English patois, but plain English—and that should have been the surprise: not that I spoke, but that I spoke English, a language I had never heard anyone speak" (7). Like her language, the question itself underscores her orientation toward the paternal sources of social power.

In order to understand how this is possible, it is helpful to turn one final time to Silverman's analysis of how race, gender, and sexuality are all integral to subject formation within culture. In her reading of Lacan's *Seminar XI*, she notes that subjectivity denotes being recognizable as well as recognizing one's self in the images currently available (which means being illuminated by the gaze). Race, gender, and other corporeal markers may disrupt this three-way process of identification by presenting markers not of the ideal but of its negative. Thus, the coherent ideal subject has as its opposite, not a fragmentary image, but a negative one caught in the slippage between the visual and sensational egos. Moreover, since the subject always holds a multiplicity of identifications and discursive positions, such slippages occur regularly. They continually displace the subject from culture's idealizing terms, spawning the desire for restitution and recognition.

Even though ideology works by naturalizing its terms, the subject's repeated experiences of displacement simultaneously produce the condition of self-reflexivity or critical distance that Xuela manifests so completely. Critical distance entails, then, awareness of one's own position within the dominant fiction as well as one's ability to change its normative ideals. At the same time, the subject's subversive potential is limited: self-reflection must always stop short of comprehending the foundational lack itself. Instead of attempting to satisfy lack, the subject may challenge its *effects* through critical distance.

* * *

Xuela's first words initiate her lifelong "questioning," as Alison Donnell writes, "of how ethical it is to position yourself as eternally, unalterably sinner or sinned upon, preserving the 'natural' hierarchy of colonial superior/inferior and consequently stabilising national boundaries around a model of historical conflict and exclusionary practices" ("Writing for Resistance," 34). Instead, Xuela challenges the validity of the model itself, using the very terms with which it would condemn her. That she knowingly assumes an active role in the Symbolic Order that structures her own subjugation is clear, even beyond her use of English. She is bombarded by lessons, drawn from Victorian morality, Christianity, and British history, of her own supposed worthlessness, and those lessons are presented by the people of color around her (her father, her teacher, Eunice Paul). The first words she learns to read in school are "The British Empire," she is severely punished for breaking Eunice's prized plate that depicts Heaven as the English countryside, and she is taught in school that she should be ashamed of her race and her sexuality. Claiming English as her own is her way of assuming control of the very forces that would otherwise erase her: "I came to love myself in defiance, out of despair, because there was nothing else" (*AMM*, 56–7). In an interview with Moira Ferguson, Kincaid explains how "claiming yourself" may signal at once insecurity and self-determination: "I do come from this tradition of possessing and claiming yourself, because if you don't possess and claim yourself, someone else will. You keep declaring that you are in full possession, which is to say you are on guard" (184).

Butler's explication of the two forms of the power the subject possesses becomes helpful here in explaining Xuela's autonomy. Butler invokes these terms, subjection (*assujetissement*) and the power the subject wields (*pouvoir*), which resonate materially and psychically, to explain the duality of subordination and empowerment that Xuela so clearly manifests. By separating agency and power, while insisting that the former derives from the latter, Butler allows us to conceptualize agency "constrained by no teleological necessity" (*The Psychic Life of Power*, 15). Xuela's agency, as with that of any subject, has its foundation in the social structure in which she lives. For Xuela that means assuming the dominant discourse in order to challenge its most debilitating effects on its most oppressed subjects.

Mastery of English facilitates self-mastery as it allows her to contest the web of oppressions she finds at home and at school. Her teacher and schoolmates, who find their own African heritage a "source of humiliation and self-loathing," see in Xuela's features the Carib people: "The Carib people had been defeated and then exterminated, thrown away like the weeds in a garden; the African people had been defeated but survived. When they looked at me, they saw only the Carib people. They were wrong but I did not tell them so" (15–16). Instead of directing her discourse outward, she talks to herself, assuaging her loneliness, and, in the process, taking pleasure in the sound of her voice. Soon she learns that by directing her discourse outward she can effect even greater change. After learning to write a proper form letter (a lesson that initially appears as an absurd remnant of colonial schooling meant only to emphasize the lack of opportunities available to a poor, black girl), she writes secret letters to her father, begging to be taken into the home where he lives with his new wife. When a schoolmate finds the stash and the teacher in anger mails them, her father retrieves Xuela and she first senses the potential of her agency: "I had, through the use of some words, changed my situation; I had perhaps even saved my life. To speak of my own situation, to myself or others, is something I would always do thereafter. It is in this way that I came to be so extremely conscious of myself, so interested in my own needs, so interested in fulfilling them, aware of my grievances, aware of my pleasures" (22). Throughout the novel, Xuela cultivates multiple voices—biographical, historical, philosophical, directed inward as well as outward—in an attempt to satisfy the desire for pleasure inaugurated by her foundational loss.

In *The Autobiography of My Mother*, the framing of the loss that cannot be thought or compensated takes place through a series of displacements which enhance Xuela's agency. As in Rushdie's novels, we as readers must sustain some form of identification with the narrator in order to reap the pleasures of the text and the critical distance from loss that it fosters. The novel encourages this through its strident critique of the dominant fiction, such that we, as readers, wish, at least temporarily, to suspend belief in it. While Xuela's mother is the most immediate sign of loss, she stands in for the historical wounds suffered by the Carib and African peoples as well as the island itself and for the colonial education both Xuela and Kincaid received. That education, devoted to the history and exploits of the English, was its own form of oppression. As Kincaid writes of her own life in "On Seeing England for the First Time,"

> I did not know then that the statement [which began every school exam], 'Draw a map of England' was something far worse than a declaration of war, for in fact a flat-out declaration of war would have put me on alert, and again in fact, there was no need for war—I had long ago been conquered. I did not know then that this statement was part of a process that would result in my erasure, not my physical erasure, but my erasure all the same. (34)

The alternative, she continues, "was to fall back into the something from which I had been rescued, a hole filled with nothing, and that was the word for everything about me" (35). Xuela experiences the same education, as she and her classmates are taught not only of English superiority but also to mistrust one another. These holes, these wounds cannot be healed, as Kincaid argues stridently regarding Antigua in *A Small Place*: "Nothing can erase my rage—not an apology, not a large sum of money, not the death of the criminal—for this wrong can never be made right, and only the impossible can make me still: can a way be found to make what happened not have happened?" (32). Full compensation is impossible in part because there exists no prior, originary identity to which to return. Instead Kincaid offers the partial compensation afforded by aesthetic pleasure and historical responsibility.

* * *

Although Xuela initially tries to recover her mother's past as a key to Xuela's own present, this, too, is impossible. Abandoned outside a nunnery as an infant, Xuela's mother was raised and named by the nuns who "baptized her a Christian, and demanded that she be a quiet, long-suffering, unquestioning, modest, wishing-to-die-soon person." Xuela concludes, "She became such a person" (199), thereby signaling the reader that Xuela's own or another's attempt to define her through her mother will only result in misidentification. Religion is, of course, another form of conquest, and her mother's Christianity silences the *obeah* traditions

Xuela associates with women's knowledge and the fierce independence of the Carib people. Xuela's father, in contrast, has the social mobility accorded only to men, and religion is just one of the vehicles he uses to resolve the discrepancy between his Scottish father and the African mother, the former self-determining and the latter already defeated: "within my father the struggle between the hyphenated man and the horde had long since been resolved, the hyphenated man as before had triumphed" (188). Within the hyphenated man "there existed at once victor and vanquished, perpetrator and victim, [and] he chose, not at all surprisingly, the mantle of the former, always the former" (192). Hybridity alone, then, does not guarantee subversion of the ongoing legacies of colonial power. What matters instead is how one wields the agencies subjectivity affords as an ideological weapon.

As a woman, Xuela lacks the freedom to make the identificatory choice her father did; yet she refuses to accept complete subjugation. For her to make a comparable, hopefully more ethical, choice, she needs to rewrite the opposition between maternal defeat and paternal power into sequence of images, identifications, and agencies. As Butler describes, this process takes place on the fringes of the conscious and unconscious and through the secondary desires such mental activity produces. To escape the harsh environment of school and home, Xuela learns to take pleasure in her natural world, which is feminized as "silent, soft, and vegetable-like in its vulnerability, subject to the powerful whims of others" (17). Sitting by the lagoon, watching the weather change and the ducks swim, she dreams her first of a recurring image of her mother: "I saw my mother come down a ladder. She wore a long white gown, the hem of it falling just above her heels, and that was all of her that was exposed, just her heels" (18). Even the fuzzy dream world fails to yield anything other than modesty and absence, yet Xuela refuses to become trapped in loss: "At first I longed to see more, and then I became satisfied just to see her heels coming down toward me." Upon waking, as when she began to speak, she actively claims her paternal legacy and with it the power to define herself in her own terms. "I was not the same child I had been before I fell asleep," she notes. "I longed to see my father and to be in his presence constantly" (18). By substituting the insatiable desire for her mother's image with the desire, which she meets through her letter writing, for her father's presence, Xuela transforms yearning into satisfaction and defeat into agency.

These strategies do not produce a single, totalizing subjectivity modeled on the coherence often ascribed to the Western self; nor do they transform Xuela into her father's weak mimic. For example, detailing the specific histories of her parents, Xuela emphasizes the gaps. "I don't know," "I don't know," she often says to underscore how history ignores the personal stories of those it conquers. Rather than fill those gaps with a counter-history, she uses them to show the failure of the colonial past to determine completely its contemporary descendants as well as to underscore the inevitable failures of writing history. As she matures, whenever she faces indeterminacy, negativity, and lack, Xuela turns to her own body as a source of power and pleasure. Already relishing the pleasure she can give herself, when her first employer, Monsieur LaBatte, extends a sexual "invitation," she retains a measure of control, as she says, "knowing what it was I wanted" (70). In this case, laying claim to her desires disrupts any simplistic reading of the power dynamics between them. It also demands our continued wariness regarding any claims to female solidarity. While Lise LaBatte initially served as a maternal figure to Xuela, Lise's joy from the liaison between her servant and husband and the pregnancy that results from it teaches Xuela that the only link the two women share under such circumstances is one of oppression. By insisting on her own sexual pleasure and by terminating the pregnancy, Xuela rejects both the one female companion she has had in favor of her own autonomy as well as the seemingly inevitable link between female sexuality and procreation.

Her rejection of any position of romantic subjugation grows stronger as the novel progresses. In narrating her first encounter with the white doctor, Philip, who would eventually become her husband, Xuela provides only questions—"Did he knock at the door? Did I say come in?" (149)— to undermine any such turn toward the romantic. She remains steadfastly focused instead on guaranteeing her own pleasure: "He was like most of the men I had known, obsessed with an activity he was not very good at, but he took directions very well and was not afraid of being told what to do, or ashamed that he did not know all the things there were to do" (143). Finally, she refuses the requests of Roland, her one genuine lover whom, like herself, she identifies with the islands, to bear his children as proof of her desire, and chooses instead to terminate their relationship. In all these ways she acknowledges, in Angela Carter's words, that "no bed, however unexpected, no matter how apparently gratuitous, is free from the de-universalising facts of real life" (9). "Real life," in this case, includes the colonial and slave-holding history of control over women's sexuality and children, which finds its current expression in the novel in black and white men's sexual power over women.

* * *

Sexual pleasure and control do not equal happiness nor transform Xuela into an adherent of the law of the father. They do, however, provide, alongside her use of English, a measure of self-determination that translates into the auto/biography itself. It is in these strategic uses of language and sexuality that Kincaid most clearly obscures the distinctions between her roles as novelist, auto/biographer, and critic. Alison Donnell encourages us to see these slippages as "an opportunity to understand that there is a way of restor(y)ing agency through representing an other." Donnell cites "bell hook's condemnatory phrase 'Re-writing you, I write myself anew' " to argue that Kincaid translates this statement of selfish appropriation into one "of positive possession of selves previously denied ownership of their stories" ("When Writing the Other" 130). The strategy calls up the subaltern ghost, introduced at the beginning of this chapter, whose voice(s) struggle to emerge in postcolonial criticism. In the story of Xuela and her mother, through its echoes of Kincaid's grandmother's life, and in the shifting narrative stances Kincaid adopts, the silence of the defeated is broken. At the same time, the critical distance maintained by both author and subject demand more than just willing readers. It demands a kind of conscience that, like Xuela's, is anything but simple and that, Butler specifies, is produced by the melancholia underpinning subjectivity (*PLP*, 177).

Implicit in Butler's schema is the irony that melancholia arises from a loss ("located" in the split between the ego and super-ego) that cannot be articulated, yet may lead to a challenge of dominant ideology (otherwise sustained by the super-ego). That critical faculty to challenge does not in and of itself promise happiness. The identifications Xuela consciously chooses (particularly her claim on the English language and sexual agency) do not cure melancholia; melancholia persists despite her agency because melancholia is at once individual and historical. Xuela recognizes the link, commenting that "all that is impersonal I have made personal" (228). Even in old age with her husband Philip, she cannot evade historical legacy. Philip chose her in an attempt to atone for the past and exist wholly in the present, and in doing so he accepts his own defeat: "He grew to live for the sound of my footsteps, so often I would walk without making a sound; he loved the sound of my voice, so for days I would not utter a word" (217–18). Despite her control, she asks, "Did so much sadness ever enclose two people?" (224), for the history of colonization ultimately robbed them both of victory. Race, gender, and national identities have become crimes, which she notes, "I know now more than ever," adding, "I do not have the courage to bear [those identities]. Am I nothing, then? I do not believe so" (226). Although seemingly caught between historical erasure and oppression, she retains her commitment to speaking out for her own preservation. The only option that remains for her is to negotiate the complicated path between power and victimhood, goodness, evil, and revenge.

Such a path is the "price" Butler identifies of gaining critical consciousness, as the existence of critical consciousness demands that the ego itself also become available for self-scrutiny (*PLP*, 180). Xuela's idealized and antagonistic images of her parents produce her ability to champion herself without losing that critical distance. The melancholia or loss that enables her subjectivity and spurs her anger simultaneously turns inward, refusing self-identifications exclusively with the good. Rather than separate the loved and hated aspects of the ideal, in Xuela's case her mother and her father, into what has been forever lost and what regulates all possible compensation, respectively, we might find both within conscience.

For Xuela, that conscience is both personal and national, yet it seeks to undermine rather than embrace the workings of the nation as family metaphor. As opposed to Philip whose future is bounded by "a past he had inherited" (215), Xuela says of herself:

> I am of the vanquished, I am of the defeated. The past is a fixed point, the future is open-ended; for me the future must remain capable of casting a light on the past such that in my defeat lies the seed of my great victory, in my defeat lies the beginning of my great revenge. My impulse is to the good, my good is to serve myself. I am not a people, I am not a nation. I only wish from time to time to make my actions be the actions of a people, to make my actions be the actions of a nation. (216)

Xuela makes this statement at the end of her life when her father has died, she has purposely remained childless and her body is "withering like fruit dying on a vine" (225), and Philip is reduced to "bus[ying] himself with the dead" (224). In doing so, she portrays the dominant nation as family metaphor heading for extinction. At the same time, she maintains her right to speak on behalf of the nation and some of its constituents, to speak of historical trauma and the potential for change.

Here Xuela is engaged in the active process of affiliation Said describes in *The World, the Text and the Critic*. Affiliation offers an alternative social network to filiative networks, as the biological underpinnings of filiation and the nation as family metaphor, not to mention their paternal slant, are particularly inappropriate in past slave-holding colonies such as Dominica whose population and various languages (English, English patois, French patois) reflect a history of familial, cultural, and sexual violence. Kincaid stretches the conditions of affiliation far beyond the liberating notion of choice that seems to be implicit in Said's model; for Kincaid, affiliation arises from historically traumatic conditions of necessity. *The Autobiography of My Mother* accounts for that violent past while it approaches affiliation through a narrative that is at once lyrical and political. It participates, along with the earlier novels, *Annie John* and *Lucy*, in what Moira Ferguson calls "the process of historical reclamation" (*JK*, 164). The novel does not abandon or limit itself to the shared history of Caribs and Africans it represents, rather it seeks to establish a web of historical understanding and critical engagement among its readers that includes both Dominican history and broader issues of colonization.

Despite their emphasis on the historical constraints on affiliation, Kincaid and Xuela attempt its radical gesture of crossing traditional boundaries (here between genres). They also articulate the subtleties of this approach, the difficulties in claiming both agency and defeat in a postcolonial context. In her interview with Ferguson, conducted during the writing of *The Autobiography of My Mother*, Kincaid describes how her own history has enabled her to see from these two seemingly conflicted perspectives: "I am interested in the defeated and identify with the defeated even though I don't feel defeated myself [. . .] Actually, the great thing about being the victim is that you identify with the victim, and that may save you from victimizing. If you can keep in mind who suffers, it might prevent you from suffering" (171). Such a position is not an evasion of situated knowledge, but rather an acceptance of the shifting subject positions and identifications we can cultivate.

Xuela adopts the same dual perspective when she realizes "that many things which reminded me that [Philip], too, was human and frail caused a great feeling of anger to swell up in me; for if he, too, was human, then would not all whom he came from be human, too, and where would that leave me and all that I came from?" (220). She eventually accepts both her (justifiable) anger—"for the first step to claiming yourself is anger"[1]—and the inability to "be a part of anything that is outside history [. . .] that can deny the wave of the human hand, the beat of the human heart, the gaze of the human eye, human desire itself" (218). We are caught in the web of desire in all of its intricacy. Rather than seek to escape those desires, whether beneficent or harmful, she suggests we must foster the critical consciousness to understand and employ them.

* * *

The question remains of how new images of subjective and national identity might emerge from the alliances Kincaid/Xuela attempts to initiate with the reader. Writing the nation requires, as does the auto/biographical subject, a precarious balance of idealization and practicality to avoid the abyss of foundational loss. For Homi Bhabha, the ideal image of the nation, like that of the subject, is one beyond the discursive order and its loss (for which narratives of the nation try to compensate). Nevertheless, Bhabha argues that through "another time of *writing*" (*Location of Culture*, 141) the nation we might learn to see the ambivalence of both our desires and the narratives they spawn. Bhabha's focus on the enunciation rather than the epistemology of the nation is a useful guide to the multiple voices Kincaid creates. Because these two temporalities oppose one another and because the "nation as narration" is a text that must be continuously written and read, there are, despite the obvious success of the nation as an imaginary ideal, repeated breaks in its coherence. For Bhabha, the temporal rather than spatial dimension of those slippages constitutes the realm of politics— of ideological domination and resistance.

* * *

I want to conclude with the argument that Kincaid's "autobiography" enacts just such another time, producing identities of subject and nation that are feminized but not necessarily maternal, representative but not totalizing. In *A Poetics of Women's Autobiography*, Sidonie Smith argues that "[w]omen who do not challenge those gender ideologies and the boundaries they place around women's proper life script, textual inscription, and speaking voice do not write autobiography. Culturally silenced, they remain sentenced to death in the fictions of woman surrounding them" (44). For Smith, those fictions or false autobiographies take two main forms, both of which "derive from the erasure of female sexuality": a woman most often presents herself as either a "representative man" (requiring "the repression of the mother") or a de-eroticized and "good" " 'representative' woman" (55). Although Xuela chooses the identification with her father and his discourse, she does so as a sexual woman in search of what Smith terms "a new sentence." As Kincaid insists in her interview with Ferguson, only those who will remain trapped by history "cling to their narrow definitions of themselves [. . .] What you ought to do is take back. Not just reclaim. Take—period. Take anything. Take Shakespeare . . . Just take it" (168).

Such an author (or subject), Smith writes, "traces her origins to and through, rather than against the mother who has been repressed in order for the symbolic contract to emerge. Through the marginalized space inhabited by actual mothers and daughters, she pursues the source of patriarchy's reproduction of woman as a means to discovering some new truth about her sexuality" (57). In Xuela's case, the absence of her mother enables Xuela to claim her father's language as her own source of power. She takes a similar approach to her sexuality, insisting upon her right both to sexual control and pleasure. Both linguistically and sexually, she refuses to abide by the social rules that would disenfranchise her, and instead seeks to rewrite them.

Nominally fiction, yet blurring the lines between genres, Kincaid's writing uses long lyrical passages that transform logical oppositions into grammatical companions in order to insist as much on a shared history of black Caribbean women as it does on the speaker's right to define herself beyond that history. For example, she describes her father's face as "a map of the world":

> His cheeks were two continents separated by two seas which joined an ocean (his nose); his gray eyes were bottomless and sleeping volcanoes; between his nose and his mouth lay the equator; his ears were the horizons, to go beyond was to fall into the thick blackness of nothing; his forehead was a range of mountains known to be treacherous; his chin the area of steppes and deserts. Each area took on its appropriate coloring: the land mass a collection of soft yellows and blues and mauves and pinks, with small lines of red running in every direction as if to deliberately confound; the waters blue, the mountains green, the deserts and steppes brown. (92)

She concludes this studied cartography by stating, "I did not know this world, I had only met some of its people." She transforms the familiar tool of the colonizer, adventurer, conqueror, and knowledge-maker into a topographical screen that masks a reality that presumably lies beneath it. This transformation simultaneously alters her identity from mapmaker to mapreader, desperately trying to make sense of the now unfamiliar territory.

Kincaid frequently undermines such models of knowledge and possession in order to point to the narrator's agency rather than her defeat. By insisting again and again that knowledge is only ever partial, "truth is always full of uncertainty" (223), loss is ever-present, and we all as victors and victims must share history as well as a common humanity, Kincaid reclaims multiple voices for the otherwise silenced. The goal is one of historical responsibility, pleasure, and meaning, not total control. The text refuses any nostalgic return to coherent subjectivity, essential gender or racial identifications, or singular narrative of national identity, offering instead a voice at once assertive, self-critical, questioning, and angry whose "very composure [. . .] is so unsettling" (Donnell, "When Writing the Other," 131) to our fixed notions of subject and nation. This composure allows Xuela to ask "What makes the world turn?" in imitation of the great European religious and philosophical thinkers she studies in school, as well as "Who would need an answer to such a question?" (131). Holding her right to speak—Butler's *pouvoir*—inalienable, she shows how to utilize that power to challenge traditional hierarchies. "What makes the world turn?" thus becomes in a few sentences, "What makes the world turn against me and all who look like me?" (132). Each of these narrative shifts, particularly when played out against the layered lives of multiple subjects (Xuela, her mother, Kincaid's grandmother), disrupts the linearity of the nation and subject's story. We can only be certain that identities are always in process and always tied to their historical conditions.

The changes in meaning, at once subtle and aggressive, and so lyrically conveyed, break down the aesthetic foundations that uphold the dominant metaphors of colonial and postcolonial writing as well as the gender divisions upon which those metaphors depend. Without those interventions, "[i]t is as if [. . .] the beauty—the beauty of the sea, the land, the air, the trees, the market, the people, the sounds they make—were a prison, and as if everything and everybody inside it were locked in and everything and everybody that is not inside it were locked out," Kincaid writes in *A Small Place* (79). What she offers instead is a narrator who speaks from within and outside of that prison in order to dismantle its walls. In place of the struggle between the coherent subject—so often white, male, and propertied—and the injured object—so often a person of color, female, and poor, Kincaid asks us to recognize *in one another* our commonalties: the lack that initiates subjectivity, the historical traumas girding national identity, the mutual responsibility for the future. Just as Silverman calls for the ethical look that bestows the "active gift of love" on whoever is "not me," Kincaid writes on behalf of the pleasure of seeing "experience collect in the eyes" of another, a pleasure that comes from "an invisible current between the two, the observed and observer, beheld and beholder [. . .] which is in many ways a definition of love" (*AMM*, 56).

Conclusion

Postcolonialism, Provisionality, and Alternative Modernities

I have argued throughout these chapters that the metaphor of the paternal family plays a central role in our understanding of modern subjects and nations and that the aesthetic, by blurring the boundaries between conscious and unconscious desires and identifications, may enable us to achieve a critical distance from the injurious identifications the metaphor fosters. That distance produces an ethical responsibility to re-imagine our relationships with others and, thus, our understanding of ourselves. In order to look deeply at how the ideology of the paternal family sustains belief (as both a metaphor and an instrument of imperialism) in postcolonial contexts, as well as where, when, and why belief falters, I have turned to psychoanalysis, despite its long engagement with the dominant fiction. A key objective in this approach has been to explore and to stretch the limits of psychoanalytic theory in responding to postcolonial concerns. My model of subjectivity, drawn from Silverman and Butler, emphasizes the foundational lack at the subject's core. While the application of this model to postcolonial subjects and texts might seem inevitably to re-inscribe the hegemonic terms of imperialism, by reading the postcolonial condition as inherently damaged or lacking, I have tried instead to offer a critique of those terms immanent to them. By insisting on the provisionality of *all* subject positions while analyzing the failures of the nation as family metaphor in maintaining its subjects' allegiance, I have focused on postcolonial sites of resistance to rather than yearning for dominant identities.

Resistance in these readings is not limited to a dialectic response from the oppressed margins to the imperial center, but configured as a constellation of practices used to subvert the center–periphery model by showing the provisionality and instability at the heart of both positions. Those practices vary according to the specificities of the novels and their historical contexts, yet all constitute a form of what has been called creative adaptation to—and I would add appropriation of—the challenges of modernity. Dilip Parameshwar Gaonkar describes creative adaptation as the "manifold ways in which a people question the present. It is the site where a people 'make' themselves modern, as opposed to being 'made' modern by alien and impersonal forces, and where they give themselves an identity and a destiny" (18). This is an ambivalent process, caught between the agency of self-production and the realization that one's potential identities are always constrained by the need to be recognizable to an other.

The novels, in differing ways, throw that glance of recognition back on itself, casting shadows on dominant subjective and national identities while illuminating those heretofore barred. Through an examination of the most vulnerable features of the psychic topography—the sites of unremitting desire, lack, and melancholia and—I have tried to show how such shifts in value may occur, how we may unlearn our own positions of privilege or subjugation in favor of building affinity with others. The insistence that it is a profound melancholia and yearning that founds our common humanity is a surprisingly uplifting conclusion in the novels. It invites us to follow the lead of Beigh Masters, Hannah Easton, Saleem, Nadia Wadia, and even Xuela in discovering the pleasure of an other through the revelatory potential of the aesthetic.

NOTES

Chapter 1 Subjectivity, National Identity, and the Aesthetic

1. In *Imperial Leather*, e.g., McClintock reminds us that sexuality as a metaphor for imperialism does not account for all of its gendered effects: "Sexuality as a trope for other power relations was certainly an abiding aspect of imperial power. The feminizing of 'virgin' land [. . .] operated as a metaphor for relations that were very often not about sexuality at all, or were only indirectly sexual [. . .]. But seeing sexuality only as a metaphor runs the risk of eliding *gender* as a constitutive dynamic of imperial and anti-imperial power" (14). This reminder is a useful caveat to Silverman's psychoanalytic model. McClintock, in her own traversings of the line between public and private, insists that we not substitute an understanding of discursive metaphors for that of material experience. Although we inevitably read one category through the other, they are not identical.

2. Silverman turns to the psychoanalytic work of Paul Schilder and Henri Wallon in order to explain how socially inscribed corporeality is linked to sensation and thus to experience and identification. Drawing on Schilder's 1935 *The Image and Appearance of the Human Body*, she describes how the child's understanding of his or her corporeality is intimately connected with the emotions and desires received upon the body from parents or caretakers. This provides an added cultural dimension to the formation of the ego through the visual (and sensual) recognition in the mirror stage, and it renders parental desire "a privileged site for the articulation of cultural differences" (*TVW*, 14). Schilder's explication of the parental role in the child's ego formation contributes to our understanding of how the dominant fiction and the Oedipus complex are culturally "inherited" and literally domesticated.

   Wallon adds another important component to Silverman's model. In his 1934 reading of the mirror stage, *Les Origines du caractère chez l'enfant*, he presents the internalization of the wholistic, idealized image as a much more laborious process than does Lacan, a process produced by cultural norms after a struggle to unite what Wallon sees as the two separate images the child maintains of corporeality and the mirror reflection. The child's recognition of the reflection in the mirror, Silverman's "identity-at-a-distance," means that the child identifies him- or herself as "other" and, thus, as an image not only loved (because it is his or her own) but also hated (because it is always removed) (*TVW*, 15).

Chapter 2   Mimicry and Reinvention: Female Desire and National Identity
in Bharati Mukherjee's *The Holder of the World*

1. To describe her changing aesthetic and its celebration of the "exuberance" of immigration, Mukherjee has frequently named Eastern European Jewish immigrant writers such as Bernard Malamud and Isaac Babel as her literary models (replacing Naipaul). In an interview with Alison B. Carb, Mukherjee states, "I view myself as an American author in the tradition of other American authors whose ancestors arrived at Ellis Island" (650). At the same time, she notes that her fiction is different from Malamud or Babel's because it "has to consider race, politics, religion, as well as certain nastiness that other generations of white immigrant American writers may not have had to take into account" (651). Despite these claims of local specificity, however, the citations above make clear that her primary concern is with immigration as a process of adaptation and transformation, rather than as a response to particular socioeconomic conditions in the host and home countries.

2. For example, when Hannah decides to marry Gabriel Legge, the narrator elides the possibility of self-determination: "We do things when it is our time to do them. They do not occur to us until it is time; they cannot be resisted, once their time has come. It's a question of time, not motive" (70).

3. Crucial to my understanding of *The Scarlet Letter*, and hence *The Holder of the World*, is Lauren Berlant's work in *The Anatomy of National Fantasy: Hawthorne, Utopia, and Everyday Life*. Berlant provides a reading of *The Scarlet Letter* that shows "how the bond between erotic desire and the desire for collective political existence serves the nation, by connecting national identity with more local and personal forms of intimacy" (7). She invokes the term "National Symbolic" to identify the configuration of land, language, law, and experience that must produce the fantasy of collective national experience. The National Symbolic shares with Silverman's dominant fiction a way of conceptualizing the foundations of our strongest assumptions and world views. Both concepts link language, ideology, law, and the subject in order to help explain how we come to hold our fundamental beliefs, and both focus on the role of memory in maintaining those collective beliefs. Berlant and Silverman differ in the specific fields their terms define. The National Symbolic addresses citizenship as the link between the personal and the national: "By passing into citizenship through inscription in the National Symbolic of the body politic that expresses him/her, the citizen reaches another plane of existence, a whole unassailable body, whose translation into totality mimics the nation's permeable yet impervious spaces. According to this logic, disruptions in the realm of the National Symbolic create a collective sensation of almost physical vulnerability: the subject without a nation experiences her/his own mortality and vulnerability because s/he has lost control over physical space and the historical time that marks that space as a part of her/his inheritance" (24). The dominant fiction, on the other hand, pinpoints the psychic structures underlying ideology, structures that impact on the formation of national identity as one of many identificatory sites. While Silverman's approach is more germane to my project as a whole, the National Symbolic does facilitate an understanding of how privileged social signifiers connect subject and nation.

4. For two insightful discussions of Hawthorne's place in the formation of an American literary canon, see Richard H. Brodhead, *The School of Hawthorne*, New York: Oxford University Press, 1986 and Jane Tompkins, *Sensational Designs: The Cultural Work of American Fiction, 1790-1860*. Both authors see canonicity as a reflection of changing literary cultures rather than as timeless judgment. They also situate Hawthorne within the broader literary culture of his time to show the relationship between publishing, marketing, and literary value. As Brodhead notes, "Hawthorne moves through our past like a kind of tracer-dye, baring the changing contours both of what it has included and of the terms and processes by which it has been built" (10).

5. In "Dealing with Differences," Christina Crosby sums up the danger implicit in the rhetoric of pluralism. Unless we are willing to "read the processes of differentiation," she writes, "differences will remain as self-evident as identity once was, and just as women's studies once saw woman everywhere, the academy will recognize differences everywhere, cheerfully acknowledging that since everyone is different, everyone is the same" (140).

6. Silverman, *Male Subjectivity at the Margins*, 149. Silverman is distinguishing here between two forms of mimicry outlined by Lacan. The first, passive form he ascribes to the entire animal kingdom whereas the second requires the conscious intervention of the human subject.

7. Shirley Geok-lin Lim, in "Assaying the Gold: Or, Contesting the Ground of Asian American Literature," describes defamiliarization as "the radicalizing technique by which the complacent majority are made uncomfortable" (160). Defamiliarization does not necessarily avoid the dangers she noted earlier, however, that face a self-described "ethnic" or "Asian" or "Asian-American" text: conflation of content and style into a standard of ethnic authenticity, pressure to define ethnicity in "socially desirable" terms, an inability to create means of textual affiliation across cultural boundaries.

8. Jonathan Rosen, writing in the *New York Times Book Review*, suggests, "King David's conquest of the city of Jerusalem 3,000 years ago should perhaps be considered the true starting point of American literature—if not America itself. The Pilgrim Fathers mapped out this country Bible in hand, and American writers have been reading the image of Jerusalem into our culture ever since." Rosen notes that the links between Jerusalem and its "New World" namesake, Salem, extend through and beyond Hawthorne's text: "[Hawthorne's] great-great-great-grandfather had helped settle the city [Salem] and, as Hawthorne wrote in his preface to 'The Scarlet Letter', he was forever haunted by the image of a 'grave, bearded, sable-cloaked and steeple-crowned progenitor—who came so early with his Bible and his sword'. The progenitor's son served as a judge of the Salem witch trials. No wonder Salem, though its name means 'peace', became an inspiration for Hawthorne's darkest tales, a place where America's longings for spiritual purity often yielded to their dangerous opposite." Mukherjee, too, maintains the thematic connections between Jerusalem and Salem as historical guides to the conflict between purity and transgression. For Beigh, speaking for her author, revision of history to include ethnicity and passion is a necessary precursor to a better future: "Before you build another city on the hill, first fill in the potholes at your feet" (91).

9. Hannah imagined, at age 12

an ocean, palm trees, thatched cottages, and black-skinned men casting nets and colorfully garbed bare-breasted women mending them; native barks and, on the horizon, high-masted schooners. Colonial gentlemen in breeches and ruffled lace, buckled hats and long black coats pacing the shore. In the distance, through bright-green foliage, a ghostly white building—it could even be the Taj Mahal—rising. (44)

That Hannah portrays desire in colonial terms allows for a paradoxical reading of this passage. First, it aligns Rebecca with the victims of colonial expansion on two continents. At the same time, it foreshadows Hannah's own landing in colonial India. There the white building suggests less the Taj Mahal than White Town where she and the other "Europeans" sequestered themselves in Fort St. Sebastian. This foreshadowing also implicates Hannah in the project of colonial expansion, an implication that negates the potential of a series of mnemonic displacements leading eventually to the productive look. In this sense, her embroidery may be read as a means of literally domesticating the exotic that she has seen and will see.

10. This passage reveals the same paradoxical relationship to colonial power as does the embroidery example. Mukherjee positions the fisherman boy's account as part of a historical revision from a non-European perspective: In London, "he chanced upon John Dryden's *Aureng-Zebe* and was incensed by its Eurocentric falsity. That fisherman's boy composed his own heroic play, *The World-Taker*, in rhyming couplets as a corrective. In the extant fragment, the anonymous fisherman–poet claimed that when he first came upon Dryden's confession that 'true passion is too fierce to be in fetters bound', he was wracked by the vision that had befallen him years before on a sandy strip in neglected Fort St. Sebastian" (161). The fisherman boy's revision is validated to the extent that it complies with European aesthetic norms, yet it does not sanction recognition of his own identity via the same standards. He remains a nameless imitator and reinventor who can only expose the limitations of Dryden's view by still deferring to the authority of his language and form.

11. John F. Kasson's description, in *Amusing the Million*, of Coney Island's appeal nearly a century ago could just as easily apply to virtual reality in *The Holder of the World*:

In various ways all these rides were designed to throw people off balance, literally and imaginatively, to sweep patrons up in their grasp and momentarily overwhelm them before allowing order to be restored at the end. Such rides served in effect as powerful hallucinogens, altering visitors' perceptions and transforming their consciousness, dispelling everyday concerns in the intense sensations of the present moment. They allowed customers the exhilaration of whirlwind activity without physical exertion, of thrilling drama without imaginative effort. Riders could enjoy their own momentary fright and disorientation because they knew it would turn to comic relief; they could engage in what appeared dangerous adventure because ultimately they believed in its safety. (81–2)

Chapter 3 Traumatic Legacy and the Psychoanalysis of Race: African American Masculinity in Darryl Pinckney's *High Cotton*

1. It is useful to maintain a distinction between the phallus and privileged signifier in order to avoid inadvertently reproducing the patriarchal signification of the phallus. Particularly if our goal is to open up psychoanalytic models to attend to racial subjectivities that are not subordinate to sexual difference, it is crucial to free the terms of subjectivity from that binary opposition.

2. Bhabha, in *The Location of Culture* (131), is quoting Michel Foucault, *The Archaeology of Knowledge* (London: Tavistock, 1972), 92, 111.

3. Fuss's chapter, "Interior Colonies: Frantz Fanon and the Politics of Identification," provides an excellent analysis of the historical context of Fanon's loyalty to dominant codes of heterosexual masculinity. As she notes, "Fanon's resolutely masculine self-identifications, articulated through the abjectification of femininity and homosexuality, take shape over and against colonialism's castrating representations of black male sexuality" (160).

4. Silverman builds on Freud's definition of "war trauma" to explain how an "outside" event may trigger neurosis in those who experience it. Her own examples are drawn from films produced just after World War II which show the war's potentially traumatic effects on masculine subjectivity.

5. I use the term "legacy" purposely here to underscore the legitimation of historically denied inheritance and genealogy. Communal memories, then, form the basis for familial identifications that may be elided on the level of kinship and patronymic markers. As such they constitute a wellspring of possible alternative signifying images.

6. Sigmund Freud, "Beyond the Pleasure Principle," *The Freud Reader*, ed. Peter Gay (New York: W.W. Norton, 1989), 598. The most succinct and direct literary expression of trauma as fright and surprise that I know of is in Art Spiegelman's graphic novel, *Maus I* and *II*. In the second volume, Art tells his "shrink" (a survivor of Terezin and Auschwitz) of his difficulties trying to capture his parents' experiences at Auschwitz. Explaining his writer's block, Art says, "I can't BEGIN to imagine what it felt like." Pavel responds, "What Auschwitz felt like? Hmm . . . How can I explain? . . . **BOO!**" and sends Art out of his chair. "It felt a little like **that**," Pavel adds, "But ALWAYS! From the moment you got to the gate until the very end" (41).

7. Freud explains this transformation with the example of his grandson's *fort-da* game. The game, in Freud's reading, re-enacts the child's experience of his mother's departure and allows him to control the longed for return (of his toy, and thus his mother), even if the pleasure of the return necessitates the trauma of the departure. As Freud says, "At the outset, he was in a *passive* situation—he was overpowered by the experience; but, by repeating it, unpleasurable though it was, as a game, he took on an *active* part" (600).

8. It is important to note that a complete conscious revision is inconceivable. As Bhabha's formulation emphasizes, what is unknowable will always partially remain so. For example, the caves' echo (themselves a repetition of an irretrievable source) in *A Passage to India*, the resounding "ou-boum" that signals both Mrs. Moore and Adela's traumatic encounters in the cave,

cannot be satisfactorily deciphered. On the one hand, there is Adela's own comment, "I remember scratching the wall with my finger-nail, to start the usual echo" (214); on the other is her story that, in the words of the District Superintendent of Police, "[t]here was an echo that appears to have frightened her" (185). Neither the meaning nor the source of the echo (and thus the trauma) is locatable within the novel, even in the repeated retelling of the event. Caruth similarly discusses the partialness of any response to trauma. Her focus is less on trying to know the unknowable than on coming to terms with it (and hence with one's own lack).

9. Ernest Renan's 1882 essay "What is a nation?" has been recently reprinted in Homi K. Bhabha (ed.), *Nation and Narration* (New York: Routledge, 1990), 8–22. According to Renan, the sense of national cohesion depends upon a shared set of memories and a common desire to live together, both of which require that the "ancient tragedies" of nation-building (he refers to fratricide, massacres, and so forth) be somehow forgotten or integrated into the myth of the nation as unifying rather than disruptive events.

10. This is not to contradict Anderson's excellent analysis of the role of print media in creating a sense of simultaneity and shared experience for constituents of the modern nation. To my mind, Bhabha is distinguishing between a kind of shared imagination of horizontal time and the vertical time implied in the historical process.

11. I use "colonial discourse" in the broad sense described by Bhabha:

> It is an apparatus that turns on the recognition and disavowal of racial/cultural/historical differences. Its predominant strategic function is the creation of a space for a 'subject peoples' through the production of knowledges in terms of which surveillance is exercised and a complex form of pleasure/unpleasure is incited. It seeks authorization for its strategies by the production of knowledges of colonizer and colonized which are stereotypical but antithetically evaluated. The objective of colonial discourse is to construe the colonized as a population of degenerate types on the basis of racial origin, in order to justify conquest and to establish systems of administration and instruction. (70)

12. Caruth, *Unclaimed Experience*, N21, 136.

Chapter 4   Postcolonial Lack and Aesthetic Promise in Salman Rushdie's *Midnight's Children* and *The Moor's Last Sigh*

1. Jawaharlal Nehru, "A Tryst with Destiny," *India's Freedom* (London: Unwin, 1962), 94–5.

2. Perhaps the most widely noted critique issues from Aijaz Ahmad's chapter on Jameson in *In Theory*. Ahmad focuses on the ways in which the "Three Worlds" model necessarily privileges questions of nationalism at the expense of those of material and economic collectivities. As Ahmad notes, "If this Third World is *constituted* by the singular 'experience of colonialism and imperialism,' and if the only possible response is a nationalist one, then what else is there that is more urgent to narrate than this 'experience'? In fact, there

is *nothing else* to narrate" (102). Neil Lazarus, reviewing Ahmad's book in "Postcolonialism and the Dilemma of Nationalism," points out that Ahmad is critiquing not the "Three Worlds" model as such, but Jameson's definition of it "in terms not of production but of imperialism" (376). Thus, Ahmad disputes Jameson's paradigm of "First World"/capitalism, "Second World"/socialism, and "Third World"/nationalism on the grounds that it ignores differences between nationalist movements and defines the "Third World" only according to the effects of colonialism and imperialism (Jameson's foundation for "Third World" nationalism). Madhava Prasad argues that Ahmad, in subscribing to the same set of terms despite their different definitions, fails to offer a viable alternative to Jameson.

3. Madhava Prasad, e.g., suggests abandoning the "Three Worlds" model in favor of redefining "the libidinal/private in its allegorical status (its relation to particular nations but especially to particular classes—a class allegory) and collapsing the distinction which originates in capitalist ideology" (78). By replacing the nationalistic effects of public/private distinctions with class ones, Prasad exposes one of the foundational dualities of bourgeois thinking. This approach has the advantage of rethinking public and private, although it does so at the expense of analyzing the national or aesthetic. Sangeeta Ray, in her introduction to *En-Gendering India*, argues that Prasad's theoretical approach also lacks a means of addressing "how gender intersects with class to confound and contradict class affiliations." Neil Lazarus's recent book, *Nationalism and Cultural Practice in the Postcolonial World*, makes the most sustained argument for a Marxist approach, and it positions itself in relation to Ahmad's *In Theory*.

4. Much of the scholarship on *Midnight's Children* focuses on traces in the text of *The Tin Drum, Tristram Shandy*, and *Kim*, among others. See, e.g., Michael Gorra's *After Empire: Scott, Naipaul, Rushdie*, Richard Cronin's "The Indian English Novel: *Kim* and *Midnight's Children*," Clement Hawes's "Leading History by the Nose: The Turn to the Eighteenth Century in *Midnight's Children*," Michael Harris's *Outsiders and Insiders: Perspective of Third World Culture and British Post-Colonial Fiction*, Colin Smith's "The Unbearable Lightness of Salman Rushdie," K.J. Phillips's "Salman Rushdie's *Midnight's Children*: Models for Storytelling, East and West," and Rudolph Bader's "Indian *Tin Drum*." In "Caught in a Strange Middle Ground: Contesting History in Salman Rushdie's *Midnight's Children*," David Lipscomb also provides a detailed analysis of Rushdie's historiographic borrowings from Stanley Wolpert's *A New History of India*. Criticism of *The Moor's Last Sigh* is similar in its tracings of intertext from sources as diverse as *Othello, Don Quixote*, and *Orlando*. See, e.g., Ania Loomba's "Local-manufacture made-in-India Othello fellows," Paul A. Cantor's "Tales of the Alhambra: Rushdie's Use of Spanish History in *The Moor's Last Sigh*," and Jonathan Greenberg's "The Base Indian' or 'The Base Judean'? *Othello* and the Metaphor of the Palimpsest in Salman Rushdie's *The Moor's Last Sigh*."

5. Timothy Brennan, Cosmopolitans and Celebrities, *Race and Class* 31.1 (1989): 2, 4. It is important to note that while Brennan here groups Mukherjee and Rushdie into a single category of international cosmopolitan

writers, they see themselves quite differently. Mukherjee at the time of Brennan's article had already moved from defining herself as an expatriate Indian to an American. Rushdie, during the same period, considered himself Indian first.

6. In *Questions of Cinema*, Stephen Heath notes that the shot/reverse shot formation, as described in Oudart and Dayan's systems of suture, does not account for the multiplicity of techniques used to create the identificatory relationship between viewer and cinematic subject (98). At the same time, Heath warns against reading all editing techniques that construct a narrative out of a series of shots (a definition that empties suture of any significance); he maintains a strict reading of suture as the name of the relationship of lack to its ideological system of signification (100–1).

7. Anthony D. Smith, *National Identity* (Reno: University of Las Vegas Press, 1991): 11–12. Smith emphasizes that both legal-political and ethnic nationalisms depend for success upon shared collective historical memories: "Transcending oblivion through posterity; the restoration of collective dignity through an appeal to a golden age; the realization of fraternity through symbols, rites and ceremonies, which bind the living to the dead and fallen of the community; these are the underlying functions of national identity and nationalism in the modern world, and the basic reasons why the latter have proved so durable, protean and resilient through all vicissitudes" (163). I want to push this model a step further to look at the way the rhetoric of the family binds the nation, legal-political and ethnic, as a site of collective meaning. Rushdie's work is especially good at showing the struts and rivets that hold these two models together, and it is this exposure of construction itself that makes it possible to imagine other models.

8. See, e.g., Partha Chatterjee's *Nationalist Thought and the Colonial World: A Derivative Discourse?* (London: Zed Books, 1986) for a discussion of Gandhi's use of kinship rhetoric in support of Indian nationalism.

9. Neil Ten Kortenaar, "'Midnight's Children' and the Allegory of History," *ARIEL* 26.2 (April 1995): 45.

10. See David W. Price, "Salman Rushdie's 'Use and Abuse of History' in 'Midnight's Children'," *ARIEL* 25.2 (April 1994): 91–107. Price uses Nietzsche's division of antiquarian, monumental, and critical history to discuss competing historical narratives within the novel. In Price's schema, William Methwold (Saleem's British progenitor) represents the antiquarian, Indira Gandhi the monumental, and Saleem the critical historian. Whereas the first two betray the ideals of the nation, Saleem represents "the potential to contribute to life" (92). Price discusses Saleem's imaginative construction of the past as a way of making "true narratives" (102) to counter the official "truths" proffered by the government. While this celebration of the imaginary and the metaphoric is in keeping with Rushdie's own faith, captured in narrative form, in "the Indian talent for non-stop regeneration" (*Imaginary Homelands*, 16), it elides the way in which Saleem's errors, lies, and impending dissolution undercut his own authority.

11. Rushdie invokes Hindu deities throughout the novels to establish a link between the mythic, narrative, and national "realities." We see this not only

in the relationship between Kali and Parvati, but also in Parvati and Shiva's child Adam (described in terms of his mythological counterpart, Ganesh) and in the relationship between Saleem and Shiva. These rivals for leadership over the MCC, both of whom share the distinction of being born at the exact moment of Indian independence, represent the dichotomy between Brahma and Shiva. As Timothy Brennan says in *Salman Rushdie and the Third World*, "Brahma, as we know, is the god who *dreams* the world. Shiva, we learn, is the god who allows it to exist by declining to use his immeasurable power for destroying it" (113).

12. Bruce Robbins's collection, *The Phantom Public Sphere* provides an excellent overview of the limits and continued usefulness of the term "public sphere." Contributors show how Habermas's model constitutes the participatory public as white, male, literate, and propertied even while it claims to be non-corporeal and open. Robbins and Nancy Fraser, in particular, respond to the restrictions of the Habermasian public sphere with their own models of multiple, shifting spheres. Negt and Kluge's *Public Sphere and Experience* provides one of the fullest elaborations of Habermas, although it falls prey to the same gender exclusions. They rework the ideal public sphere into three overlapping spheres—the liberal bourgeois sphere, public sphere of production, and the proletarian public sphere—in order to show how public opinion is constituted in multiple commercial, social, and political domains rather than in the idealized (no) place between public and private. They also keep these publics firmly attached to contemporary social conditions and media technologies. Arguing that bourgeois society replicates the patriarchal family structure, Negt and Kluge say that the decline of the family and/or entry into the labor force transfers control of patriarchal fantasy-production to the "consciousness industry" (a conglomeration of macro-capitalist interests and media that address the consumer). The "consciousness industry" provides consumers with the "libidinal compensation" for desires constructed in patriarchal terms.

13. As Chatterjee notes in his introduction, "If the nation is an imagined community and if nations must also take the form of states, then our theoretical language must allow us to talk about community and state at the same time. I do not think our present theoretical language allows us to do this" (11).

14. In a further revision of gender roles, when Adam and the pickle factory reappear in *The Moor's Last Sigh* he, at only 17, has assumed control of entering the pickles in the global market. With his flair for slogans and marketing, he is the epitome of the self-made man. Mary Periera and her sister are reduced to the "old ladies" (*MLS*, 343).

15. In "*The Satanic Verses* as a Cinematic Narrative," Nicholas D. Rombes, Jr. quotes a 1983 interview with Rushdie in *Contemporary Authors*. Telling Jean W. Ross about his use of cinematic techniques and terminology, Rushdie notes, "The whole experience of montage technique, split screens, dissolves, and so on, has become a film language which translates quite easily into fiction and gives you an extra vocabulary of literature." Rombes uses this quote to launch his analysis of cinematic techniques in *The Satanic Verses*.

According to Rombes, Rushdie creates a "dichotomy between the narrator's omniscient point of view and the constricted point of view of the 'camera eye'" (50). Understanding and truth come from the narrator's ability to look within characters. The camera's point of view, on the other hand, is limited by the economic and physical conditions of production. Rombes attributes this dichotomy to Rushdie in order to argue that it distinguishes "between seeing as a method of discovering the truth and seeing as a means of recording to speculate on the dangerous potential for manipulating what we see and how we see it via technology" (52). I have a completely different reading of Rushdie's use of the cinematic. As I argue in this chapter, Rushdie appropriates these techniques in celebration, not in criticism. While Rombes sees the coexistence of a narrator and a camera's "eye" as a mark of their difference, I see them as parallel functions. Rushdie uses these "eyes" to underscore the partiality of all vision, regardless of any claims of omniscience. We find this partiality not only in the fallibility of all of Rushdie's narrators, but also in his exuberant magic realism where truth and perception are always in play.

16. Lipscomb is particularly helpful in filtering out Rushdie's references and borrowings from Wolpert's *A New History of India* in *Midnight's Children*.

17. See, e.g., Keith Wilson's analysis (33) of the reader's relationship to Padma in *Midnight's Children*.

18. Interview, *Le Croix* (April 30, 1984), 24. Quoted in and translated by Jean-Pierre Durix, "Salman Rushdie's Declaration of Kaleidoscopic Identity," *Declarations of Cultural Independence in the English Speaking World*, ed. Luigi Sampietro (Milan: D'Imperio Editore Novaram 1989), 173. Rushdie has been critiqued for his celebration of plurality on the grounds that it represents his own class privilege. See, e.g., Timothy Brennan, "Cosmopolitans and Celebrities," *Race and Class* 31.1 (1989): 1–19. There Brennan describes Rushdie's exoticism as a marketable mark of difference in the Western literary marketplace. Whereas as Brennan reads Rushdie as "deny[ing] the old pattern of the need to create a national *mythos* in the country of origin" (4), I see him as pointing out just how difficult that process is.

19. See Jonathan Greenberg's " 'The Base Indian' or 'the Base Judean'?: Othello and the Metaphor of the Palimpsest in Salman Rushdie's *The Moor's Last Sigh*" and J.M. Coetzee's "Palimpsest Regained" for two additional discussions of Rushdie's use of the palimpsest.

20. Richard Fletcher, in his description of the transfer of power, notes that, "curiously enough [the Catholic monarchs] had chosen to dress themselves in Moorish costume for the ceremony" (165). This idiosyncratic appropriation of Moorish dress finds its way into *The Moor's Last Sigh* in Miranda's portrait and Aurora's thematic paintings.

In "Christopher Columbus and Queen Isabella Consummate Their Relationship (*Santa Fe*, AD 1492)," from his *East, West* collection, Rushdie plays on the interstices of colonial narratives with an eroticized story of colonizing appetites. He represents a frustrated Columbus imagining the Queen at the take-over: "*See: there at the gates of Alhambra is Boadbil the*

Unlucky, the last Sultan of the last redoubt of all the centuries of Arab Spain. Behold: now, at this very instant, he surrenders the keys to the citadel into her grasp . . . there! And as the weight of the keys falls from his hand into hers, she . . . she . . . yawns" (114). The story sexualizes imperial desire so that Columbus and the Queen need each other for their conquests. "The loss of money and patronage," Columbus says, "is as bitter as unrequited love" (115). Columbus, resenting his dependence on the Queen, fantasizes about refusing her if she calls for him. When the summons finally arrives, however, he answers, *"Yes. I'll come"* (119).

21. Thanks to Vikram Chandra for introducing me to the history of the original Nadia Wadia.

22. Both Tharoor and Khilnani read Nehru's image as an attempt to satisfy the condition of historical amnesia (amnesia of a fractured populace) Ernst Renan says is necessary for modern nationhood.

Chapter 5   Family Matters in Jamaica Kincaid's *The Autobiography of My Mother*: The Decline of the Nation as Family and the Regeneration of the Aesthetic

1. Donna Perry, ed., "Jamaica Kincaid," *Backtalk: Women Writers Speak Out: Interviews by Donna Perry* (New Brunswick, NJ: Rutgers University Press, 1983), 127–41. Quoted in Diane Simmons, *Jamaica Kincaid* (New York: Twayne Publishers, 1994), 19.

BIBLIOGRAPHY

Abel, Elizabeth. "Black Writing, White Reading: Race and the Politics of Feminist Interpretation." *Critical Inquiry* 19.3 (Spring 1993): 470–98.

Afzal-Khan, Fawzia. *Cultural Imperialism and the Indo-English Novel.* University Park, PA: Pennsylvania State University Press, 1993.

——— "Myth De-Bunked: Genre and Ideology in Rushdie's *Midnight's Children* and *Shame.*" *The Journal of Indian Writing in English* 14.1 (January 1986): 49–60.

Ahmad, Aijaz. *In Theory: Classes, Nations, Literatures.* New York: Verso, 1992.

Alam, Faruk. *Bharati Mukherjee.* New York: Twayne Publishers, Simon & Schuster Macmillan, 1996.

Ali, Tariq. "*Midnight's Children.*" *New Left Review* 136 (November–December 1982): 87–95.

Anderson, Benedict. *Imagined Communities: Reflections on the Origin and Spread of Nationalism.* New York: Verso, 1991.

Appadurai, Arjun. "The Heart of Whiteness." *Callaloo* 16.4 (1993): 796–807.

Appiah, K. Anthony. "The Postcolonial and the Postmodern." *The Post-Colonial Studies Reader.* Ed. Bill Ashcroft, Gareth Griffiths, and Helen Tiffin. New York: Routledge, 1995. 119–24.

——— "Is the Post- in Postmodernism the Post- in Postcolonial?" *Critical Inquiry* 17.2 (1991): 336–57.

——— "Giving Up the Perfect Diamond." Review of *The Holder of the World. New York Times Book Review* October 10, 1993: 7.

Appignanesi, Lisa and Sara Maitland. *The Rushdie File.* Syracuse: Syracuse University Press, 1990.

Awkward, Michael. "Negotiations of Power: White Critics, Black Texts, and the Self-Referential Impulse." *American Literary History* 2.4 (Winter 1990): 581–606.

——— "Race, Gender, and the Politics of Reading." *Black American Literature Forum* 22.1 (Spring 1988): 5–27.

Bader, Rudolph. "Indian Tin Drum." *International Fiction Review* 11.2 (Summer 1984): 75–83.

Ball, John Clement. "Acid in the Nation's Bloodstream: Satire, Violence, and the Indian Body Politic in Salman Rushdie's *The Moor's Last Sigh.*" *International Fiction Review* 27 (2000): 37–47.

Banville, John. "An Interview with Salman Rushdie." *New York Review of Books* 40.5 (March 4, 1993): 34–6.

Benston, Kimberly W. "I yam what I yam: the topos of (un)naming in Afro-American literature." *Black Literature and Literary Theory.* Ed. Henry Louis Gates, Jr. New York: Methuen, 1984. 151–72.

Berlant, Lauren. *The Anatomy of National Fantasy: Hawthorne, Utopia, and Everyday Life.* Chicago: University of Chicago Press, 1991.

——— "National Brands/National Body." *The Phantom Public Sphere.* Ed. Bruce Robbins. Minneapolis: University of Minnesota, 1993. 173–208.

Bhabha, Homi K. *Nation and Narration.* New York: Routledge, 1990.

——— "Interrogating Identity: The Postcolonial Prerogative." *Anatomy of Racism.* Ed. David Theo Goldberg. Minneapolis: University of Minnesota Press, 1990.

——— *The Location of Culture.* New York: Routledge, 1994.

——— "Of Mimicry and Man: The Ambivalence of Colonial Discourse." *October* 28 (Spring 1984): 125–33.

——— " 'Race', Time and the Revision of Modernity." *Oxford Literary Review* 13.1–2 (1991): 193–219.

——— "Signs Taken for Wonders: Questions of Ambivalence and Authority Under a Tree Outside Delhi, May 1817." *Race, Writing, and Difference.* Ed. Henry Louis Gates, Jr. Chicago: University of Chicago Press, 1986. 163–84.

Birch, David. "Postmodernist Chutneys." *Textual Practice* 15.1 (Spring 1991): 1–7.

Blaise, Clark. *Resident Alien.* Ontario, Canada: Penguin Books, 1986.

Bodnar, John E. *Remaking America: Public Memory, Commemoration and Patriotism in the Twentieth Century.* Princeton: Princeton University Press, 1992.

Boehmer, Elleke. "Post-colonial Literary Studies: A Neo-Orientalism?" *Oriental Prospects: Western Literature and the Lure of the East.* Atlanta, GA: Rodopi, 1998. 239–45.

Booker, M. Keith. "Beauty and the Beast: Dualism as Despotism in the Fiction of Salman Rushdie." *English Literary History* 57.4 (Winter 1990): 977–97.

Booth, Wayne. *The Company We Keep: An Ethics of Fiction.* Berkeley: University of California Press, 1988.

Brennan, Timothy. "Cosmopolitans and Celebrities." *Race and Class* 31.1 (1989): 1–19.

——— "India, Nationalism, and Other Failures." *South Atlantic Quarterly* 87.1 (Winter 1988): 131–46.

——— *Salman Rushdie and the Third World: Myths of Nation.* New York: St. Martin's Press, 1989.

Brodhead, Richard H. *The School of Hawthorne.* New York: Oxford University Press, 1986.

Brooks, David. "An Interview with Salman Rushdie." *Helix* 19 (1984): 55–69.

Buell, Frederick. *National Culture and the New Global System.* Baltimore: Johns Hopkins University Press, 1994.

Butler, Judith. *Bodies That Matter: On the Discursive Limits of "Sex."* New York: Routledge, 1993.

——— *Excitable Speech: A Politics of the Performative.* New York: Routledge, 1997.

——— *Gender Trouble: Feminism and the Subversion of Identity.* New York: Routledge, 1990.

——— "Imitation and Gender Insubordination." *The Lesbian and Gay Studies Reader.* Ed. Henry Abelove, Michèle Aina Barale, and David Halperin. New York: Routledge, 1993. 307–20.

────── The Psychic Life of Power. Stanford: Stanford University Press, 1997.

Butler, Thomas. Ed. Memory: History, Culture and the Mind. Oxford: Basil Blackwell, 1989.

Butts, Dennis. "From Newbury to Salman Rushdie: Teaching the Literature of Imperialism in Higher Education." Literature and Imperialism. Ed. Robert Giddings. New York: St. Martin's Press, 1991: 64–74.

Campbell, Elaine. "Beyond Controversy: Vidia Naipaul and Salman Rushdie." Literary Half-Yearly 27 (July 1986): 42–9.

Cantor, Paul A. "Tales of the Alhambra: Rushdie's Use of Spanish History in The Moor's Last Sigh." Studies in the Novel 29.3 (Fall 1997): 239–60.

Carter, Angela. "Polemical Preface: Pornography in the Service of Women." The Sadeian Woman. New York: Pantheon Books, 1978.

Carter-Sanborn, Kristin. " 'We Murder Who We Were': Jasmine and the Violence of Identity." American Literature 66.3 (September 1994): 573–93.

Caruth, Cathy. Unclaimed Experience: Trauma, Narrative, and History. Baltimore: The Johns Hopkins University Press, 1996.

Caton, Louis F. "Romantic Struggles: The Bildungsroman and Mother–Daughter Bonding in Jamaica Kincaid's Annie John." MELUS 21.3 (Fall 1996): 125–42.

Caygill, Howard. The Art of Judgment. Oxford: Basil Blackwell, 1989.

Chakrabarty, Dipesh. "Postcoloniality and the Artifice of History: Who Speaks for 'Indian' Pasts?" Representations 37 (1992): 1–26.

Chakravarty, Sumita S. National Identity in Indian Popular Cinema, 1947–1987. Austin: University of Texas Press, 1993.

Chatterjee, Partha. The Nation and Its Fragments: Colonial and Postcolonial Histories. Princeton: Princeton University Press, 1993.

────── Nationalist Thought and the Colonial World: A Derivative Discourse? London: Zed Books, 1986.

Chrisman, Laura. "The Imperial Unconscious?" Critical Quarterly 32.3 (1990): 38–58.

Christian, Barbara. "Community and Nature: The Novels of Toni Morrison." Journal of Ethnic Studies 7.4 (1980): 65–78.

Chua, C.L. "Passages from India: Migrating to America in the Fiction of V.S. Naipaul and Bharati Mukherjee." Reworlding: The Literature of the Indian Diaspora. Ed. Emmanuel S. Nelson. New York: Greenwood Press, 1992. 51–61.

Cincotti, Joseph A. "Same Trip, Opposite Direction." New York Times Book Review October 10, 1993: 7.

Coetzee, J.M. "Palimpsest Regained." Review of The Moor's Last Sigh, by Salman Rushdie. New York Review of Books. March 21, 1996: 13–16.

Connerton, Paul. How Societies Remember. Cambridge: Cambridge University Press, 1989.

Connolly, William E. Identity/Difference: Democratic Negotiations of Political Paradox. Ithaca: Cornell University Press, 1991.

────── Political Theory and Modernity. New York: Basil Blackwell, 1988.

Cornwell-Giles, JoAnne. "Afro-American Criticism and Western Consciousness: The Politics of Knowing." Black American Literature Forum 24.1 (Spring 1990): 85–98.

Crighton, S. and L. Shapiro. "An Exclusive Talk with Salman Rushdie." *Newsweek* (February 12, 1990): 46–9.

Cronin, Richard. "The Indian English Novel: *Kim* and *Midnight's Children*." *Modern Fiction Studies* 33.2 (Summer 1987): 201–13.

Crosby, Christina. "Dealing with Differences." *Feminists Theorize the Political*. Ed. Judith Butler and Joan W. Scott. Routledge: New York, 1992. 130–43.

Cunningham, Valentine. "Nosing Out the Indian Reality." *Times Literary Supplement* May 15, 1981: 38.

Danto, Arthur C. "Mughal Art." *The Nation* (February 2/9, 1998): 64–7.

Dayal, Samir. "Talking Dirty: Salman Rushdie's *Midnight's Children*." *College English* 54.4 (April 1992): 431–45.

Degabriele, Maria. "Trafficking Culture in Postcolonial Literature: Postcolonial Fiction and Salman Rushdie's *Imaginary Homelands*." *SPAN* (October 1992): 60–70.

Derrida, Jacques. "Economimesis." *Diacritics* 11 (June 1985): 3–25.

———— *The Truth in Painting*. Trans. Geoff Bennington and Ian McLeod. Chicago: University of Chicago Press, 1987.

Deleuze, Gilles and Felix Guattari. *Anti-Oedipus: Capitalism and Schizophrenia*. Minneapolis: University of Minnesota Press, 1996.

Dharker, Rani. "An Interview with Salman Rushdie." *New Quest* 42 (November–December 1983): 351–60.

Dingwaney, Anuradha. "Author(iz)ing *Midnight's Children* and *Shame*: Salman Rushdie's Constructions of Authority." *Reworlding: The Literature of the Indian Diaspora*. Ed. Emmanuel S. Nelson. New York: Greenwood Press, 1992. 157–67.

Donnell, Alison. "She Ties Her Tongue: The Problems of Cultural Paralysis in Postcolonial Criticism." *ARIEL: A Review of International English Literature* 26.1 (January 1995): 101–16.

———— "When Writing the Other is Being True to the Self: Jamaica Kincaid's *The Autobiography of My Mother*." *Women's Lives into Print: The Theory, Practice and Writing of Feminist Auto/Biography*. Ed. Pauline Polkey. New York: St. Martin's Press, 1999. 123–36.

———— "Writing for Resistance: Nationalism and Narratives of Liberation." *Framing the Word: Gender and Genre in Caribbean Women's Writing*. Ed. Joan Anim-Addo. London: Whiting and Birch, 1996. 28–36.

Donzelot, Jacques. *The Policing of Families*. New York: Random House, 1979.

DuBois, W.E.B. *The Souls of Black Folk*. New York: Signet, 1969.

Durix, Jean Pierre. "Magic Realism in Midnight's Children." *Commonwealth Essays and Studies* 8.1 (Autumn 1985): 57–63.

———— "Salman Rushdie's Declaration of Kaleidoscopic Identity." *Declarations of Cultural Independence in the English-Speaking World: A Symposium*. Ed. Luigi Sampietro. Milan: D'Imperio Editore Novare, 1989: 173–84.

Eagleton, Terry. *The Ideology of the Aesthetic*. Oxford: Basil Blackwell, 1990.

Esonwanne, Uzo. " 'Race' and Hermeneutics: Paradigm Shift—From Scientific to Hermeneutic Understanding of Race." *African American Review* 26.4 (1992): 565–81.

Ewing, Katherine Pratt. *Arguing Sainthood: Modernity, Psychoanalysis, and Islam.* Durham: Duke University Press, 1997.

Fanon, Frantz. *Black Skin, White Masks.* Trans. Charles Lam Markmann. New York: Grove Press, 1967.

———— *The Wretched of the Earth.* Trans. Constance Farrington. New York: Grove Press, 1963.

Fenton, James. "Keeping up with Salman Rushdie." *New York Review of Books* 38.6 (March 28, 1991): 26–34.

Ferguson, Moira. *Jamaica Kincaid: Where the Land Meets the Body.* Charlottesville: University Press of Virginia, 1994.

———— "A Lot of Memory: An Interview with Jamaica Kincaid." *The Kenyon Review* 16.1 (1994): 163–88.

Feroza, Jussawalla. "Chiffon Saris: The Plight of South Asian Immigrants in the New World." *The Massachusetts Review* 29.4 (1988): 583–95.

Finney, Brian. "Suture in Literary Analysis." *LIT: Literature Interpretation Theory* 2 (1990): 131–44.

Fischer, Michael M.J. "Ethnicity and the Post-Modern Arts of Memory." *Writing Culture: The Poetics and Politics of Ethnography.* Ed. James Clifford and George Marcus. Berkeley: University of California Press, 1986. 194–233.

Flanagan, Kathleen. "The Fragmented Self in Salman Rushdie's *Midnight's Children.*" *The Commonwealth Novel in English* 5.1 (Spring 1992): 38–45.

Fletcher, D.M. Ed. *Reading Rushdie: Perspectives on the Fiction of Salman Rushdie.* Atlanta, GA: Rodopi, 1994.

Fletcher, Richard. *Moorish Spain.* Berkeley: University of California Press, 1992.

Forster, E.M. *A Passage to India.* New York: Harcourt Brace, 1924.

Freud, Sigmund. *The Freud Reader.* Ed. Peter Gay. New York: W.W. Norton and Co., 1989.

———— *The Interpretation of Dreams.* Trans. and Ed. James Strachey. New York: Avon Books, 1965.

———— *Moses and Monotheism.* Trans. Katherine Jones. New York: Alfred A. Knopf, 1939.

Friedlander, Saul, Geulie Arad, and Dan Diner. Eds. *History and Memory: Studies in Representation of the Past.* Bloomington: Indiana University Press, 1994.

Fuss, Diana. *Essentially Speaking: Feminism, Nature & Difference.* New York: Routledge, 1989.

———— *Identification Papers.* New York: Routledge, 1995.

Gaonkar, Dilip Parameshwar. Ed. *Alternative Modernities.* Durham: Duke University Press, 2001.

Gates, Henry Louis, Jr. *Figures in Black: Words, Signs, and the "Racial" Self.* Oxford: Oxford University Press, 1987.

———— Ed. *"Race," Writing, and Difference.* University of Chicago Press: Chicago, 1985.

———— *The Signifying Monkey: A Theory of African-American Literary Criticism.* Oxford: Oxford University Press, 1988.

Gilroy, Paul. *The Black Atlantic: Modernity and Double Consciousness.* Cambridge, MA: Harvard University Press, 1993.

Glendenning, Victoria. "A Novelist in the Country of the Mind." *Sunday Times* October 25, 1981: 28.

Gorra, Michael. *After Empire: Scott, Naipaul, Rushdie.* Chicago: University of Chicago Press, 1997.

——— "Call it Exile, Call it Immigration." Review of *Jasmine. New York Times Book Review.* September 10, 1989: 9.

Gramsci, Antonio. *Selections from the Prison Notebooks.* Ed. and Trans. Quintin Hoare and Geoffrey Nowell Smith. New York: International Publishers, 1971.

Greenberg, Jonathan. " 'The Base Indian' or 'the Base Judean'? Othello and the Metaphor of the Palimpsest in Salman Rushdie's *The Moor's Last Sigh.*" *Modern Language Studies* 29.2 (Fall 1999): 93–107.

Greene, Gayle. "Feminist Fiction and the Uses of Memory." *Signs* 16.2 (1991): 290–321.

Habermas, Jürgen. *The Philosophical Discourse of Modernity.* Cambridge: MIT Press, 1978.

——— *The Structural Transformation of the Public Sphere.* Trans. Thomas Burger with Frederick Lawrence. Cambridge: MIT Press, 1991.

Haffenden, John. *Novelists in Interview.* New York: Methuen, 1985.

Hall, Stuart. "Ethnicity: Identity and Difference." *Radical America* 23.4 (1991): 9–20.

Haraway, Donna. "Ecce Homo, Ain't (Arn't) I a Woman, and Inappropriate/d Others." *Feminists Theorize the Political.* Ed. Judith Butler and Joan W. Scott. New York: Routledge, 1992. 86–100.

——— *Simians, Cyborgs, and Women.* New York: Routledge, 1992.

Harpham, Geoffrey Galt. "Aesthetics and the Fundamentals of Modernity." *Aesthetics & Ideology.* Ed. George Levine. New Brunswick, New Jersey: Rutgers University Press, 1994. 124–49.

Harris, Michael. *Outsiders and Insiders: Perspectives of Third World Culture and British Post-Colonial Fiction.* New York: Peter Lang, 1992.

Harvey, David. *The Condition of Postmodernity.* Oxford: Blackwell, 1990.

Hawes, Clement. "Leading History by the Nose: The Turn to the Eighteenth Century in *Midnight's Children.*" *Modern Fiction Studies* 39.1 (Winter 1993): 147–68.

Hawthorne, Nathaniel. *The Great Short Works of Hawthorne.* New York: Harper Row, 1967.

Healey, Beth. "Mosaic vs. Melting Pot." *New York Times Book Review.* June 1988: 22.

Heath, Stephen. *Questions of Cinema.* Bloomington: Indiana University Press, 1981.

Henderson, Mae Gwendolyn. "Speaking in Tongues: Dialogics, Dialectics, and the Black Woman Writer's Tradition." *Reading Black, Reading Feminist.* Ed. Henry Louis Gates, Jr. New York: Meridian, 1990. 116–42.

Hewson, Kelly. "Opening Up the Universe a Little More: Salman Rushdie and the Migrant as Story-Teller." *SPAN: Journal of the South Pacific Association for Commonwealth Literature and Language Studies* 29 (October 1989): 82–93.

Holston, James and Arjun Appadurai. "Cities and Citizenship." *Public Culture* 8.2 (Winter 1966): 187–204.

Homans, Margaret. " 'Women of Color' Writers and Feminist Theory." *New Literary History* 25.1 (Winter 1994): 73–94.

hooks, bell. "Choosing the Margin as a Space of Radical Openness." *Yearning: Race, Gender and Cultural Politics*. Boston: South End Press, 1990.

Hutcheon, Linda. *A Poetics of Postmodernism*. New York: Routledge, 1988.

——— "Subject in/of/to History and His Story." *Diacritics* 16.1 (Spring 1986): 78–91.

Irving, T.B. "The Rushdie Confrontation: A Clash in Values." *Iowa Review* 20.1 (Winter 1990): 175–84.

Iyer, Nalini. "American/Indian: Metaphors of the Self in Bharati Mukherjee's 'The Holder of the World.' " *ARIEL: A Review of International English Literature* 27.4 (1996): 29–44.

Jameson, Fredric. *The Political Unconscious*. Ithaca: Cornell University Press, 1981.

——— "Third World Literature in the Era of Multinational Capitalism." *Social Text* 15 (Fall 1986): 65–88.

Joyce, James. *A Portrait of the Artist as a Young Man*. New York: Penguin, 1964.

Juan-Novarro, Santiago. "The Dialogic Imagination of Salman Rushdie and Carlos Fuentes: National Allegories and the Scene of Writing in *Midnight's Children* and *Cristobal Nonato*." *Neohelicon* 20.2 (1994): 257–311.

Jussawalla, Feroza. "Beyond Indianness: The Stylistic Concerns of '*Midnight's Children*'." *Journal of Indian Writing in English* 12.2 (July 1984): 26–47.

Kammen, Michael. *Mystic Chords of Memory: The Transformation of Tradition in American Culture*. New York: Knopf, 1991.

Kasson, John F. *Amusing the Million*. New York: Hill and Wang, 1978.

Kaufman, Michael T. "Author from Three Countries." *New York Times Book Review* 3 November 13, 1983: 22–3.

Kehde, Suzanne. "Colonial Discourse and Female Identity: Bharati Mukherjee's *Jasmine*." *International Women's Writing: New Landscapes of Identity*. Ed. Anne E. Brown and Marjanne E. Goozé. Westport, CT: Greenwood Press, 1995: 70–7.

Khilnani, Sunil. *The Idea of India*. New York: Farrar, Straus, Giroux, 1997.

Kincaid, Jamaica. *The Autobiography of My Mother*. New York: Plume, 1996.

——— "In History." *Callaloo* 20.1 (1997): 1–7.

——— "On Seeing England for the First Time." *Transition: An International Review* 51 (1991): 32–40.

——— *A Small Place*. London: Virago Press, 1988.

Kinsley, David. *Hindu Goddesses: Visions of the Divine Feminine in the Hindu Religious Tradition*. Berkeley: University of California Press, 1986.

Kolodny, Annette. "The Integrity of Memory: Creating a New Literary History of the United States." *American Literature* 57 (1985): 291–307.

Kortenaar, Neil Ten. " 'Midnight's Children' and the Allegory of History." *ARIEL: A Review of International English Literature* 26.2 (April 1995): 41–62.

Krishnaswamy, Revathi. "Mythologies of Migrancy: Postcolonialism, Postmodernism and the Politics of (Dis)location." *ARIEL: A Review of International English Literature* 26.1 (January 1995): 25–146.

Lacan, Jacques. *Ecrits: A Selection*. New York: W.W. Norton, 1977.

Lacan, Jacques. *Four Fundamental Concepts of Psycho-Analysis*. Ed. Jacques-Alain Miller. Trans. Alan Sheridan. New York: W.W. Norton and Co., 1981.

Lakshmi, Vijay. "Rushdie's Fiction: The World Beyond the Looking Glass." *Reworlding: The Literature of the Indian Diaspora*. Ed. Emmanuel S. Nelson. New York: Greenwood Press, 1992. 149–55.

Laplanche, J. and J.-B. Pontalis. *The Language of Psychoanalysis*. New York: W.W. Norton, 1973.

Lazarus, Neil. *Nationalism and Cultural Practice in the Postcolonial World*. New York: Cambridge University Press, 1999.

——— "Postcolonialism and the Dilemma of Nationalism: Aijaz Ahmad's Critique of Third-Worldism." *Diaspora* 2.3 (1993): 373–400.

Leong, Liew-Geok. "Bharati Mukherjee." *International Literature in English: Essays on the Modern Writers*. Ed. Robert L. Ross. New York: St. James Press, 1991. 487–500.

Levine, George. Ed. *Ideology and Aesthetics*. New Brunswick, NJ: Rutgers University Press, 1994.

Liddle, Joanna and Rama Joshi. *Daughters of Independence: Gender, Caste and Class in India*. London: Zed Books, 1986.

Lim, Shirley Geok-Lin. "Assaying the Gold; or, Contesting the Grounds of Asian-American Literature." *New Literary History* 24 (1993): 147–69.

Lipscomb, David. "Caught in a Strange Middle Ground: Contesting History in Salman Rushdie's *Midnight's Children*." *Diaspora* 1.2 (1991): 163–89.

Loomba, Ania. " 'Local-Manufacture made-in-India Othello fellows': Issues of race, hybridity and location in post-colonial Shakespeares." *Post-Colonial Shakespeares*. Ed. Ania Loomba and Martin Orkin. New York: Routledge, 1998. 143–63.

Low, Gail Ching-Liang. "In a Free State: Post-Colonialism and Postmodernism in Bharati Mukherjee's Fiction." *Women: A Cultural Review* 4.1 (Spring 1993): 8–18.

Majid, Anouar. *Unveiling Traditions: Postcolonial Islam in a Polycentric World*. Durham: Duke University Press, 2000.

Marzorati, Gerald. "Salman Rushdie: Fiction's Embattled Infidel." *New York Times Magazine* January 29, 1989: 24.

Mason, Roger Burford. "Salman Rushdie." *PN Review* 15.4 (1989): 15–19.

McClintock, Anne. *Imperial Leather: Race, Gender and Sexuality in the Colonial Context*. New York: Routledge, 1995.

——— " 'No Longer in a Future Heaven': Gender, Race and Nationalism." *Dangerous Liaisons: Gender, Nation, and Postcolonial Perspectives*. Ed. Anne McClintock, Aamir Mufti, and Ella Shohat. Minneapolis: University of Minnesota Press, 1997. 89–112.

McNab, Chris. "Derrida, Rushdie and the Ethics of Mortality." *The Ethics in Literature*. Ed. Andrew Hadfield, Dominic Rainsford, and Tim Woods. New York: St. Martin's Press, 1999. 136–51.

Meer, Ameena. "Bharati Mukherjee: An Interview." *BOMB* 29 (1989): 46–7.

——— "Salman Rushdie: An Interview." *BOMB: Interviews*. New York: New Art Publications, 1992. 61–74.

Messud, Claire. "The Emperor's Tear." Review of *The Holder of the World*. *Times Literary Supplement*, November 12, 1993: 23.

Michaels, Walter Benn. "Race into Culture: A Critical Genealogy of Cultural Identity." *Critical Inquiry* 18 (1992): 655–85.

Miller, Donald. "Omnipotence and Its Enemies." *Third Text* 11 (1990): 135–43.

Miller, Jacques-Alain. "Suture (elements of the logic of the signifier)." *Screen* 18.4 (Winter 1977–78): 24–34.

Mishra, Vijay. "Postcolonial Differend: Diasporic Narratives of Salman Rushdie." *ARIEL: A Review of International English Literature* 26.3 (July 1995): 7–45.

Morrison, Toni. *Beloved*. New York: Plume Books, 1987.

——— *Sula*. New York: Plume Books, 1973.

Moss, Laura. " 'Forget those damnfool realists!' Salman Rushdie's Self-Parody as the Magic Realist's 'Last Sigh'." *ARIEL: A Review of International English Literature* 29.4 (October 1998): 121–39.

Mouffe, Chantal. "Citizenship and Political Identity." *October* 61 (Summer 1992): 28–32.

Mukherjee, Arun. *Towards an Aesthetics of Opposition: Essays on Literature, Criticism, and Cultural Imperialism*. Stratford, Ontario: Williams-Wallace, 1988.

Mukherjee, Arun P. "Characterization in Salman Rushdie's *Midnight's Children*: Breaking out of the Hold of Realism and Seeking the 'Alienation Effect'." *The New Indian Novel in English: A Study of the 1980s*. Ed. Virney Kirpal. New Delhi: Allied Publishers, 1990: 109–19.

Mukherjee, Bharati. "After the Fatwa." With Clark Blaise. *Mother Jones* 15.3 (April–May 1990): 28–31, 61–65.

——— *Conquering America with Bharati Mukherjee*. Videocassette. Produced by Bill Moyers. Public Affairs Television, 1990.

——— "A Conversation with V.S. Naipaul." With Robert Boyers. *Salmagundi* 50–1 (Fall 1980–Winter 1981): 153–71.

——— *Darkness*. New York: Fawcett Crest, 1985.

——— *Days and Nights in Calcutta*. With Clark Blaise. New York: Doubleday and Co., 1977.

——— "A Four-Hundred-Year-Old Woman." *Critical Fictions: The Politics of Imaginative Writing*. Ed. Philomena Mariani. Seattle: Bay Press, 1991. 24–8.

——— *The Holder of the World*. New York: Fawcett Columbine, 1993.

——— "Immigrant Writing: Give Us Your Maximalists!" *New York Times Book Review* August 28, 1988: 1, 28–9.

——— "An Interview with Bharati Mukherjee." With Alison B. Carb. *Massachusetts Review* 29.4 (1988): 645–54.

——— "An Interview with Bharati Mukherjee." With Michael Connell, Jessie Grearson, and Tom Grimes. *Iowa Review* 20.3 (Spring 1990): 7–32.

——— "An Interview with Bharati Mukherjee." With Geoff Hancock. *Canadian Fiction Magazine* 59 (May 1987): 30–44.

——— "An Interview with Bharati Mukherjee." *View* 20.3 (1990).

——— "An Invisible Woman." *Saturday Night* 96 (March 1981): 36–40.

——— *Jasmine*. New York: Fawcett Crest, 1989.

Mukherjee, Bharati. *The Middleman and Other Stories*. New York: Fawcett Crest, 1988.

Mukherjee, Bharati. "Prophet and Loss: Salman Rushdie's Migration of Souls." *Village Voice Literary Supplement* 72 (March 1989): 9–12.

———— *The Tiger's Daughter*. New York: Fawcett Crest, 1971.

———— *Wife*. New York: Fawcett Crest, 1975.

Mulvey, Laura. "Visual Pleasure and Narrative Cinema." *Screen* 16.3 (1975): 8–18.

Naik, M.K. "A Life in Fragments: The Fate of Identity in *Midnight's Children*." *Indian Literary Review* 3.3 (October 1985): 63–8.

Nasta, Susheila. "Motherlands, Mothercultures, Mothertongues: Women's Writing in the Caribbean." *Shades of Empire in Colonial and Post-Colonial Literatures*. Ed. C.C. Barfoot and Theo D'haen. Amsterdam: Rodopi, 1993. 211–20.

Natarajan, Nalini. "Woman, Nation, and Narration in *Midnight's Children*." *Scattered Hegemonies*. Ed. Inderpal Grewal and Caren Kaplan. Minneapolis: University of Minnesota Press, 1994. 76–89.

Nazareth, Peter. "Total Vision." *Canadian Literature* 110 (Fall 1986): 84–191.

Needham, Anurdha Dingwaney. "The Politics of Post-Colonial Identity in Salman Rushdie." *Massachusetts Review* 29.4 (Winter 1988–89): 609–24.

Negt, Oskar and Alexander Kluge. *The Public Sphere and Experience*. Minneapolis: University of Minnesota Press, 1993.

Nehru, Jawaharlal. *The Discovery of India*. New York: Asia Publishing House, 1961.

Nelson, Cecil. "New Englishes, New Discourses, New Speech Acts." *World Englishes: Journal of English as an International Language* 10.3 (Winter 1991): 317–23.

Nelson, Emmanuel S. Ed. *Bharati Mukherjee: Critical Perspectives*. New York: Garland Publishing, Inc., 1993.

———— "Kamala Markandaya, Bharati Mukherjee, and the Indian Immigrant Experience." *Toronto South Asian Review* 9 (Winter 1991): 1–9.

———— "Troubled Journeys: Indian Immigrant Experience in Kamala Markandaya's *Nowhere Man* and Bharati Mukherjee's *Darkness*." *From Commonwealth to Post-Colonial*. Ed. Anna Rutherford. Sydney, Australia: Dangaroo Press, 1992: 53–9.

Newman, Judie. "Spaces In-Between: Hester Prynne as the Salem Bibi in Bharati Mukherjee's *The Holder of the World*." *Borderlands: Negotiating Boundaries in Post-Colonial Writing*. Ed. Monika Reif-Hulser. Atlanta, GA: Rodopi, 1999. 69–87.

Nietzsche, Friedrich. "On the Truth and Lies in a Nonmoral Sense." *Philosophy and Truth: Selections from Nietzsche's notebooks of the Early 1870's*. Ed. and Trans. Daniel Breazeale. New Jersey: Humanities Press, 1979. 79–100.

Nussbaum, Martha C. *Poetic Justice: The Literary Imagination and Public Life*. Boston: Beacon Press, 1995.

Ondaatje, Michael. "Michael Ondaatje: Interview by Linda Hutcheon." *Other Solitudes: Canadian Multicultural Fictions*. Ed. Linda Hutcheon and Marion Richmond. Toronto: Oxford University Press, 1990. 196–202.

Onega, Susana. "Postmodernist Re-Writings of the Puritan Commonwealth: Winterson, Ackroyd, Mukherjee." *Intercultural Encounters—Studies in English Literatures*. Ed. Heinz Antor and Kevin L. Cope. Heidelberg: Universitatsverlag C. Winter, 1999. 439–66.

Parameswaran, Uma. "Handcuffed to History: Salman Rushdie's Art." *ARIEL: A Review of International English Literature* 14.4 (October 1983): 34–45.

———— "'Lest He Returning Chide': Saleem Sinai's Inaction in Salman Rushdie's *Midnight's Children*." *Literary Criterion* 18.3 (1983): 57–66.

Pathak, R.S. "Identity Crisis in the Novels of Salman Rushdie." *Language Forum* 18.1–2 (1992): 112–34.

Pattanayak, Chandrabhanu. "Interview with Salman Rushdie." *Literary Criterion* 18.3 (1983): 19–22.

Phillips, K.J. "Salman Rushdie's *Midnight's Children*: Models for Storytelling, East and West." *Comparative Literature East and West: Traditions and Trends. Selected Conference Papers*. Ed. Cornelia N. Moore and Raymond A. Moody. Honolulu: University of Hawaii Press, 1989. 202–7.

Pinckney, Darryl. *High Cotton*. New York: Penguin, 1992.

———— "Slouching Toward Washington." *New York Review of Books* December 21, 1995: 73–82.

Piwiniski, David J. "Losing Eden in Modern Bombay: Rushdie's *Midnight's Children*." *Notes on Contemporary Literature* 23.3 (May 1993): 10–12.

Prakash, Gyan. "Writing Post-Orientalist Histories of the Third World: Perspectives from Indian Historiography." *Comparative Studies in Society and History* 32.2 (April 1990): 383–408.

Prasad, Madhava. "On the Question of a Theory of (Third World) Literatures." *Social Text* 31/32 (1992): 57–83.

Price, David W. "Salman Rushdie's 'Use and Abuse of History' in 'Midnight's Children'." *ARIEL: A Review of International English Literature* 25.2 (April 1994): 91–107.

Raban, Jonathan. "Savage Boulevards, Easy Streets." Review of *The Middleman and Other Stories*. *New York Times Book Review* June 19, 1988: 1, 22–3.

Radhakrishnan, R. "Nationalism, Gender, and the Narrative of Identity." *Nationalisms and Sexualities*. Ed. Andrew Parker, Mary Russo, Doris Somer, and Patricia Yaeger. New York: Routledge, 1992. 77–95.

Rahman, Tariq. "Politics in the Novels of Salman Rushdie." *Commonwealth Novel in English* 4.1 (Spring 1991): 24–37.

Rai, Amit S. *Rule of Sympathy: Sentiment, Race, and Power, 1750–1850*. New York: Palgrave, 2002.

———— "'Thus Spake the Subaltern . . . ': Postcolonial Criticism and the Scene of Desire." *The Psychoanalysis of Race*. Ed. Christopher Lane. New York: Columbia University Press, 1998. 91–119.

Rajan, Gita. "Bharati Mukherjee." *Writers of the Indian Diaspora: A Bibliographical Critical Sourcebook*. Ed. Emmanuel S. Nelson. Westport, CT: Greenwood Press, 1993. 235–42.

———— "Fissuring Time, Suturing Space: Reading Bharati Mukherjee's *The Holder of the World*." *Generations: Academic Feminists in Dialogue*. Ed. Devoney Looser and Ann E. Kaplan. Minneapolis: University of Minnesota Press, 1997. 288–308.

Rao, K.B. "Asia and the Pacific: Midnight's Children." *World Literature Today* 56 (Winter 1982): 181.

Rao, Madhusudana. "Quest for Identity: A Study of the Narrative in Rushdie's *Midnight's Children*." *Literary Criterion* 25.4 (1990): 31–42.

Ray, Sangeeta. *En-Gendering India*. Durham: Duke University Press, 2000.

Reimenschneider, Dieter. "History and the Individual in Anita Desai's *Clear Light of Day* and Salman Rushdie's *Midnight's Children*." *World Literature Written in English* 23.1 (Winter 1984): 196–207.

Renan, Ernest. "Qu'est-ce qu'une nation?" *Oeuvres Complètes* (Paris, 1947–61), vol. 1, pp. 887–907. Reprinted as "What is a nation?" Transl. Martin Thom. *Nation and Narration*. Ed. Homi K. Bhabha. New York: Routledge, 1990: 8–22.

Robbins, Bruce. Ed. *Intellectuals: Aesthetics, Politics, Academics*. Minneapolis: University of Minnesota, 1990.

———— "Introduction." *The Phantom Public Sphere*. Minneapolis: University of Minnesota, 1993.

Rombes, Nicholas D., Jr. "*The Satanic Verses* as a Cinematic Narrative." *Literature/Film Quarterly* 21.1 (1993): 47–53.

Rosen, Jonathan. "Our Jerusalem." *New York Times Book Review* June 23, 1996: 91.

Ross, Bruce M. *Remembering the Personal Past: Descriptions of Autobiographical Memory*. New York: Oxford University Press, 1991.

Ross, Jean W. "Interview with Salman Rushdie." *Contemporary Authors* 111 (1983): 414–17.

Roy, Anindo. "The Aesthetics of an (Un)willing Immigrant: Bharati Mukherjee's *Days and Nights in Calcutta* and *Jasmine*." *Bharati Mukherjee: Critical Perspectives*. Nelson, Emmanuel S. New York: Garland Publishing, Inc., 1993.

Rush, Norman. "Doomed in Bombay." Review of *The Moor's Last Sigh*. *New York Times Book Review* January 14, 1996: 7.

Rushdie, Salman. "Damme, This Is the Oriental Scene for You!" *New Yorker* (June 23 and 30, 1997): 50–61.

———— "A Dangerous Art Form." *Third World Book Review* 1 (1984): 3–5.

———— *East, West*. New York: Pantheon Books, 1994.

———— "Goodness: The American Neurosis." *The Nation* 242 (March 22, 1986): 344.

———— *Imaginary Homelands*. New York: Penguin Books, 1991.

———— "In Conversation: 'Fictions are Lies that Tell the Truth.' " With Günter Grass. *The Listener* (June 27, 1985): 14–15.

———— "The Indian Writer in England." *The Eye of the Beholder: Indian Writing in English*. Ed. Maggie Butcher. London: Commonwealth Institute, 1983. 75–83.

———— "Interview." National Public Radio, 'All Things Considered', January 17, 1996.

———— "Interview." National Public Radio, 'Talk of the Nation', January 15, 1996.

———— "Introduction." Ali, Tariq. *An Indian Dynasty*. New York: G.P. Putnam's Sons, 1985.

———— *Midnight's Children*. New York: Penguin Books, 1980.

———— "*Midnight's Children* and *Shame*." *Kunapipi* 7 (1985): 1–19.

———— "Introduction." *Mirrorwork: 50 Years of Indian Writing, 1947–1997*. Ed. Salman Rushdie and Elizabeth West. New York: Henry Holt and Co., 1997. vii–xx.

——— *The Moor's Last Sigh*. New York: Pantheon Books, 1995.
——— "The Riddle of Midnight." Videocassette. Public Media Video, 1988.
——— "Salman Rushdie." With Charlotte Cornwall. *Writers Talk—Ideas of Our Time*. Writers in Conversation Series. ICA Video, 1989.
——— "Salman Rushdie: *The Satanic Verses*." With W.L. Webb. *Writers Talk—Ideas of Our Time*. Writers in Conversation Series. Videocassette. ICA Guardian Video, 1989.
Rustomji-Kerns, Roshni. "Expatriates, Immigrants, and Literature: Three South Asian Women Writers." *Massachusetts Review* 29.4 (Summer 1988): 655–65.
Sage, Vic. " 'The God-Shaped Hole': Salman Rushdie and the Myth of Origins." *Hungarian Studies in English* 22 (1991): 9–21.
Said, Edward. "Third World Intellectuals and Metropolitan Culture." *Raritan* 9.3 (Winter 1990): 27–50.
——— *The World, the Text and the Critic*. Cambridge, MA: Harvard University Press, 1983.
Saldívar, José. *The Dialectics of Our America: Genealogy, Cultural Critique, and Literatary History*. Durham: Duke University Press, 1991.
Sangari, Kumkum. "The Politics of the Possible." *Cultural Critique* 7 (Fall 1987): 157–86.
Sant-Wade, Arvindra and Karen Marguerite Radell. "Refashioning the Self: Immigrant Women in Bharati Mukherjee's New World." *Studies in Short Fiction* 29 (1992): 11–17.
Scarry, Elaine. *The Body in Pain: The Making and Unmaking of the World*. New York: Oxford University Press, 1985.
Scott, Joan W. "Multiculturalism and the Politics of Identity." *October* 61 (1992): 12–19.
Sen, Suchismita. "Memory, Language, and Society in Salman Rushdie's *Haroun and the Sea of Stories*." *Contemporary Literature* 36.4 (Winter 1995): 654–75.
Sennett, Richard. "The Identity Myth." *New York Times* January 30, 1994: 17.
Sethi, Sunil. "After Midnight." *India Today* April 15, 1983: 136–7.
Shapiro, Alan. *In Praise of the Impure*. Evanston, IL: TriQuarterly Books, 1993.
Shepherd, Ron. "*Midnight's Children* as Fantasy." *Commonwealth Review* 1.2 (1990): 33–43.
Shulman, Polly. "Home Truths: Bharati Mukherjee, World Citizen." *Voice Literary Supplement* June 1988: 19.
Silverman, Kaja. *Male Subjectivity at the Margins*. New York: Routledge, 1992.
——— *The Subject of Semiotics*. New York: Oxford University Press, 1983.
——— *Threshold of the Visible World*. New York: Routledge, 1995.
Simmons, Diane. "Coming-of-Age in the Snare of History: Jamaica Kincaid's *The Autobiography of My Mother*." *The Girl: Constructions of the Girl in Contemporary Fiction by Women*. New York: St. Martin's Press, 1998. 107–18.
——— *Jamaica Kincaid*. New York: Twayne Publishers, 1994.
Singh, Amritjit, Joseph T. Skerrett, Jr., and Robert E. Hogan, Eds. *Memory & Cultural Politics: New Approaches to American Ethnic Literatures*. Boston: Northeastern University Press, 1996.

Singh, Amritjit, Joseph T. Skerrett, Jr., and Robert E. Hogan *Memory, Narrative, and Identity: New Approaches in Ethnic American Literatures*. Boston: Northeastern University Press, 1994.

Singh, Sushila. "Salman Rushdie's Novels from Fantasy to Reality." *Commonwealth Review* 1.1 (1989): 111–23.

Slemon, Stephen. "Post-Colonial Allegory and the Transformation of History." *Journal of Commonwealth Literature* 23.1 (1988): 157–68.

Smith, Anthony D. *National Identity*. Reno: University of Las Vegas Press, 1991.

Smith, Colin. "The Unbearable Lightness of Salman Rushdie." Selected Papers of the 10th Annual Conference on Commonwealth Literature and Language Studies, Konigstein, June 11–14, 1987. *Critical Approaches to the New Literatures in English*. Ed. Dieter Riemenschneider. Essen: Die Blau Eule, 1989. 104.

Smith, Sidonie. *A Poetics of Women's Autobiography: Marginality and the Fictions of Self-Representation*. Bloomington, Indiana: Indiana University Press, 1987.

Spiegelman, Art. *Maus: A Survivor's Tale, II: And Here My Troubles Began*. New York: Pantheon, 1991.

Spillers, Hortense J. " 'All the Things You Could Be by Now, If Sigmund Freud's Wife Was Your Mother': Psychoanalysis and Race." *Boundary 2* 23.3 (Fall 1996): 75–141.

——— *Comparative American Identities: Race, Sex, and Nationality in the Modern Text*. New York: Routledge, 1991.

——— "Mama's Baby, Papa's Maybe." *Diacritics* 17.2 (Summer 1987): 65–81.

Spivak, Gayatri Chakravorty. *Outside in the Teaching Machine*. New York: Routledge, 1993.

——— *The Post-Colonial Critic*. Ed. Sarah Harasym. New York: Routledge, 1990.

——— "Reading *The Satanic Verses*." *Public Culture* 2.1 (Fall 1989): 79–99.

Srivastava, Aruna. " 'The Empire Writes Back': Language and History in *Shame* and *Midnight's Children*." *Past the Last Post: Theorizing Post-Colonialism and Post-Modernism*. Ed. Ian Adam and Helen Tiffin. Alberta: University of Calgary Press: 1990. 65–77.

St. Andrews, B.A. "Co-Wanderers Kogawa and Mukherjee: New Immigrant Writers." *World Literature Today* 66.1 (1992): 56–8.

Steinberg, Sybil. "Bharati Mukherjee." *Publisher's Weekly* August 25, 1989: 46–7.

Stoler, Ann Laura. "Making Empire Respectable: The Politics of Race and Sexual Morality in Twentieth-Century Colonial Cultures." *Dangerous Liaisons: Gender Nation, and Postcolonial Perspectives*. Ed. Anne McClintock, Aamir Mufti, and Ella Shohat. Minneapolis: University of Minnesota Press, 1997. 344–73.

Suleri, Sara. "Contraband Histories: Salman Rushdie and the Embodiment of Blasphemy." *Yale Review* 78.4 (Summer 1989): 604–24.

——— "Woman Skin Deep: Feminism and the Postcolonial Condition." *The Post-Colonial Studies Reader*. Ed. Bill Ashcroft, Gareth Griffiths, and Helen Tiffin. New York: Routledge, 1995. 273–80.

Sunder Rajan, Rajeswari. *Real and Imagined Women: Gender, Culture and Postcolonialism*. New York: Routledge, 1993.

Swann, Joseph. " 'East Is East and West Is West'? Salman Rushdie's *Midnight's Children* as an Indian Novel." *World Literature Written in English* 26.2 (Autumn 1986): 353–62.

Tapping, Craig. "South Asia/North America: New Dwellings and the Past." *Reworlding: The Literature of the Indian Diaspora.* Ed. Emmanuel S. Nelson. Westport, CT: Greenwood Press, 1992. 35–42.

Taylor, Charles. *Sources of the Self: The Making of the Modern Identity.* Cambridge: Harvard University Press, 1989.

Tharoor, Shashi. *India: From Midnight to Millennium.* New York: Arcade Publishing, 1997.

Tompkins, Jane. *Sensational Designs: The Cultural Work of American Fiction, 1790–1860.* New York: Oxford University Press, 1985.

Vergès, Françoise. *Monsters and Revolutionaries: Colonial Family Romance and Metissage.* Durham: Duke University Press, 1999.

Viswanathan, Gauri. *Masks of Conquest: Literary Study and British Rule in India.* New York: Columbia University Press, 1989.

Walcott, Derek. *Collected Poems, 1948–1984.* New York: Noonday Press, 1992.

Wall, Cheryl. A. Ed. *Changing Our Own Words: Essays on Criticism, Theory, and Writing by Black Women.* New Brunswick: Rutgers University Press, 1990.

Walton, Jean. "Re-Placing Race in (White) Psychoanalytic Discourse: Founding Narratives of Feminism." *Critical Inquiry* 21 (Summer 1995): 775–804.

Warner, Michael. "The Mass Public and the Mass Subject." *The Phantom Public Sphere.* Ed. Bruce Robbins. Minneapolis: University of Minnesota, 1993. 234–56.

Wieseltier, Leon. "Midnight's Other Children." *New Republic* (December 1983): 32–4.

West, Cornel. "Black Culture and Postmodernism." *Remaking History.* Ed. Barbara Kruger and Phil Mariani. Seattle: Bay Press, 1989. 87–96.

———— "The Dilemma of the Black Intellectual." *Breaking Bread: Insurgent Black Intellectual Life.* Ed. bell hooks and Cornel West. Boston: South End Press, 1991. 131–46.

———— *Race Matters.* New York: Vintage Books, 1994.

White, Jonathan. "Politics and the Individual in the Modernist Historical Novel." *Recasting the World: Writing After Colonialism.* Baltimore: The Johns Hopkins University Press, 1993: 208–40.

Wickramagamage, Carmen. "Relocation as Positive Act: The Immigrant Experience in Bharati Mukherjee's Novels." *Diaspora* 2.2 (1992): 171–200.

Wilson, Keith. "*Midnight's Children* and Reader Responsibility." *Critical Quarterly* 26.3 (Autumn 1984): 23–37.

Wolpert, Stanley. *A New History of India.* New York: Oxford University Press, 1993.

Yates, Frances Amelia. *The Art of Memory.* Chicago: Chicago University Press, 1966.

Žižek, Slavoj. *The Sublime Object of Ideology.* New York: Verso, 1989.

INDEX